Advanced
ActionScript 3 with
Design Patterns

Joey Lott and Danny Patterson

Adobe

Advanced ActionScript 3 with Design Patterns

Joey Lott and Danny Patterson

Peachpit Press

1249 Eighth Street
Berkeley, CA 94710
510/524-2178
800/283-9444
510/524-2221 (fax)

Find us on the World Wide Web at: www.peachpit.com
To report errors, please send a note to errata@peachpit.com

Peachpit Press is a division of Pearson Education

Project Editor: Matt Purcell
Production Editor: Becky Winter
Development Editor: Alice Martina Smith
Copy Editor: Nancy Sixsmith
Tech Editor: Roger Braunstein and Paul Newman
Compositor: Danielle Foster
Indexer: Larry Sweazy
Cover design: Charlene Will

ISBN 0-321-42656-8

9 8 7 6 5 4 3 2 1

Printed and bound in the United States of America

DEDICATION

JOEY:

To what is here, always in support.

DANNY:

This book is dedicated to Melissa, Adia and Murphy. Thanks for inspiring me to be my best.

ACKNOWLEDGMENTS

Both Joey and Danny would like to acknowledge the following people for their help with this book:

We'd like to thank Matt Purcell for helping with all aspects of this book.

Thanks also go to Angela Kozlowski for her initial work coordinating this book project. We wish you the best in your new career.

We'd like to thank our copy editor, Nancy Sixsmith, and our development editor, Alice Martina Smith.

Additionally, we'd like to thank our technical editors, Paul Newman and Roger Braunstein.

The Adobe Flash Player and Flex teams are always extremely helpful. Thank you.

And, of course, thanks to the Flash Platform community.

Joey would like to acknowledge the following people:

Thank you, Danny, for co-writing this book.

Thanks to my partner, my family, and my friends for your support, kindness, strength, and encouragement.

Danny would like to acknowledge the following people:

My thanks goes out to Joey. You're an incredible programmer and author and I'm honored to work with you on this book.

Thank you to all the programming influences in my life. There are far to many to list, but you know who you are.

And finally, my wonderful wife. Thanks for all your support and patience.

DEDICATION

JOEY:

To what is here, always in support.

DANNY:

This book is dedicated to Melissa, Adia and Murphy. Thanks for inspiring me to be my best.

ACKNOWLEDGMENTS

Both Joey and Danny would like to acknowledge the following people for their help with this book:

We'd like to thank Matt Purcell for helping with all aspects of this book.

Thanks also go to Angela Kozlowski for her initial work coordinating this book project. We wish you the best in your new career.

We'd like to thank our copy editor, Nancy Sixsmith, and our development editor, Alice Martina Smith.

Additionally, we'd like to thank our technical editors, Paul Newman and Roger Braunstein.

The Adobe Flash Player and Flex teams are always extremely helpful. Thank you.

And, of course, thanks to the Flash Platform community.

Joey would like to acknowledge the following people:

Thank you, Danny, for co-writing this book.

Thanks to my partner, my family, and my friends for your support, kindness, strength, and encouragement.

Danny would like to acknowledge the following people:

My thanks goes out to Joey. You're an incredible programmer and author and I'm honored to work with you on this book.

Thank you to all the programming influences in my life. There are far to many to list, but you know who you are.

And finally, my wonderful wife. Thanks for all your support and patience.

CONTENTS AT A GLANCE

CONTENTS

Introduction

As the Flash platform has grown, the size and scope of Flash-based applications has increased. That growth has called for an ever-increasing maturity in ActionScript developers. Flash applications have gained a new stature, and the increasing demand means that more developers must step up to the plate to hone their craft and take steps to evolve their understanding of and relationship with the code they write and the applications they build. Design patterns are a resource to help with just that.

ActionScript itself is really quite simple. It involves memorization of a basic syntax, a good API reference, and a decent IDE. What is challenging is not the ActionScript, but the architecture for an application. The real challenge is in deciding what classes to write and what the APIs for those classes should be. Yet as you build more and more applications, you'll start to find that there are patterns that emerge time and time again. There are certain ways to accomplish tasks and solve common problems that occur frequently. These common solutions are the foundations of design patterns. Many of these design patterns exist already. If you don't bother to recognize them and apply them consciously, you will simply be writing applications the hard way. You might still end up with good results, but you'll be reinventing the wheel each time. Learning the design patterns helps you more quickly identify intelligent and effective ways to structure each new application.

The design patterns discussed in this book are but a subset of the many patterns that developers have created over the years. We've selected what we feel are some of the most useful and applicable patterns to ActionScript application development. These patterns—and what we have to say about the patterns—is not intended to be held as gospel. It is intended to serve as a guide and an inspiration for your own application development. The patterns we discuss are patterns that have been identified and recognized by programming experts over the years; by studying them, you can stand on the shoulders of giants. However, it's important to understand that these patterns are not rules. Just because an expert found something useful doesn't mean you are obligated to do so. Read everything with an open and alert, yet critical, mind.

Design patterns run gambit from those that require strict adherence to a specific interface to those that simply specify a generalized structure. Regardless of the ways in which specific design patterns play out or look, the intention is always the same: to solve a design problem. One example of a common design problem is that you need a way to create an object without specifying the concrete type at compile time. For example, a graphing application might need to be able to create and display a graph where the specific type (bar chart, line graph, and so on) is decided at runtime. If you specify a concrete type at compile time (for example, create a new BarChart object), then you are locked into a rigid structure, and you cannot easily change the type or add new types later. Because this is a common problem in many applications, developers have had to create solutions many times over the years. The solutions that have proven to be most useful, most elegant, most flexible, and simple to implement have emerged as design patterns that are learnable. One solution to the concrete type problem just described is a pattern we call the Factory Method pattern (discussed in Chapter 5.)

One of the fortunate side-effects of working with design patterns is that they help you build a common vocabulary to effectively communicate with other developers. Imagine if you didn't have the word "car" in your vocabulary. Every time you wanted to talk about a car, you'd have to describe the object, perhaps saying "the object with wheels, an engine, and doors that typically seats 2 to 5 people and allows one person to conduct it by way of a steering mechanism." That would obviously make it rather difficult to have a quick and effective conversation about anything involving a car. Having a word for something makes communication faster and more effective. For this reason, all the design patterns we talk about in this book have names. Rather than talking about "the pattern that allows you to capture and set state while maintaining good encapsulation," you can simply say "the Memento pattern."

About This Book

The title of this book says that it is about advanced ActionScript 3.0 with design patterns. It's always a little misleading to call something *advanced*. What we mean when we say that this book is about advanced ActionScript 3.0 is that it steps beyond the standard introductions and API references to discuss topics not normally within the scope of those basic texts. As such, we necessarily make some assumptions about you, the reader. We assume that you already understand basic programming and ActionScript 3.0 principles, including, but not limited to, variables, expressions, statements, objects, inheritance, and how to write basic classes.

In many ways, this book starts where most books leave off in regards to object-oriented Action-Script. Although many books might discuss how to write a class, this book talks about the different ways you can design a class. This book talks about when, why, and how to use composition and inheritance, and how classes relate to one another to form patterns.

This book is organized in the following way:

1. Introduction to application design principals

2. Design pattern descriptions

3. Advanced concepts

Throughout the book, we'll present lots of examples, and we encourage you to follow along.

You can find additional information and updates at the official Web site for this book: http://www.rightactionscript.com/aas3wdp. This is also where you'll be able to find the AAS3WDP class library which you can download. Several classes from this library are used in various examples throughout the book, and you'll want to download the library if you want to follow along with the examples.

PART I

Successful Projects

CHAPTER 1

Designing Applications

One of the most frequent questions ActionScript developers ask is, "How do I know what constitutes a class?" This question strikes at the heart of a larger dilemma, which is: What are the steps for building a successful application from start to finish—from concept to completion? This is a big topic to tackle. Many people dedicate themselves to understanding and improving methodologies to answer this question.

The difficulty with teaching someone how to design and build an application from start to finish is that it requires elements that are difficult to talk about much less teach. It requires being able and willing to look at the big picture as well as looking at things from many perspectives. It requires creative thinking as well as abstraction. It requires practice and experience. But there are steps you can follow to help with the learning process. There are technologies you can use to assist you in developing your ActionScript classes. This chapter outlines some of the steps and technologies that have proven useful for many ActionScript developers.

Some methodologies say there are five steps for building applications; other methodologies say there are eight steps; still others can't decide how many steps it takes. In general, most developers agree that there are at least three phases to building successful applications:

1. Analysis

2. Design

3. Implementation

In addition, most developers also agree that testing is a vital part of the application development process. Although not always considered a core phase we'll also look at testing as a fourth important phase.

As we look at each of these phases, remember that they are not necessarily linear. You can go back to an earlier step at any point if necessary. During the design phase, for example, you might realize that you forgot about an important use case for your application. At that point, you can return to the analysis phase. However, you should be as thorough as possible at each step. Don't jump to the design phase too early just because you can. The more thorough and complete you are with each phase before moving to the next, the more successful your application is likely to be. Additionally, thoroughness at each phase helps minimize the risk that you'll have to make major architectural changes later on, which could severely impact schedules and project success.

The Analysis Phase

The analysis phase is concerned exclusively with what the application is supposed to do. The question of how the application will accomplish the goal is deferred to the design and implementation phases. In many ways, the analysis phase can be the most challenging because it requires that you take (often vague) ideas and translate them into specific functional requirements. You must create a map of what the application looks like from a distance. Although you can get away with a minimal analysis phase for a small project, the analysis phase becomes increasingly important for a project's success as the project increases in size and scope. Although you might be able to walk around your neighborhood without a map, if you wanted to cross the country, you'll undoubtedly agree that you need a map. This is true of application development as well.

All too often, the analysis phase is glanced over or deemphasized. Poor analysis leads to frustration for all parties involved (the developers who have to constantly make guesses and refector, the managers who have the responsibility to see the project through to a successful completion, the client who wants the working application, customers that have to use the application that may suffer from limited feature sets and bugs due to poor analysis, etc.). The goal of analysis is to provide a clear specification that outlines the needs of the user. Unlike later phases, the analysis phase should be as non-technical as possible.

The outcome of the analysis phase is generally a document that outlines the functional requirements. However, it's important to understand that there are many ways to approach gathering these requirements, and the resultant document has no one required format. What is most important is that you, your team, and/or your company uses an approach and document format that works best for you while still achieving the goal of clearly defining this map for the application you want to build.

Although there's no one required approach or format, we'll present one common approach to analysis using use cases. If you are new to the idea of doing formalized analysis then you may find it useful to try using use cases. We also encourage you to research other techniques and document formats to find what works best for you.

Introducing Use Cases

One way to define the functional requirements of an application is simply to list everything that the application should be able to do. Although that approach is not necessarily wrong, it is naïve in that it fails to take into account the real-world use of the application. Applications don't exist in isolation; they interface with all sorts of users. Therefore, it's much more realistic and useful to approach the functional requirements from the standpoint of how the application is used. This approach naturally leads to a kind of functional requirement called *use cases*.

Use cases present the application requirements by showing various ways in which users might interact with the application. The following is an example of a simple use case:

- **Generate Map:** The user submits a form with a street address. The system displays a physical map of the street address, with the map zoomed in at the default level.

Use cases can be formatted in many ways. Generally, use case experts talk about three basic formats.

Brief: One paragraph outlining the main success scenario. The preceding example was in the brief format.

Casual: Multiple paragraphs outlining not only the main success scenario, but also alternative scenarios. The following is an example of a casual format use case:

- **Generate Map**

  - *Main success scenario*: The user submits a form with a street address. The system displays a physical map of the street address, with the map zoomed in at the default level.

  - *Alternative scenarios*:

    If the address is invalid, the address form is redisplayed with an error message notifying the user why the operation failed.

    If the default zoom level is unavailable for the requested address, display a map at the greatest zoom level available for the location.

Formal: The most elaborate of the formats for a use case document. This format lists all the steps for the use case as well as supporting data such as actors and conditions. The formal use case is discussed in more detail in the next section.

Writing Formal Use Cases

Typically you'll want to create formal use cases for a functional requirements document. In this section we'll look at how to create a formal use case. A formal use case can include the following sections:

- *Primary actor*: A description of the user who drives the operations outlined by the use case. The description of the primary actor can include things such as the role of the user (e.g. anonymous, basic, administrator, etc.) as well as characteristics of the user that may be relevant to how they interact with the application (e.g. age, disabilities, etc.)

- *Preconditions*: Those conditions that must be met for the use case to proceed.

- *Main success scenario*: A more granular, step-based description of the way the application works than is given in the basic or casual formats.

- *Alternative scenarios*: More granular, step-based descriptions of the ways the application will handle alternative uses than are given in the casual format.

- *Special requirements*: A list of requirements for the use case that don't fit as part of the main or alternative scenarios.

- *Open issues*: A list of notes including questions that must be answered to fully implement a solution for the use case.

The following is an example of a formal use case. Note that this example does not have any open issues.

- **Generate Map**

  Primary actor: Customer

  Preconditions: Customer is already viewing the form that allows the user to specify an address and click a button to submit the form.

- **Main success scenario:**

  1. Customer fills out address form.

  2. Customer submits address data.

  3. System requests map data from mapping service.

  4. System draws map at default zoom level.

- **Alternative Scenarios:**

  3a. System detects invalid address format and redisplays form with error message.

  3b. Mapping service is unavailable and system displays error message.

  4a. Data is not available for default zoom level and system displays map at next highest available zoom level.

- **Special Requirements:**

  This portion of the application must be accessible (508 compliant).

Now that we've had a chance to see the structure of a formal use case, we'll next look at how to start writing these use cases for an application.

Forming Use Cases

Now that you've seen how to write a use case, it follows that you'll want to know how to start forming these use cases. For example, what level of granularity is appropriate? Should you have ten uses cases or a hundred? The answer to these questions is subjective. There is no one correct set of use cases for an application. However, you will likely find the following guidelines to be helpful:

1. Determine the types of users. An application can have many types of users. Each user will have different use cases. A simple example is one in which an application has a standard, anonymous user type and an administrative user type. The administrative user typically expects additional features that are not enabled for standard users. Your application might have additional tiers of users as well. For example, in addition to standard and administrative users, your application might have registered users who have access to features not available to standard users.

2. Determine the basic goals each type of user can achieve. For example, all users might be able to generate maps, but only registered users can save maps. Additionally, only administrative users might be able to view the logs and analytics for the application.

3. Fill out each use case with the appropriate sections.

4. Evaluate the use cases. It's important that you take your time with the use cases to make sure they are correct and appropriate before moving to the design phase. Getting the use cases correct helps ensure the best possible result of the design and implementation phases. It's much easier to make changes to the use cases before you've designed or implemented the application than to revise them afterward and have to redesign and re-implement the application.

Using UML in Analysis

UML (Unified Modeling Language) is a language in common use for modeling applications. Although UML is perhaps most frequently used during the design phase (as we'll see in the next section) it is not uncommon to use UML during analysis as well. One of the three parts of a system model in UML is what's called the functional model. The functional model allows you to create use case diagrams, which can be very helpful. UML use case diagrams generally are not detailed enough to be used apart from written use cases. However, they are often a nice addition to written use cases as they provide a visual representation of the uses cases, actors, and systems. Figure 1.1 illustrates actors and uses cases for a common system, a store.

Figure 1.1

An example of use cases in UML.

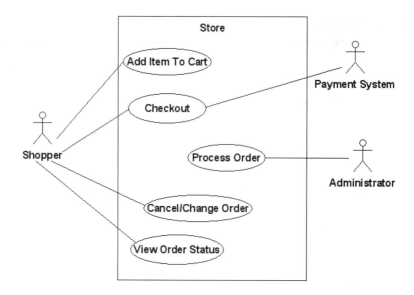

The Design Phase

After you've completed the analysis phase of an application, you have a map for what the application is supposed to do. However, that map is at such a high level that you cannot use it to begin writing code. The result of the analysis phase may be a map, but it doesn't tell you how you're going to get from point a to point b. For example, are you going to walk, drive, fly, or take the train? For that you need the next step, which we call the design phase.

In the design phase, you take the functional requirements documentation from the analysis phase and start to look at it from an architectural standpoint—looking to identify subsystems and eventually classes. During the design phase you'll parse out the elements that should be written as classes. Then you determine the responsibilities for those classes as well as the relationships between the classes.

The goal of the design phase is to generate some sort of technical document that provides a blueprint of the application you intend to build, including all the specific subsystems and classes that you will use and the relationships between them. You should expect to use this technical document to help you break up the application development into individual tasks. You should also expect that the technical document clearly identifies dependencies and collaborations between classes.

As with the analysis phase, the design phase has no rule dictating what techniques and tools you must employ. There are many ways that different people approach the design phase, and we encourage you to find the one that works best for you. However, we have found that class responsibility and collaboration (CRC) cards are a technique that proves very helpful in the design phase. In the next section we'll discuss CRC cards in more detail.

Introducing CRC Cards

CRC cards are a low-tech, yet very effective, way to determine exactly what classes you need to write, what those classes need to be able to do, and how those classes relate.

Typically, you'll find that 3x5 or 4x6 lined index cards work best as CRC cards. At the top of the index card, write the name of the class. On the left side of the index card, list the responsibilities for the class. On the right side of the card, list the classes with which the class needs to collaborate to accomplish those responsibilities. Figure 1.2 illustrates the format for a CRC card.

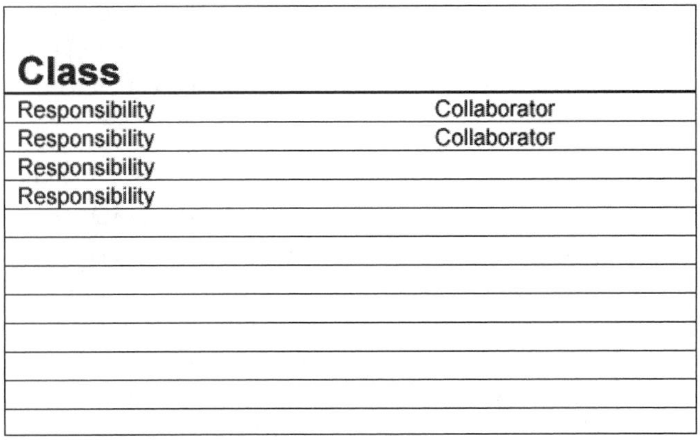

Figure 1.2

The typical format for a CRC card.

Class	
Responsibility	Collaborator
Responsibility	Collaborator
Responsibility	
Responsibility	

CRC cards are useful because you can draw them up quickly and make changes just as quickly. Using CRC cards, you can rapidly map out the functionality of an application; when you decide to split a single class into two classes, combine two classes, or change a class name, you can do that with your CRC cards in a few seconds. You can also sit around a table with a team and work together on the cards.

Now that you know the format of CRC cards, you'll undoubtedly have a few questions regarding how to decide what constitutes a *class*, what *responsibilities* are, how to know what classes are *collaborators*, and so forth. The next few sections address each of these questions.

Determining Classes

Deciding what constitutes a class is as much an art as it is a science. Just as every painter has different ideas about composition, use of color, and so on, so too does every application designer have different ideas about how to build an application. However, you'll likely find certain guidelines helpful when you try to determine what classes your application needs.

It's often a good idea to look at your use cases to find classes. Classes are nouns. You can scan use cases for all the significant nouns and use those as classes in your application. For example, consider the Generate Map use case we described earlier in this chapter. From that use case we can easily identify these relevant nouns which are natural candidates for classes: "address form," "address data," "mapping service," "map data," and "map."

When you have selected all the candidates for classes, write them down on your CRC index cards. The next step is to determine the responsibilities for each class.

Determining Class Responsibilities

After you've decided on the initial candidates for classes, you can assign responsibilities to those classes. Assigning responsibilities is an important step because it helps you determine the viability of the class candidate. If a class candidate doesn't have any responsibilities, it must be unnecessary, and you can discard it. If the candidate seems to have too many responsibilities, it probably needs to be divided into two or more classes. There are some schools of thought that state that a class should have no more than one responsibility. While we respect that standpoint, we find it to be severe. A general rule of thumb that we use is that a class should have between one and three responsibilities.

It's important to understand what a responsibility is (and what it is not). A responsibility is essentially what a class (or an instance of the class) should be able to do or facilitate. Although there is a relationship between a class's methods and its responsibilities, they are not identical. You should not think of a class's responsibilities in terms of methods or method names. A class may require many methods to accomplish just one responsibility. At this point in the design, it's too early to map out the actual methods. Responsibilities are higher-level abstractions than methods.

A responsibility is usually something that can be written out in plain language in a few words. The following are examples of possible class responsibilities:

- Create user input form

- Validate user input

- Encapsulate data model for a map

- Handle requests and responses to and from server-side service

- Draw vector map from data model

As you work on determining the responsibilities for the classes in your application, you will most likely drop classes, add classes, and change existing classes. These revisions are a desirable part of the process, which result in a well-considered design.

Although you *can* go through each class candidate and try to think of the responsibilities each class might have, that approach can be problematic. It encourages you to add responsibilities based on what you think the class candidate *ought to do* rather than based on what *the application requires*. A better approach is to scan the use cases for verbs—both explicit and implicit verbs. Explicit verbs are obvious because they are written in the use case steps. Implicit verbs are the verbs that are not written in the steps but are necessary for the successful completion of a step.

Determining Collaborators

Many, if not most, classes cannot fulfill all their responsibilities on their own. They must rely on other classes to assist them. The assisting classes are called *collaborators*. Collaborators generally lend a hand either by providing data or by enabling the class to offload functionality.

After you have defined classes and class responsibilities, the next step in the design phase is to determine what each class's collaborators are. This is extremely helpful in finding additional classes that you hadn't previously thought of. For example, consider a Map class whose responsibilities include drawing a vector map based on a data model. It might be immediately obvious that in such a case a MapData class would be a collaborator since Map would want to query MapData for the data needed to draw the map. Locating collaborators is useful for us in terms of determining relationships between existing classes. In this case, because we likely already have a CRC card for the MapData class – derived from the "map data" noun we spotted in the use cases – this collaborator did not help us find a new class. However, when we think about the Map class still more, we'll probably realize that drawing all the different types of elements on a map would probably be far too much for the Map class itself to handle. Instead we can rely on collaborators that draw the specific map elements, and we realize that these collaborators become new classes we missed before: Street, Highway, River, and CityMarker.

Elaborating on Relationships Between Classes

Classes have relationships with one another. When finding collaborating classes, you are finding the classes that have relationships. However, it's possible and necessary to determine what type of relationship these collaborating classes have. Although every relationship between classes will be unique, it is possible to generalize those relationships into the following categories:

- Association
- Aggregation
- Inheritance

Association and aggregation are types of relationships that can more generally be called composition. Later in this chapter (in the section titled, "Inheritance and Composition"), we'll compare and contrast the generalized principals of composition and inheritance as they apply to implementation.

The Association Relationship

Association is the weakest of these relationships. Association relationships are also sometimes called dependency relationships. When two classes are related in this way, one of the classes relies on its collaborator to help with one or more of its responsibilities.

An example of an association relationship is the relationship between a Map and a MapData class. The Map class has a dependency on the MapData class. Without a MapData instance, a Map object wouldn't be able to draw the map.

Associations are perhaps the most common sort of relationship between classes. You can think of associations as "uses" relationships, meaning that Map "uses" MapData.

The Aggregation Relationship

Aggregation is a stronger form of composition relationship than the association relationship. When classes are related by aggregation, the life cycles of the classes are linked. When classes are related by association, one class instance can be created or destroyed without necessarily affecting the other. However, when classes are related by aggregation, it implies that one class is the owner of the collaborator class. If the owner class is destroyed, so too are the aggregate collaborator classes.

An example of an aggregation relationship is that of the Map and Street classes. You can think of aggregations as "has a" relationships, meaning that Map "has a" Street. That doesn't mean that all Street objects are owned by Map objects. But this relationship does state that Map objects can have Street objects, and when the Map object is destroyed, so too are the Street objects it owns.

The Inheritance Relationship

Inheritance is the strongest sort of relationship between classes. When a class inherits from an existing class, it initially looks exactly like the class from which it inherits. The entire interface and implementation (more on these topics in the next chapter) of the existing class (what we call the *superclass* or *base class*) are passed down to the new class (what we call the *subclass*.) The relationship is so strong between superclasses and subclasses that subclass instances can even stand in for superclass instances in many cases. Because of the strength of inheritance relationships we say that inheritance defines an "is a" relationship such that the subclass "is a" superclass.

Inheritance relationships allow you to create abstractions that are shared by many similar classes. For example, Street, Highway, River, and CityMarker are all types of map elements. If all the classes share common interfaces and implementations, these classes might have a lot of duplicate and redundant code. You can abstract that code by placing it into a new MapElement class. Street, Highway, River, and CityMarker can then all inherit from the MapElement class. They will automatically inherit the interface and implementation from MapElement, which will remove the need to repeat that code in each of the subclasses. It also means that you can begin to use *polymorphism*. Although we'll talk about this topic in more detail in the next chapter, the idea behind polymorphism is that a more specific type can substitute for a more general type. In other words, the Map class can have an aggregation relationship with MapElement rather than having aggregation relationships with Street, Highway, River, and CityMarker. That distinction is very important because if you later wanted to add a Bridge class, you could simply define it such that it inherits from MapElement, and the Map object would automatically work with Bridge objects without your having to rewrite any of the Map code.

Although inheritance relationships are very powerful, they also tend to create very rigid relationships. Inheritance has its place and deserves credit for all that it can do. However, so much emphasis has been placed on inheritance relationships in many programming communities that it is often overused and misused. Inheritance relationships should generally be the least frequent type of relationships in your applications. Inheritance enables polymorphism, which is extremely valuable. However, inheritance is not the only way to enable polymorphism, as you'll read in the next chapter. We'll compare and contrast inheritance with composition relationships in the "Inheritance and Composition" section later in this chapter.

Formalizing Public APIs

By this point, you've decided on the classes your application requires as well as the responsibilities of each class, the class collaborators, and the relationships each class has with those collaborators. Although you might be anxious to start coding right now, there are still some steps to complete in the design phase.

The next step is to formalize the public APIs (Application Programming Interface, which means the public methods) of the classes.

Formalizing the API for a class is a matter of translating the responsibilities into method signatures. Not all responsibilities necessarily translate into public methods because some of what a class is responsible for might be private. For example, the AddressForm class might have a responsibility to validate user input. That is probably not something that translates into a public method. Rather, it is far more likely that this responsibility is handled internally by the class when the user clicks a button. However, some class responsibilities might translate into several public methods. For example, in the case of our map example, the responsibility "handle request and responses to and from server-side service" might translate into the following methods (depending on the application requirements):

```
function getMapDataForAddress(address:AddressData):void;
function getSavedMapData(id:uint):void;
```

NOTE

In the preceding example, the two methods are purely based on speculation as to what sorts of methods such an application might require for a server-side service proxy (often called a remote proxy). Furthermore, both methods are declared with void return types because the assumption is that the class is a proxy to a server-side service that works asynchronously with Flash Player, and responses will be handled by event listeners.

Using UML for Design

We first mentioned UML in relation to analysis. However, one of the most common uses of UML is during the design phase because you can use UML class diagrams to visually represent all the classes, their APIs, and the relationships between the classes. UML class diagrams are really useful because they allow you to look at all the classes and there relationships all at one time in a relatively succinct format. Usually a UML class diagram doesn't replace the need for technical documentation. However, UML class diagrams can often supplement technical documentation and serve as a useful tool both during the design phase as well as during the implementation phase when you must actually write all the classes shown in a UML class diagram. Figure 1.3 shows a very simple UML class diagram that shows two classes and an interface.

Figure 1.3

A simple UML class diagram.

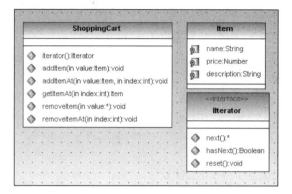

Note that this figure shows only public class members, yet you can also represent private and protected members.

Not only does UML provide a nice way to visualize the classes used by an application, but it also provides the possibility to export stub code for all the necessary classes and interfaces. At the time of this writing there is no known ActionScript 3.0 stub code generator for UML. However, since this is a common feature for many other languages (Java, C#, etc.) it is reasonable to think that there will be an ActionScript 3.0 generator for UML in the near future.

The Implementation Phase

Following the design phase is the implementation phase. In the implementation phase, you actually write the code you have planned out. If you've had successful analysis and design phases, the implementation of your application should be relatively straightforward—simply a matter of coloring in the lines, so to speak. By the time you get to the implementation phase, you should already have decided on the classes, their relationships, their responsibilities, and their APIs.

Much of the implementation phase simply involves writing ActionScript code, and as the one step you can't skip, it is the phase with which everyone is familiar. As such, we're not going to focus on the details of how to write classes. However, there are several topics that bear further discussion, namely:

- Coding conventions
- Encapsulation
- Composition and inheritance
- Coupling

Coding Conventions

There are few rules for naming classes, packages, variables, functions, and interfaces in Action-Script. In each case, you can use only letters, numbers, dollar signs ($), and underscores (_) and the first character must not be a number. Although the rules are few, there are still conventions for naming that you might find useful. At the very least, you will find it useful to know what conventions we use in this book. You should know that the conventions we use aren't the only conventions, and you aren't obligated to use them. We introduce this topic here because consistent and conscious coding conventions are a boon to application development. By applying conventions consistently you can expect to write code that is easily read by you and anyone else during team development. Remember that classes can involve hundreds of lines of code, and using consistent conventions helps you to more quickly identify parts of the code and their purposes.

Variables and Functions

For variables, it is a convention to use initial lowercase letters. Consider this example:

```
var city:Map;
```

Generally, it is advisable to use as the name words and phrases that describe the variable. For example, `city` is probably a much better name for a `Map` variable than `m` would be. Often times, it's possible to more accurately describe a variable using several words. In such cases, the convention is to use a style called camel case (sometimes called inter caps) in which the first letter of each word (except the first) is capitalized, as in this example:

```
var cityMap:Map;
```

Class properties are special sorts of variables, and as such they use the same naming convention as variables. However, to better distinguish between local variables and class properties, it is a convention to name all private properties with an initial underscore, as in this example:

```
private var _cityMap:Map;
```

NOTE

The issue of underscores for private properties is a contentious one among developers. It is our preference to use underscores as we feel they help clearly differentiate between private properties and local variables. However, some developers will argue vehemently against the use of underscores as they feel there is no significant benefit in their use.

Functions (and methods) also follow the same naming conventions as variables. Function names should start with lowercase letters and use camel case formatting when the function name consists of more than one word. Consider this example:

```
public function getMapDataForAddress(address:AddressData):void;
```

Parameters are also special variables, and as such they use the same naming conventions as variables, as you can see in the preceding example.

Unlike private properties it is not common to use underscores for private methods. The logic behind this is that a method is not generally defined within another method as a local variable might be defined within a method. Therefore, it's always clear that a method is a method without having to use underscores.

NOTE

> The variable and function/method naming conventions presented here are not intended to be comprehensive of all possible naming conventions. Many developers like to use additional conventions such as using variable prefixes to denote type. We are presenting the conventions that we find useful and that we use in this book. You are always welcome to use whatever conventions you find helpful.

Constants

Constants are special types of fields; you can define them with a value, but you cannot change the value subsequently. You've likely seen many constants in the Flash Player events API such as `Event.COMPLETE` and `MouseEvent.CLICK`. As you can see, constants use all uppercase characters by convention. If a constant name uses more than one word, the words are delimited by an underscore, as in `MouseEvent.MOUSE_MOVE`.

NOTE

> Constants are a new feature in ActionScript 3.0.

Classes and Interfaces

By convention, class names always start with an uppercase character. Class names also use camel case when necessary. In addition, class names should always be nouns.

Interfaces use the same naming conventions as classes except that they have one additional convention: Interface names always start with the letter *I* (meaning interface.) Additionally, interfaces do not always have to use nouns as names. Although it's not uncommon to name an interface with a noun (e.g. `ICollection`) it's equally common to use an adjective ending in -able. For example, the Flash Player API includes the following ActionScript 3.0 interfaces: `IExternalizable` and `IBitmapDrawable`.

Packages

For the most part, package names follow the same conventions as variables: They start with lowercase letters. There are two schools of thought regarding the use of camel case in package names. One group uses camel case while the other group uses exclusively lowercase characters in package names. In this book we do not employ camel case in package names.

There's yet another important convention when it comes to package names. One of the functions of packages is to ensure that classes exist within unique namespaces. For example, two classes called `Example` cannot be created in the same package, but may exist in two separate packages. When you decide on package names, try to ensure that the package name guarantees uniqueness. That way, if you happen to use your `Example` class in a project with an `Example` class from an existing library, the two classes can coexist.

By convention, package names can guarantee uniqueness by using subpackages in order of descending order of specificity. When a class is part of a library belonging to a company or organization, the convention is to name the packages starting with the organization's domain name in reverse order. The first part of most package names is the top-level domain such as `com` or `org`. The second part of most package names is the domain such as `google` or `amazon`. If the classes are specific to a project, the project name follows the company's domain name. The classes themselves are generally placed in subpackages that group them by classification. For example, utility classes might go in a `utils` subpackage and service proxy classes might go in a `services` package. As an example, imagine that you're writing a class called `LoggingService` that is specific to a project with a code name of JediKnight for your company called ExampleCompany (with a domain name of examplecompany.com.) You might place that class in the following package:

```
com.examplecompany.jediknight.services
```

Encapsulation

One of the rules of good object-oriented design is that all classes should be black boxes: you can put things in and take things out, but you can't determine how it operates. In other words, the only way to interact with a class instance is to use its public methods. You should never be able to look into an object or change the object's state except by asking the object to tell you about itself or to change its own state. The object must always maintain sovereignty. The minute an object is no longer in charge of its own internal world, the entire object-oriented universe starts to crumble and fall apart into an unmanageable train wreck.

This idea of classes being black boxes is a fundamental principle of object-oriented design called encapsulation. Encapsulation is absolutely necessary for an object-oriented design to succeed because it enables objects to interact with one another in known and well-defined ways. This approach models the world in which we live in many ways. Every object in the physical world has boundaries that define it and its interface with the world around it. Your body interacts with the air by way of respiration, for example. Without these well-defined interfaces there would be chaos, and it would be impossible to interact with anything in a useful or meaningful way.

Implementing classes so that they adhere to the principle of encapsulation is quite simple. To achieve this goal, there are just two basic rules:

1. Don't use any public properties.

2. Don't reference objects outside the class unless the reference was passed to the class as a parameter.

Public Properties

Properties store an object's state. As we've already said, an object must be in control of its own state. Public properties allow other objects to directly change an object's state without the object being in control. The implications of this can be far-reaching, but we can see the problem with a simple example. Consider a Student class that models a student at a school. One of the fields that comprise a Student object's state is the GPA (grade point average). It might seem like a good idea to simply define the class with a public gpa property. However, consider that GPAs are generally constrained to a specific range of values (0 to 4, for example). With a public property, there's no way for the application to guarantee that a student's GPA will always be in the valid range. If the property is public, you can simply set the value to any numeric value regardless of whether or not it is within the valid range, as this example does:

```
student.gpa = 400;
```

As if that wasn't bad enough, there are further ramifications. What if there are other collaborating objects that must be updated with a student's GPA changes? For example, a SchoolRecord object might need to know when a GPA changes in general, and a Parent object might need to know when the GPA drops below or raises above a certain level. If the Student object doesn't even know when its own state changes, it can not very well notify other objects when its state changes.

The solution to public properties is to use private properties with accessor methods. In Action-Script, we call the accessor methods getter and setter methods, and ActionScript enables two types of getters and setters: explicit and implicit. An explicit getter or setter is a normal method, typically using the word get or set in the name of the method. For example, rather than declaring a public gpa property, you can declare a private _gpa property and then use methods called getGPA() and setGPA(). Consider this example:

```
public function getGPA():Number {
   return _gpa;
}
public function setGPA(value:Number):void {
   if(value > 4) {
      _gpa = 4;
   }
   else if(value < 0) {
      _gpa = 0;
   }
   else {
      _gpa = value;
   }
   dispatchEvent(new Event(Event.CHANGE));
}
```

Notice that the setter method uses boundary testing to verify that the value is always in the valid range between 0 and 4. This example simply corrects values outside the valid range, but another implementation might throw an error. The method also dispatches an event that can notify listeners (such as a SchoolRecord or Parent object). When you want to set the GPA for a student, you can simply call the setGPA() method and pass it the value, as shown here:

```
student.setGPA(4);
```

When you want to retrieve the value you can call `getGPA()`, as in this example:

```
textfield.text = "GPA: " + student.getGPA();
```

Implicit getters and setters are similar to explicit getters and setters. In fact, the implementation of implicit methods can look almost identical to that for explicit getters and setters. The difference is that implicit getters and setters are defined as methods, but they look like properties when used. The syntax for implicit getters and setters uses the keywords `get` and `set` after the function keyword. The following example rewrites the preceding explicit methods as implicit methods:

```
public function get gpa():Number {
   return _gpa;
}
public function set gpa(value:Number):void {
   if(value > 4) {
      _gpa = 4;
   }
   else if(value < 0) {
      _gpa = 0;
   }
   else {
      _gpa = value;
   }
   dispatchEvent(new Event(Event.CHANGE));
}
```

When you want to call the implicit setter method, you use it as part of an assignment statement. The value you assign to the "property" is passed to the setter method, like this:

```
student.gpa = 4;
```

You can call the getter method when you reference the "property" in a context that attempts to read the value, as shown here:

```
textfield.text = "GPA: " + student.gpa;
```

External References

A class should never directly reference any object that is outside of itself unless it obtains that reference through its public interface. A class *can* declare private properties and local variables and can reference those objects internally because they exist within the class. A class can also reference an outside object if the reference was passed into it via a public method. For example, a `Student` class might define a method called `attendClass()` that accepts an `AcademicClass` parameter. The `Student` object can then reference that object because it was passed in as part of a method call.

```
public class Student {

   public function _classes:Array;

   public function Student() {
      _classes = new Array();
   }

   public function attendClass(class:AcademicClass):void {
```

```
            _classes.push(class);
            // Now that the class was passed in as a parameter the
            // Student instance can store that reference in the array
            // and use it later. This doesn't break encapsulation
            // because the reference was passed in via the public API.
        }

        // Remainder of implmentation.

    }
```

Designing for Encapsulation

Encapsulation is an extremely important principle, and it can have far-reaching consequences. Consider a School class that has a private property called _students, an array of all the students who attend the school. If you need to make the students available to collaborators with the School object (for example, a SchoolDistrict class might need to know about all the students at all the schools in the district), you can make the array accessible using a getter method, as shown here:

```
public function get students():Array {
    return _students;
}
```

Even though you aren't using a public property, the design in this example breaks the principle of encapsulation. Consider what happens when you retrieve the _students array and make changes to it directly:

```
school.students.splice(10, 5);
```

The preceding code removes five students from a school, but the school never receives notification about the removal of the students. That is obviously not the behavior you would want (a school should always know when students have been removed). You can address this issue in several ways. One way is to simply return a copy rather than a reference, as shown here:

```
public function get students():Array {
    return _students.concat();
}
```

Another solution is to employ the Iterator pattern (described in Chapter 7, "Iterator Pattern"). Regardless of which solution you use, you are solving the design flaw that broke the principle of encapsulation.

Most design patterns are solutions to problems relating to encapsulation. In many cases, encapsulation might appear to be in direct opposition to other important design principles. For example, many applications need to have globally accessible objects of specific types. An application might need a globally accessible User object that represents the current user of the application. As we've already discussed, it would break encapsulation if all the other classes in the application had hard-coded references to that one specific User object. However, using the Singleton pattern (described in Chapter 4), you can achieve the goal of a globally accessible object without having to directly reference a specific object.

Inheritance and Composition

One class can leverage the functionality of another class in one of two basic ways: inheritance or composition. Both are powerful techniques. Inheritance allows you to define a new class so that it automatically gets the interface and implementation of an existing class. The following code declares a class called `Employee`:

```
public class Employee {
   public function Employee() {}
   public function work():void {
      trace("working");
   }
}
```

The new class, which we call the subclass, can build on the foundation of the existing class, which we call the superclass or base class, without needing to rewrite the original code or write any new code to use the superclass code. There are different types of employees, and we can define different subtypes by inheriting from the `Employee` superclass. For example, the following `Executive` class inherits from `Employee` by using the `extends` keyword:

```
public class Executive extends Employee {
   public function Executive() {}
   public function attendMeeting():void {
      trace("attending meeting");
   }
}
```

Furthermore, inheritance automatically enables polymorphism because the subclass inherits the interface of the superclass. That means that an `Executive` object is also an `Employee`…just a more specific type. An `Executive` object can be used any time an `Employee` object is expected although the reverse is not true:—an `Employee` object cannot stand in for an `Executive` object. Note that the `Executive` class defines another method called `attendMeeting()`. Because `Executive` objects inherit from the `Employee` superclass, you can call the `work()` method for an `Executive` and you can also call the `attendMeeting()` method which is specific to `Executive`.

In contrast with inheritance, composition allows you to write a new class (a front-end class) that has an instance of an existing class (the back-end class). Every time you define a class with a property whose type is another class, you are using composition in some sense. The following example is a rewrite of the `Executive` class example just shown so that it uses composition rather than inheritance:

```
public class Executive {
   private var _employee:Employee;
   public function Executive() {}
   public function attendMeeting():void {
      trace("attend meeting");
   }
   public function work():void {
      _employee.work();
   }
}
```

When you use composition, the new (front-end) class does not automatically inherit the interface of the existing (back-end) class. The front-end class can use the back-end class instance only by way of its public interface. If the front-end class needs to have part or all of the same interface as the back-end class, you must write code that defines the interface as well as its implementation. That is the reason that this rewrite of the Executive class has to define a work() method. Unlike the example that used inheritance, the composition version of the Executive class does not inherit the work() method. If you want the work() method to be part of the Executive interface, you must define it. The preceding example uses a technique called delegation to pass along the method call to the composed object.

Because a class that composes an instance of another class does not automatically inherit the object's interface, composition does not automatically enable polymorphism. In other words, using composition, an Executive object is not an Employee, and it cannot stand in for an Employee. (The solution to this issue is to use interface constructs as discussed earlier in this chapter.)

In reading the preceding paragraphs, you might think that inheritance sounds like a much better technique for reusing existing functionality. It sounds like composition requires much more work with little or no advantage. Yet both inheritance and composition have their advantages and disadvantages.

Advantages and Disadvantages of Inheritance

As you've seen already, inheritance has the following advantages:

- Simplicity of use: Inheritance is a concept built into the language. All you have to do is use the extends keyword in order to define one class so that it inherits both the interface and the implementation of an existing class.

- Ability to change inherited implementation: By using the overrides keyword, you can change the implementation inherited for a particular method.

Yet inheritance also has its disadvantages:

- Implementations are fixed at compile-time: For example, if a Chart3D class inherits from the BarChart class, then it's impossible at runtime to apply the 3D functionality to a LineGraph object.

- Supports weak encapsulation and fragile structures: Subclasses have privileged access to a superclass's implementation. Anything that is marked as public, internal, or protected is accessible to a subclass. This means that encapsulation is weak in inheritance relationships. Because of this, it's possible that a change to a superclass implementation could break subclasses even if the public interface does not change.

- Superclass interface changes necessarily change subclasses: If you change the signature of a superclass method the change will ripple to all subclasses.

- ActionScript allows a class to inherit directly from just one class (as opposed to multiple inheritance, a concept utilized by very few languages): Suppose that all `Executive` objects share the functionality of both `Employee` and `DecisionMaker` classes. ActionScript allows `Executive` to inherit from just one of those classes, not both.

Advantages and Disadvantages of Composition

Although we haven't yet mentioned the advantages of composition, they are numerous. Some of the most prominent advantages are as follows:

- Implementations are configurable at runtime: For example, if a `Chart3D` class operates on an object typed as `Chart` (of which there are many subtypes such as `BarChart` and `LineGraph`), the `Chart3D` class can operate on any of those subtypes. The specific subtype can be set at runtime.

- Supports good encapsulation and adaptable structures: Classes that use composition are forced to go through the back-end class public interfaces. That means that they enforce good encapsulation. That also means that changes in implementation of the back-end classes are less likely to break classes that use them. As long as the interface remains the same, the front-end classes won't break.

- Interface changes have limited ripple effect: When the interface of a back-end class changes, it will break front-end classes that rely on the old version of the interface. However, the damage is contained and generally fairly trivial to correct. Because interfaces are not inherited when using composition, the changes affect only the front-end class, but not classes that in turn compose instances of the front-end class. In other words, if `Executive` is a front-end class for `Employee` and the interface for `Employee` changes, you will most likely have to make changes to `Executive`. However, the interface for `Executive` does not change. That means that if a `Company` class composes an `Executive` object, the `Company` class does not have to change.

- Composition allows a front-end class to have relationships with many back-end classes: Using composition, an `Executive` class can have both an `Employee` and a `DecisionMaker` property.

Yet composition is not without its disadvantages:

- Frequently requires more code than inheritance: If a front-end class needs to use some or all of a back-end class's interface, it must re-create it.

- Often more difficult to read than inheritance: Inheritance establishes a very straightforward relationship. Composition is often less direct and presents a trail that's more difficult to follow if you're not familiar with the code.

Which to Use: Inheritance or Composition

Generally, the rule of thumb is to favor object composition over inheritance. The advantages of object composition outnumber the disadvantages. Furthermore, the disadvantages of composition are not obstacles as much as they are simply inconveniences. Because inheritance is so much more straightforward, it's a lot easier to teach and learn in many cases, and it tends to be overemphasized and overused by many people in the ActionScript development community. For this reason, it's often beneficial for ActionScript developers to determine whether composition is the best option for establishing a relationship between classes.

With that said, it's also worth noting that with the surge of interest in object-oriented design and design patterns in the ActionScript community, inheritance has been maligned in many circles. It's important to understand several things about this conflict:

- Inheritance is not wrong: Just because you should favor composition does not mean that inheritance is never appropriate. Inheritance is a better solution in some cases. It's difficult to make rules that tell you when to use inheritance and when to use composition. However, as a general guideline, it's advisable to use inheritance in the following situations: When a new class really does define a subtype of an existing class, when the new class is not likely to have subclasses itself (limiting inheritance chains keeps some of the disadvantages of inheritance at bay), when the new class would benefit greatly by inheriting part of the existing class's implementation that is hidden from the public, and when the new class does not have special requirements (for example, it needs to be adaptable to significant changes at runtime).

- Inheritance and composition are not competitors: Although it is true that in almost all cases two classes will be related by either inheritance or composition (and not both), that does not mean that these two types of relationships can not work together. In fact, most classes that use inheritance also use composition.

Conventional teaching says that to determine whether two classes should be related by inheritance or composition, you should use the "is a/has a" test. The "is a/has a" test says that you should answer the following question: Is (new class) a (existing class) or does (new class) have a (existing class)? If the new class *is a* more specific version of the existing class, the relationship is inheritance. If the new class simply *has an* instance of the existing class as a property, the relationship is composition. Although that guideline can be useful, it is not definitive. Consider an example using an existing class called Student and a new class called School. If we ask whether School *is a* Student, the answer is obvious: a School is not a Student. Therefore, the relationship must be composition, not inheritance. Yet just because we can answer that a new class is a more specific version of an existing class doesn't mean that the relationship should necessarily be inheritance. For example, consider the relationship between a HighSchool class and a School class. If you use only the "is a/has a" test, you might determine that a HighSchool is a School and therefore the relationship is inheritance. Yet consider what happens if you need to have a HighSchool object that uses experimental administration structure and teaching techniques. We can assume that the implementation for School deals with traditional school systems and infrastructure and would not meet the needs of an experimental school. An inheritance relationship between School and HighSchool is rigid. If you use composition to define the relationship, it's possible to create an experimental high school type at compile type by substituting an ExperimentalSchool instance for the School property of a HighSchool object.

Coupling

Coupling refers to the degree to which two objects must know about one another. When the objects have to know a great deal about one another to work, we call that tight coupling; when they have to know little to nothing about one another, we call that loose coupling. In object-oriented design, we generally strive to have loose coupling among the objects in the system. Loose coupling creates flexible and adaptable systems. If objects are tightly coupled, the system is rigid—one change in one object can cascade and break the entire system. If objects are loosely coupled, changes are much less likely to break things, and even when changes do cause malfunctions, the malfunctions are generally contained.

Many design patterns aim to create loosely coupled systems. For example, if an object needs to ask another object to run a behavior, the traditional way to accomplish this goal is for the object to have a reference to the collaborator and to call a method of that collaborator. That way of structuring an application uses tight coupling because the calling object has to have a reference to the collaborator and it has to know the signature of the method it wants to call. It's difficult to make changes to that structure. The Command pattern described in Chapter 10 addresses this issue by completely decoupling the objects. The Command pattern adds an intermediary layer that parameterizes the behavior and allows the calling object to simply have a reference to the intermediary object and know about a standard interface. This is just one example of how design patterns can promote loose coupling or decoupling, and you'll see many more examples throughout the book as you read about each of the patterns.

Testing

Once you've completed the implementation phase the next important phase you need to consider is the testing phase. Generally testing involves a quality assurance (QA) group that runs test cases to determine that the application behaves as expected and to try to catch any bugs. This testing phase is iterative. When QA returns a list of bugs the development team must work to fix any issues. However, when fixings bugs it's possible to introduce new bugs. If you have architected the application well, favoring composition over inheritance for building flexible structures, then the risk of introducing new bugs during this phase is minimized. However, it's is almost inevitable that some new bugs will be introduced during bug fixing and old fixed bugs will re-emerge. Because of the possibility of this introduction and re-introduction of bugs testing generally involves something called regression testing—which basically means all tests that previously passed must be run again to ensure that changes didn't cause any of those tests to suddenly fail.

As you might imagine the introduction and re-introduction of bugs can be quite expensive during the testing phase if they go uncaught until the build is regression tested by a QA team. If a bug isn't caught until QA runs a regression test then it means that the development team must fix the bugs again and send yet another build to QA for regression testing.

If possible it's always best for developers to try to find new bugs and regressions before sending the build to QA. The difficulty with that strategy is that it requires the development team to be responsible for testing the application. If developers could handle testing in addition to develop-ment and bug fixes then there wouldn't be a need for a QA team in the first place, so it might almost seem ridiculous to suggest that developers should have to test an application. However, if developers can run automated tests that verify that an application continues to work correctly from a programmatic standpoint then that doesn't require a great deal more work on the part of the developer, and it enables developers to quickly identify errors before sending a build to QA. These programmatic tests are can be formalized into what is called a *unit test*.

Unit testing allows the developer to create programmatic tests that ensure that parts of the application behave in an expected way. For example, if you have a method that's supposed to convert a parameter value from radians to degrees and return that value then you want to make sure that if you pass it a value of `Math.PI` it returns 180 every time. Using this basic concept you can create a series of tests where you ensure that results of operations are as expected (i.e. `Math.PI` radians is always converted correctly to 180 degrees).

You can create unit tests without a formal unit test framework. However, using a formal frame-work for unit testing has several advantages. Specifically:

- When you use an existing framework you don't have to reinvent the wheel, saving you time

- An existing framework is likely to be tested so that bugs in the unit testing framework won't cause your tests to fail to work (which would negate the value of running unit tests in the first place.)

Although there may be additional unit testing frameworks for ActionScript 3.0 subsequent to the writing of this book the one existing unit testing framework we know of at this point is called FlexUnit. As the name implies, you can use FlexUnit for unit testing Flex applications. However, that doesn't mean that FlexUint is limited to unit testing applications that use the Flex framework. Even if you are working on a purely ActionScript 3.0 project you can use FlexUnit.

At the time of this writing FlexUnit is available for download at http://labs.adobe.com/wiki/index.php/ActionScript_3:resources:apis:libraries. If that URL changes you may not be able to find the downloads there. In such a case you can look to www.rightactionscript.com/aas3wdp for an updated URL.

Once you've located the correct URL you should download the archive containing the .swc file which contains the necessary FlexUnit framework libraries. You will want to extract the .swc file from the archive and then make sure that the .swc is included in the library path for your project for which you want to use unit tests.

If you want to write custom unit tests that don't rely on FlexUnit then you are welcome to do so. However, for the remainder of this section on unit testing we will be giving specific instructions for running unit tests using FlexUnit.

Creating Basic Unit Tests

In FlexUnit basic unit tests require the following elements:

- Classes you want to test. These are the classes that comprise your application.

- Test cases. Test cases are special classes that you write just for the purposes of unit testing.

- Test runner. A test runner is a class (or MXML file) that actually runs all the test cases and reports the results.

The first category of elements isn't specific to unit tests. That category is simply comprised of the classes you've already written. They are part of unit testing because you are testing that they actually work the way you expect. For the basic test cases we'll test the following class.

```
package example {
  public class SimpleConverter {
    public function SimpleConverter() {}
    public function convertToRadians(degrees:Number):Number {
      return (degrees / 180) * Math.PI;
    }
    public function convertToDegrees(radians:Number):Number {
      return (radians / Math.PI) * 180;
    }
  }
}
```

Test cases and test runners, on the other hand, are unique to unit testing. Since test cases and test runners are likely new to you we'll look at how to create them in the next sections.

Writing Test Cases

A FlexUnit test case is an instance of a class that extends flexunit.framework.TestCase. The test case class constructor should always accept a string parameter and then call the super constructor, passing it the parameter value.

```
package tests {
  import flexunit.framework.TestCase;
  public class SimpleTest extends TestCase {
    public function SimpleTest(method:String) {
      super(method);
    }
  }
}
```

The class should then define one or more methods that run a test. Each test should result in an assertion. An assertion is what actually determines the success of the test. You can run an assertion using any of the assert methods inherited by the Assert class which is the superclass of TestCase:

- assertEquals(): Tests if all the parameters are equal (equivalent to an == operation)

- assertStrictlyEquals(): Tests if all the parameters are strictly equal (equivalent to an === operation)

- `assertTrue()`: Test if the parameter is true

- `assertFalse()`: Test if the parameter is false (passes test if the parameter is false)

- `assertUndefined()`: Test if the parameter is undefined (passes test if the parameter is undefined)

- `assertNull()`: Test if the parameter is null (passes test if the parameter is null)

- `assertNotNull()`: Test if the parameter is not null

- `fail()`: Though technically not an assertion, the fail() method explicitly causes the test to fail, which can be useful when you need to test for a failure.

The following update to SimpleTest defines two test methods to test the conversions to and from degrees and radians.

```
package tests {
  import flexunit.framework.TestCase;
  import example.Simple;
  public class SimpleTest extends TestCase {
    public function SimpleTest(method:String) {
      super(method);
    }
    public function testConvert0ToDegrees():void {
      var simple:SimpleConverter = new SimpleConverter();
      var degrees:Number = simple.convertToDegrees(0);
      assertEquals(degrees, 0);
    }
    public function testConvertPIToDegrees():void {
      var simple:SimpleConverter = new SimpleConverter();
      var degrees:Number = simple.convertToDegrees(0);
      assertEquals(degrees, 180);
    }
    public function testConvert0ToRadians():void {
      var simple:SimpleConverter = new SimpleConverter();
      var radians:Number = simple.convertToRadians(0);
      assertEquals(radians, 0);
    }
    public function testConvert180ToRadians():void {
      var simple:SimpleConverter = new SimpleConverter();
      var radians:Number = simple.convertToRadians(180);
      assertEquals(radians, Math.PI);
    }
  }
}
```

Once you've created one or more test cases you next to create a test runner to run the tests and view the results.

Writing a Test Runner

Assuming you're using Flex you can use the FlexUnit test runner to run a suite of unit tests. First, you must create a runnable MXML document that does the following:

- Add the `flexunit.flexui.*` namespace

- Add an instance of `TestRunnerBase`, an MXML component

- Create a `flexunit.framework.TestSuite` instance, and add all the test cases to it.

- Assign the `TestSuite` instance to the test property of the `TestRunnerBase` instance.

  Call the `startTest()` method of the `TestRunnerBase` instance.

The following example MXML document runs all the tests from `SimpleTest`.

```
<?xml version="1.0" encoding="utf-8"?>
<!-- Notice that the Application tag adds the flexui namespace prefix and maps it
to flexunit.flexui.*. Also notice that it registers initializeHandler() as an event
handler for the initialize event.-->
<mx:Application xmlns:mx="http://www.adobe.com/2006/mxml" xmlns:flexui="flexunit.
flexui.*" initialize="initializeHandler(event)">

    <mx:Script>
      <![CDATA[
          import flexunit.framework.TestSuite;
          import tests.SimpleTest;

          private function initializeHandler(event:Event):void {
            // Create a new TestSuite object.
            var suite:TestSuite = new TestSuite();

            // Use the addTest() method to add each of
            // the four test cases to the suite.
            suite.addTest(new SimpleTest("testConvert0ToDegrees"));
            suite.addTest(new SimpleTest("testConvertPIToDegrees"));
            suite.addTest(new SimpleTest("testConvert0ToRadians"));
            suite.addTest(new SimpleTest("testConvert180ToRadians"));

            testRunner.test = suite;
            testRunner.startTest();
          }
      ]]>
    </mx:Script>
    <flexui:TestRunnerBase id="testRunner" width="100%" height="100%" />
</mx:Application>
```

Notice that each test case is an instance of `SimpleTest` with one of the test method names passed to the constructor. When you run the preceding test runner it should show all the tests as passing. If you make the following change to `SimpleConverter` you'll see that one of the tests fails.

```
package example {
  public class SimpleConverter {
    public function SimpleConverter() {}
    public function convertToRadians(degrees:Number):Number {
      return (degrees / 180) * Math.PI;
```

(CODE CONTINUED)

```
    }
    public function convertToDegrees(radians:Number):Number {
      return 0;
    }
  }
}
```

Note that since `convertToDegrees()` always returns 0 the `testConvertPIToDegrees` test will fail. Since the specific test fails you immediately know where the error is occurring, and you can fix the bug.

Another thing that can be useful when creating test cases is to add a static method to each `TestCase` subclass that returns a `TestSuite` of all the tests for that class. This allows you to simplify the test runner. The following is an example of such a method you could add to `SimpleConverter`.

```
public static function suite():TestSuite {
  var suite:TestSuite = new TestSuite();
  suite.addTest(new SimpleTest("testConvert0ToDegrees"));
  suite.addTest(new SimpleTest("testConvertPIToDegrees"));
  suite.addTest(new SimpleTest("testConvert0ToRadians"));
  suite.addTest(new SimpleTest("testConvert180ToRadians"));
  return suite;
}
```

The test runner `initializeHandler()` method would then simplify to the following:

```
private function initializeHandler(event:Event):void {
  testRunner.test = SimpleTest.suite();
  testRunner.startTest();
}
```

Creating Asynchronous Unit Tests

Many unit tests are synchronous—meaning that you can immediately determine if a test has passed or failed. For example, the `SimpleConverter` test in the preceding section passed or failed a test immediately. However, it's possible that some tests may depend on asynchronous operations. For example, a class may need to make a request and wait for a response from a service method before a test can be verified properly. In such cases it's important to be able to run tests asynchronously. For an example consider the following class which loads data from a text file when calling the `getData()` method.

```
package example {
  import flash.events.EventDispatcher;
  import flash.net.URLLoader;
  import flash.events.Event;
  import flash.net.URLRequest;

  public class AsynchronousExample extends EventDispatcher {

    private var _loader:URLLoader;

    public function get data():String {
      return _loader.data;
```

```
        }

        public function AsynchronousExample() {
            _loader = new URLLoader();
            _loader.addEventListener(Event.COMPLETE, onData);
        }

        public function getData():void {
            _loader.load(new URLRequest("data.txt"));
        }

        private function onData(event:Event):void {
            dispatchEvent(new Event(Event.COMPLETE));
        }

    }
}
```

With a few simple changes it's possible to run FlexUnit tests asynchronously so you can test operations like getData(). Asynchronous operations should use events to notify listeners when the operation has completed. Typically when you register a listener for a particular event you use the addEventListener() method, and you pass it a reference to the listener method. When writing test cases for asynchronous operations you should register a listener method to handle the event that signals a completed operation. However, rather than registering the listener directly, you should use an inherited TestCase method called addAsync(). The addAsync() method allows you to specify a listener method along with a time out in milliseconds. This allows you to specify what method should handle the event, but if the event doesn't occur within the timeout window then the test will fail. The event listener method should run the assertion. The following example uses these techniques. You'll see that the class extends TestCase just like a basic unit test. Furthermore, this test case class also accepts a method name as a parameter for the constructor, and it passes the parameter to the super constructor. What differs is that the test method registers a listener using addAsync() and defers the assertion to onData(). This example times out after 2000 milliseconds. That means that if the data loads in 2000 milliseconds or less then the assertion will run. However, if the data doesn't load in time then the test case assumes that it was due to a failure and the test fails.

```
package tests {
    import flexunit.framework.TestCase;
    import example.AsynchronousExample;
    import flash.events.Event;
    import flexunit.framework.TestSuite;

    public class AsynchronousTest extends TestCase {

        public function AsynchronousTest(method:String):void {
            super(method);
        }

        public function testGetData():void {
            var asynchronous:AsynchronousExample = new AsynchronousExample();
```

(CODE CONTINUED)

```
        asynchronous.addEventListener(Event.COMPLETE, addAsync(onData, 2000));
        asynchronous.getData();
    }

    private function onData(event:Event):void {
        assertNotNull(event.target.data);
    }

    public static function suite():TestSuite {
        var suite:TestSuite = new TestSuite();
        suite.addTest(new AsynchronousTest("testGetData"));
        return suite;
    }

    }
}
```

The following test runner will run both the simple tests and the asynchronous test.

```
<?xml version="1.0" encoding="utf-8"?>
<mx:Application xmlns:mx="http://www.adobe.com/2006/mxml" xmlns:flexui="flexunit.
flexui.*" initialize="initializeHandler(event)">

    <mx:Script>
        <![CDATA[
            import flexunit.framework.TestSuite;
            import tests.SimpleTest;
            import tests.AsynchronousTest;

            private function initializeHandler(event:Event):void {
                var suite:TestSuite = new TestSuite();
                suite.addTest(SimpleTest.suite());
                suite.addTest(AsynchronousTest.suite());
                testRunner.test = suite;
                testRunner.startTest();
            }
        ]]>
    </mx:Script>
    <flexui:TestRunnerBase id="testRunner" width="100%" height="100%" />
</mx:Application>
```

Summary

Although many people think of building applications as exclusively writing the code, in this chapter we have seen that writing code is just one of the phases of building successful applications. We've seen that one of the biggest challenges is knowing what to write, and the analysis and design phases of a project are the time to determine the answer to that question. The third phase, implementation, is the time to actually write the code. Following implementation is the testing phase which allows developers to use unit testing to ensure fewer regressions.

CHAPTER 2

Programming to Interfaces

Learning and mastering the fundamentals of object-oriented design and application development is no small feat, and you should undoubtedly congratulate yourself for all your accomplishments so far. And as you know, with every step taken yet another step presents itself. Our next step involves understanding interfaces in the context of good application design and pattern-based development. Although mastering basic object-oriented concepts enables an evolution in how you build applications, understanding interfaces can rapidly push your coding to take another evolutionary leap. After you've learned about using interfaces, the code you write may hardly resemble the code you used to write.

It may surprise you to learn that lurking within every class are at least two distinct layers which we call the interface and the implementation. Early on when you're learning how to write classes, it can be difficult to distinguish between the two layers. However, as you become more adept at writing good classes, it becomes easy to differentiate between the interface and the implementation.

Classes consist of methods and properties. As explained in the previous chapter, properties should never be defined as public. Properties are used by a class to store its state, and good encapsulation dictates that an instance of a class should always be responsible for managing its own state. As such, the only public interface that most classes define is comprised of methods. Looking at a class from the outside, you could describe it by its public methods and their signatures. In fact, you could even say that two classes look identical from the outside if they have the same method names and method signatures. In contrast, those two classes with the same method names and signatures could have vastly different implementations for those methods. This is the basic idea that enables something called *polymorphism*. Polymorphism is the idea that if you program to an interface rather than an implementation, the resultant code is much more flexible because any instance of any class that uses that interface can stand in for any other object that uses the same interface—even if the implementations are totally different.

We'll talk much more about interfaces, implementation, polymorphism, and all sorts of related topics throughout this chapter.

Defining Interfaces

As mentioned in the introduction to this chapter, classes have both an interface and an implementation. The interface is the way in which the outside world can communicate with an object. The interface simply says what methods are publicly available, what parameters those methods accept, and what, if any, types are returned by methods. The interface does not say anything at all about what a method does or how it does it. For example, the flash.net.LocalConnection and flash.net.NetConnection classes both define methods called connect() with identical signatures:

```
connect(value:String):void
```

However, notice that although that portion of the interface for both classes is identical, the actual implementations are quite different. LocalConnection objects listen for requests over a specified channel while NetConnection objects either make a connection to an RTMP server (if the parameter uses the RTMP protocol) or simply stores the parameter value for subsequent requests.

The class implementation is hidden from public view. When you call a method, you always call it by way of the interface, but the implementation is what runs. The implementation consists of the actual code that defines the internals of the method.

When you write code you can reference a class by typing variables and properties as the class. While that is not necessarily wrong, it does limit flexibility because it ties the code to a specific implementation—the concrete class. However, you can create more flexible code if you reference the interface instead. When you reference an interface rather than the implementation you don't lock the code into just one implementation. We'll talk more about this later in the chapter. For now what's important is to know that referencing interfaces rather than implementation is often a good strategy for creating flexible code, and we call this technique programming to interfaces.

When you program to an interface, you must write your classes so that they implement a formalized interface (more on what this means in a moment). This is essential for something called polymorphism, which we'll discuss shortly. To understand what a formal interface is, we can first look at what it is not. Just a moment ago, we mentioned that the LocalConnection and NetConnection classes have a common interface with the connect() method. However, that similarity is not part of a formalized interface. You can't declare a variable with an interface type that is generic enough to work for either LocalConnection or NetConnection. Rather, you must declare a variable as exactly LocalConnection or exactly NetConnection. This is an important distinction to make. Up to now we've said that all classes have both an interface and an implementation, and we've said that it's useful to be able to program to the interface rather than the implementation. However, unless we take steps to formalize an interface we cannot share that interface between more than class, which means we cannot polymorphically substitute one class for another in those cases. What we need to look at next is how to create a formal interface that is distinct from the implementation.

There are two ways to define formal interfaces: through inheritance and through explicit interface constructs. When you define an interface by either of these techniques, you can then define classes that implement the interface. This is an important concept that enables many of the design patterns discussed throughout this book. When you define a class that implements an interface, you can then declare variables of the *interface* type and assign to them instances of the *implementing* type. We'll be looking at this in much greater detail later in this chapter. First we'll look at how to define interfaces.

Interfaces Defined by Interface Constructs

ActionScript defines a formal interface construct that you can use to define interfaces. The syntax for defining an interface is very similar to that for defining a class, but it is simplified because it does not require (nor allow) you to provide any implementation. An interface construct defines only the interface. An interface consists of methods, including getters and setters. The basic syntax is as follows:

```
package package {
   public interface Interface {
      function method(parameter:Type):ReturnType;
      function get property():ReturnType;
      function set property(value:Type):void;
   }
}
```

The major differences between the syntax for a class and the syntax for an interface are that an interface uses the `interface` keyword rather than the `class` keyword and a semicolon appears after the return type for each method, instead of a code block defining the function body. Additionally, interfaces can describe only the *public* methods for implementing classes. That means that there is no need for a public/private/protected/internal modifier, and interfaces do not allow those modifiers.

NOTE

By convention, interface names start with I. For example `IExample` indicates that the type is an interface.

The following is an example of an interface called `IExample`:

```
package {
   public interface IExample {
      function sampleMethod(parameter1:String,
            parameter2:uint):void;
   }
}
```

When you want to define a class that implements the interface, you use the `implements` keyword following the name of the class. For example, the following defines class A as implementing an interface called `IExample`:

```
public class A implements IExample {
```

If the class extends a superclass, then the `implements` keyword follows the name of the superclass:

```
public class A extends SuperClass implements IExample {
```

When a class implements an interface, it essentially signs a contract that it will implement the methods defined in the interface. If the implementing class does not define the necessary methods with exactly the same signatures as described in the interface, the compiler throws an error. For example, the following class says it implements `IExample`, but it does not declare the necessary method `sampleMethod()`:

```
package {
   public class A implements IExample {
      public function A() {}
   }
}
```

Because A does not correctly define the necessary method, the compiler will throw an error. Also, if A is defined as follows, the compiler will still throw an error because although A defines `sampleMethod()`, it does not use the correct signature:

```
package {
   public class A implements IExample {
      public function A() {}
      public function sampleMethod(parameter1:String):void {
         trace("sampleMethod");
      }
   }
}
```

The compiler will approve the class only when the class correctly adheres to the contract and defines all the necessary methods with the correct signatures, as it does in this example:

```
package {
   public class A implements IExample {
      public function A() {}
      public function sampleMethod(parameter1:String,
         parameter2:uint):void {
         trace("sampleMethod");
      }
   }
}
```

It's also important to note that, unlike inheritance, you can implement more than one interface per class. To implement more than one interface, simply use a comma-delimited list. For example, the following code defines A so that it implements `IExample` and `ISample`:

```
public class A implements IExample, ISample {
```

Note that a class signs a contract for each interface it implements. It must implement all the methods for all the interfaces it implements.

Interfaces Defined by Inheritance

As we've already discussed, the basic definition of an interface is the set of public methods (including getters and setter) for a class minus the actual implementation. All classes have interfaces (though by default the interfaces are tied together with the implementation), and if you define a subclass, it automatically inherits the interface of the superclass (as well as the superclass's implementation). This means that you can use inheritance to define interfaces.

Although all classes define interfaces (and can be used as interfaces), when we talk about explicitly defining interfaces using classes, we generally use a specific type of class called an *abstract class*. An abstract class is one that is not intended for instantiation. For example, if Example is an abstract class, you would never instantiate an Example object as follows:

```
var example:Example = new Example();
```

Rather, abstract classes are designed strictly to be subclassed and to define an interface that is shared among all the subclasses. Classes that subclass abstract classes and fill in their implementations are called *concrete classes*.

Abstract classes generally have little implementation. They defer the majority of implementation to subclasses. However, if you don't intend to add any implementation whatsoever, it is advisable that you use an interface construct as discussed in the previous section, "Interfaces Defined by Interface Constructs." Abstract classes in ActionScript 3.0 are typically most appropriate when you want to define a class that formalizes an interface for a set of subclasses, but also define a minimal amount of implementation.

Some programming languages define ways in which you declare abstract classes in an explicit fashion. When you define an abstract class with those languages, safeguards prevent you from accidentally instantiating an abstract class (generally, an exception is thrown). However, ActionScript 3.0 does not have a formal abstract class concept. Rather, the responsibility falls on the developer not to attempt to instantiate a class that is conceptually abstract.

There is nothing syntactically unique to abstract classes that sets them apart from standard classes. That is good news in that you don't have to learn anything new in terms of syntax.

When you want to define a class that implements the interface, you simply subclass the abstract class or a concrete class that extends the abstract class. Again, this technique of defining interfaces doesn't require any new syntax. You can simply use standard inheritance.

Deciding How to Define an Interface

How do you decide whether to define an interface through inheritance or through an interface construct? Generally you should always start with an interface construct. By using an interface construct you create the greatest degree of flexibility. If you then decide that you need an abstract class (because you want concrete classes to be able to inherit basic implementation) you should create an abstract class that implements the interface. This way you can always program to the interface construct, and if you later need to add more classes that implement the interface but don't inherit from the abstract class you can do that.

Using Polymorphism

Polymorphism is a complex-sounding word. However, the concept it represents is not very complex now that you understand what an interface is. The basic idea of polymorphism is that any class that implements an interface looks a lot like any other class that implements that same interface; any object that implements an interface can stand in when that interface is expected.

If you haven't used interfaces up to now, chances are you haven't leveraged the power of polymorphism yet. However, once you understand polymorphism, you'll quickly see how flexible it makes your code. Here's an example. First the interface is defined as follows:

```
package {
   public interface ISearchable {
      function search(searchTerm:String):Array;
   }
}
```

Next we can define a class called Library which implements ISearchable:

```
package {
   public class Library implements ISearchable {
      private var _books:Array;
      public function Library(books:Array) {
         _books = books;
      }
      public function search(searchTerm:String):Array {
         var results:Array = new Array();
         for(var i:int = 0; i < _books.length; i++) {
            if(_books[i].title.indexOf(searchTerm) != - 1) {
               // Assume that each item in the array
               // is a custom Book type that has a
               // clone() method.
               results.push(_books[i].clone());
            }
         }
         return results;
      }
   }
}
```

We can also define a Help class that implements the ISearchable interface as well.

```
package {
   public class Help implements ISearchable {
      private var _helpIndex:Object;
      public function Help() {
         // Assume the _helpIndex is populated by data loaded
         // from an XML file, and that each item in
         // _helpIndex is an array where the key is
         // a search term.
      }
      public function search(searchTerm:String):Array {
         if(_helpIndex[searchTerm] != null) {
            return _helpIndex[searchTerm];
         }
         else {
```

```
                return new Array();
            }
        }
    }
}
```

Now, even though Library and Help are different classes with different implementations, either can be used any time ISearchable is expected. For example, the following assigns a new Library instance to searchCollection.

```
var searchCollection:ISearchable = new Library(books);
```

However, note that you can also substitute a Help instance. And furthermore, you can make that substitution at runtime.

```
searchCollection = new Help();
```

We'll next take a look at this concept in more detail.

Differentiating Between Type and Class

When you've declared a variable in the past, you most likely declared the variable so that the type was identical to the class for which you planned to instantiate an object to assign to the variable. For example, if you wanted to declare a variable to which you could assign an instance of class Vegetable, you probably declared the variable in the following fashion:

```
var item:Vegetable;
```

Although there's nothing inherently wrong with the preceding code, there is an inherent inflexibility in that way of declaring a variable. Because you've declared item as type Vegetable, you can assign to it only those objects that are instances of class Vegetable or its subclasses. Even if class Fruit has the exact same interface as class Vegtable, you cannot assign an instance of class Fruit to item when you declare item as in the preceding example.

To write more flexible code, you have to differentiate between class and type. In the preceding example, Vegetable is both a class and the type. However, there's a correspondence between a type and an interface and between a (concrete) class and an implementation. Although a concrete class defines both an interface and implementation, an interface defines just the interface. Likewise, a class is also a type, but a type does not have to be a class. Types can also be interfaces. By declaring variables with interface types, you create greater flexibility in your code. Consider the following example:

```
var item:IProduce;
```

Now that item is declared as type IProduce, we can assign to item any instance of any class that implements IProduce. We're no longer locked into one specific class. If both Fruit and Vegetable implement IProduce then you can assign an instance of either class to item now that it's typed as IProduce.

Making Runtime Decisions

When you declare a variable with a type of a concrete class, you generally are making a compile-time decision as to which implementation to use. That is okay when you know absolutely that you want to use only that one implementation. However, consider an example in which an application uses a fallback plan for network communications. According to the business rules for the application, it must first attempt to communicate using Flash Remoting/AMF. If that does not work, the application next must attempt the communication using an HTTP request that sends and retrieves XML data. And if that does not work, the application next must attempt to make a binary socket connection to a server. In this case, you cannot know at compile time which protocol the application will use for network communications. If everything works correctly, the application will use Flash Remoting/AMF, but if that doesn't work, the application will have to fall back on one of the alternatives. This situation presents a dilemma if you're not programming to interfaces, but it accepts a fairly trivial solution if you are.

In order to solve the dilemma presented by this hypothetical network protocol selection issue you can write three classes (one for each protocol) that implement the same interface that we'll call INetworkProtocol. You can then program to that interface rather than to any one of the specific classes. Doing so allows you to plug in an instance of any of the implementing classes. Even though the implementations are all different, they use the same interface and therefore appear the same from the outside. That allows you to change which protocol you use at runtime.

In order to better understand this concept let's look at some sample code. We'll solve the network protocol issue by creating an interface. Note that this example shows an interface that extends an existing interface (IEventDispatcher). That means that the implementing classes must implement both the INetworkProtocol and the IEventDispatcher methods.

```
package {
   import flash.events.IEventDispatcher;
   import flash.net.URLRequest;
   public interface INetworkProtocol extends IEventDispatcher {
      function setService(service:String):void;
      function sendRequest(request:URLRequest):void;
      function testConnection():void;
   }
}
```

For this example we'll also assume that the following class defines constants we'll use for event names.

```
package {
   import flash.events.Event;
   public class NetworkEvent extends Event {
      public static const CONNECT:String = "connect";
      public static const FAILED:String = "failed";
      public static const RESULT:String = "result";
      public static const ERROR:String = "error";
   }
}
```

Now that we've defined INetworkProtocol, we can define AMFService, XMLService, and BinarySocketService so that they each implement the interface. For the sake of brevity we'll omit the actual class definitions here. What's important is not the implementation in this case, but the fact that they each implement the same interface. The code that decides which protocol to use might look like the following:

```
package {
    import flash.events.EventDispatcher;
    public class Service extends EventDispatcher {
        private var _serviceURL:String;
        private var _service:INetworkProtocol;
        private var _services:Array;
        private var _hasValidService:Boolean;
        public function Service(serviceName:String) {
            _services = new Array(new AMFService(),
            new XMLService(), new BinarySocketService());
            _serviceURL = serviceName;
            tryNextService();
        }
        private function tryNextService():void {
            _service = _services.shift();
            _service.addEventListener(NetworkEvent.CONNECT,
              onConnect);
            _service.addEventListener(NetworkEvent.FAILED,
              onFailed);
            _service.setService(_serviceURL);
            _service.testConnection();
        }
        private function onConnect(event:Event):void {
            _hasValidService = true;
            _service.addEventListener(NetworkEvent.RESULT,
              onResult);
            _service.addEventListener(NetworkEvent.ERROR,
              onError);
        }
        private function onFailed(event:Event):void {
            if(_services.length > 0) {
                tryNextService();
            }
        }
        private function onResult(event:Event):void {
            dispatchEvent(event);
        }
        private function onError(event:Event):void {
            dispatchEvent(event);
        }
        public function sendRequest(request:URLRequest):void {
            _service.sendRequest(request);
        }
    }
}
```

This example is not intended to show a fully-functional, bullet-proof network communication mechanism. What it is intended to demonstrate is how programming to interfaces enables polymorphism. In this case _service is typed as INetworkProtocol. Since AMFService, XMLService, and BinarySocketService all implement INetworkProtocol, it's possible to assign instance of any of those classes to _service.

Summary

Interfaces are the backbone of good application design. Interfaces emphasize type rather than implementation. By programming to interfaces rather than to concrete implementations, you increase the flexibility in your applications. This flexibility comes about because of the reduction of dependency on implementation. When you program to interfaces, you can change the implementation of a class as long as you don't change the interface. That means that you can make significant changes without breaking your application, and even if you introduce an error, the error is generally isolated instead of cascading to other structures in the program. This emphasis on programming to interfaces is seen throughout the rest of the book.

PART II

Patterns

CHAPTER 3

Model View Controller Pattern

There was a time when computer programs had very limited user and client interfaces. In 1975, a computer program might interact with a user through a command line. Programs built today often have rich graphical user interfaces that make use of windows, mouse, and keyboard interaction, and that permit the moving and changing of elements. The increased richness of the user interface presents new challenges, and the Model View Controller (or MVC) pattern addresses those challenges to help create more flexible applications.

Applications consist of user interfaces, business logic, and data models. For example, standard UI components such as lists and combo boxes have user interface elements (clickable regions, scrollable regions, and so on), logic that knows how to respond to user input, and data models (the data that populates the component). Although these are three distinct elements, many developers write code that combines all the elements into one object rather than several objects working in combination. When the interface and the data are collapsed into just one object in rich user interfaces, it can lead to some of the following dilemmas:

- It is difficult to use the data outside that object. For example, if an object defines a user input form and also saves the user input within the object, then it is difficult to send the data to a server. The options in that case are to place the responsibility of client-server communication in the same class or to define an interface in the object that allows access to the data and provides the only means by which to access the data. Either option creates fragile and rigid structures.

- You cannot easily change the user interface while keeping the same data. If the user interface and the data are locked in the same object, to use a new user interface you'd have to create not only the new user interface, but also transfer all the data from the old user interface to the new one. Changing the user interface is not an uncommon requirement. Consider an application in which you want to chart a data set using different types of graphs. The data remains the same in each case, but the graph style changes (line, bar, and so on). If each graph is locked up with the data set, it's difficult to change graph styles.

- Multiple simultaneous views of the same data are difficult. For example, you might want to display two or more graph styles of the same data set at the same time. If the data is locked into the user interface, you have to replicate the data for each chart.

- Synchronized views are difficult. This is an extension of the previous issue. For example, if you not only want to display two or more different graph styles for the same data set at the same time, but you also want to update those graphs over time as the data changes, then you have to update each data set stored in each user interface.

All the preceding issues are problematic because the data and the user interface are locked into one object. The MVC pattern presents a manner in which you can create two or more objects that work together. This approach enables you to create more flexible applications with more reusable parts.

NOTE

Some people argue that MVC is not a design pattern, but rather an architectural pattern. Although there may be merit to that argument, we still feel that MVC is an important pattern (design *or* architectural) and we feel that it is extremely useful to ActionScript developers. For that reason, we present the pattern here in this book.

Understanding MVC Elements

The MVC pattern is composed of three subsystems as indicated by the name: the model, the view, and the controller. In the next few sections, we'll look at each of these elements. Then we'll look at how they work together. When referring to the use of a model, a view, and a controller together, we call this grouping the *MVC triad*.

The Model

The model is the element that stores the data that is used in the MVC triad. The model can be as simple as storing one primitive value such as a string, yet it can also store extremely complex structures of data. The defining aspects of the model are that it acts as a storehouse for data and that it exists independently of the view and the controller. The model should never have a reference to the view or the controller. This is absolutely essential to the functioning of the MVC pattern because the model's independence is what creates the flexibility in the MVC pattern. If a model has a reference to a view or controller then it is tightly coupled, and it is specific to a particular type of controller and/or view. However, if the model communicates without having to have references to specific types of controllers or views then it can be used with many different types of controllers and views. We'll see how a model can interact within the MVC triad in "The Relationships Between Subsystems" section, later in this chapter.

The View

The view is the visual display portion of the user interface subsystem. The view uses the data from the model to draw itself. A view can consist of an animation, a user input form, a chart, buttons, an audio player, or any sort of user interface elements you might need in your application.

The key to understanding the view is to understand that it consists only of the visual elements and the logic necessary to read the model data and use it as required by the user interface.

The Controller

The controller is the subsystem that is responsible for taking input (user input, for example) and updating the model and view as necessary. For example, if the model needs to update data, the controller is responsible for that action.

The Relationships between Elements

Each of the elements has a specific type of relationship with the other elements. The model element must always remain independent of the view and the controller. This means that the model cannot know about any other element. This does not mean that the model does not communicate with the other elements. A model can broadcast messages when the data changes. However, what's important is that the model merely broadcasts the message without having to know who is listening. This use of events allows the model to be decoupled from the other subsystems, allowing for greater flexibility.

The view always knows about the model. The view interacts with the model in two ways: It listens for update messages, and it reads from the model. The view never writes to the model. Every view keeps a reference to its model. Because a view knows about its model but a model doesn't know about a view, a single model can act as the model for many views.

The controller also knows about the model. The controller is responsible for updating the model when necessary based on user input or system events.

The relationship between the controller and the view is very tightly coupled. Although it is possible to have a controller that uses several views, it is far more common that the relationship between view and controller is one-to-one. The view contains all the user interface elements through which the user interacts. Yet the controller is the element that responds to user input. In many, if not most, ActionScript applications, the view and the controller are one class. This variation of the MVC pattern is often called a Document View implementation of MVC.

The most important key to the MVC pattern is that the model must be an independent object that does not have a reference to the view or controller. The view updates and redraws itself based on changes to the model.

Building a Simple Example

In this example, we'll build a clock model with two views—analog and digital. We'll start by building the clock model, which we'll call `ClockData`. Then we'll build the `AnalogClock` view. After the analog clock view works in conjunction with the data model, we can build a second view to see how simple it is to use the same model for two or more views. And, to prove how simple it is to change the model without affecting the views (so long as the model interface remains the same), we will update `ClockData` to handle additional responsibilities.

Clock Data Model

The `ClockData` class stores essentially one piece of data—the time. To store the time, we'll construct a simple building-block class called `Time` which has the accessor getter and setter methods for hour, minute, and second properties. We can define the `Time` class as follows:

```
package com.peachpit.aas3wdp.mvcexample.data {

  public class Time {

    private var _hour:uint;
    private var _minute:uint;
    private var _second:uint;

    public function get hour():uint {
      return _hour;
    }

    public function set hour(value:uint):void {
      _hour = value;
    }

    public function get minute():uint {
      return _minute;
    }

    public function set minute(value:uint):void {
      _minute = value;
    }

    public function get second():uint {
      return _second;
    }

    public function set second(value:uint):void {
      _second = value;
    }

    public function Time(hour:uint, minute:uint, second:uint) {
      _hour = hour;
      _minute = minute;
      _second = second;
    }

    public function clone():Time {
```

(CODE CONTINUED)

```
                    return new Time(_hour, _minute, _second);
          }

      }
   }
```

Note that the `Time` class also defines a `clone()` method that returns a new `Time` object with the same time value as the original. The `clone()` method is important so that we can assign clones of `Time` objects rather than references to the original.

Next we want to define the `ClockData` class. We'll modify the `ClockData` class later so that it is more robust and takes on more responsibilities. However, to start, the `ClockData` class will simply act as a wrapper for a `Time` object. The following is the definition for `ClockData`:

```
package com.peachpit.aas3wdp.mvcexample.data {

    import flash.events.Event;
    import flash.events.EventDispatcher;
    import com.peachpit.aas3wdp.mvcexample.data.Time;

    public class ClockData extends EventDispatcher {

        private var _time:Time;

        public function get time():Time {
          if(_time == null) {
            var date:Date = new Date();
            return new Time(date.hours, date.minutes,
            date.seconds);
          }
          else {
            return _time.clone();
          }
        }

        public function set time(value:Time):void {
          _time = value.clone();
          dispatchEvent(new Event(Event.CHANGE));
        }

        public function ClockData() {
        }

    }
}
```

As you can see in this `ClockData` class, there is one getter/setter accessor method pair called `time`. The `time` setter simply allows you to assign a clone of a `Time` object to the `_time` property. The getter method returns a clone of the `Time` object if it's defined. If not, it returns a new `Time` object with the current client clock time retrieved from a `Date` object.

In both cases where the `ClockData` class uses the `clone()` method of `Time` objects, it does so to protect encapsulation. It's important to understand that you don't always have to protect encapsulation at this level, but we demonstrate this concept here to point out the implications of using clones of objects rather than references. In this case, if the setter method assigned a reference rather than a clone of the parameter, then any change to the original object used as the parameter would also affect the data model. Likewise, and perhaps more importantly, the getter method also calls `clone()` to return a clone of the `Time` object. If it didn't call `clone()`, but returned a reference to the object, then any changes to that object outside the data model would also affect the data model. Consider the following example:

```
var data:ClockData = new ClockData();
var time:Time = new Time(12, 0, 0);
data.time = time;
time.hour = 14;
trace(data.time.hour);
```

In this example, the `trace()` statement would output 12, which is what we would probably expect. But if the setter assigned a reference rather than a clone to the _time property of the `ClockData` object, then the `trace()` statement would output 14. The same is true for the getter, as shown here:

```
var data:ClockData = new ClockData();
var time:Time = new Time(12, 0, 0);
data.time = time;
var timeValue:Time = data.time;
timeValue.hour = 20;
trace(data.time.hour);
```

In this example, if the getter returns a clone, then the `trace()` statement will output 12. If the getter returns a reference, then the `trace()` statement would output 20.

Analog Clock View

Now that we've built the model, we can build one of the views—the analog clock view. Because we know ahead of time that we're going to build more than one clock view, it makes sense to first determine whether there is any common functionality we can place in an abstract base class. Doing so provides two benefits: It results in less redundant code among clock view classes inheriting from the abstract base class, and it enables polymorphism whereby we can type variables as the abstract base class so that any of the concrete types can be substituted.

We'll call the abstract base class `Clock`, and this class constructor will require one parameter specifying the model (a `ClockData` object) to use. It will store that model in a protected instance property, and it will register to listen for change events. Here's the code for the base class called `AbstractClockView`:

```
package com.peachpit.aas3wdp.mvcexample.clock {
    import flash.display.Sprite;
    import com.peachpit.aas3wdp.mvcexample.data.ClockData;
    import flash.events.Event;

    public class AbstractClockView extends Sprite {

        protected var _data:ClockData;
```

(CODE CONTINUED)

```
            public function Clock(data:ClockData) {
              _data = data;
              _data.addEventListener(Event.CHANGE, draw);
            }

            protected function draw(event:Event):void {

            }

        }
    }
```

Notice that _data is declared as protected so that it is accessible to all subclasses. Also note that because the constructor adds a listener to the ClockData object, the class must declare the listener method, draw(). The draw() method is declared as protected as well because subclasses must be able to override the method to define the specific implementation.

Next we can define AnalogClock, a concrete subclass of AbstractClockView. The analog clock view consists of a clock face as well as the hour hand, minute hand, and second hand. The AnalogClock class is defined as follows:

```
package com.peachpit.aas3wdp.mvcexample.clock {
    import com.peachpit.aas3wdp.mvcexample.data.ClockData;
    import com.peachpit.aas3wdp.mvcexample.data.Time;
    import flash.display.Sprite;
    import flash.events.Event;

    public class AnalogClock extends AbstractClockView {

        private var _face:Sprite;
        private var _hourHand:Sprite;
        private var _minuteHand:Sprite;
        private var _secondHand:Sprite;

        public function AnalogClock(data:ClockData) {

            // Call the super constructor, passing it the
            // model parameter.
            super(data);

            // Create the clock face, and draw a circle.
            _face = new Sprite();
            _face.graphics.lineStyle(0, 0x000000, 1);
            _face.graphics.drawCircle(0, 0, 100);
            addChild(_face);

            // Create the hands.
            _hourHand = new Sprite();
            _hourHand.graphics.lineStyle(5, 0x000000, 1);
            _hourHand.graphics.lineTo(0, -50);
            addChild(_hourHand);
            _minuteHand = new Sprite();
            _minuteHand.graphics.lineStyle(2, 0x000000, 1);
            _minuteHand.graphics.lineTo(0, -80);
```

(CODE CONTINUED)

```
        addChild(_minuteHand);
        _secondHand = new Sprite();
        _secondHand.graphics.lineStyle(0, 0x000000, 1);
        _secondHand.graphics.lineTo(0, -80);
        addChild(_secondHand);

        // Call the draw() method to draw the initial view.
        draw();
    }

    // Override the draw() method. This method gets called once
    // when the object is constructed, and then it gets called
    // every time the model dispatches a change event.
    override protected function draw(event:Event = null):void {
        var time:Time = _data.time;

        // Set the rotation of the hands based on the time
        // values.
        _hourHand.rotation = 30 * time.hour + 30 *
         time.minute / 60;
        _minuteHand.rotation = 6 * time.minute + 6 *
         time.second / 60;
        _secondHand.rotation = 6 * time.second;
    }

    }
}
```

Testing the Analog Clock

The remaining step in the first part of this exercise is to see whether the analog clock really
works. For this purpose, we'll create a simple main class that creates an instance of the model
and an instance of the view that uses the model:

```
package {

    import flash.display.Sprite;
    import flash.display.StageAlign;
    import flash.display.StageScaleMode;
    import com.peachpit.aas3wdp.mvcexample.data.ClockData;
    import com.peachpit.aas3wdp.mvcexample.clock.AbstractClockView;
    import com.peachpit.aas3wdp.mvcexample.clock.AnalogClock;

    public class ClockTest extends Sprite{

        private var _clockData:ClockData;

        public function ClockTest() {

            stage.align = StageAlign.TOP_LEFT;
            stage.scaleMode = StageScaleMode.NO_SCALE;

            _clockData = new ClockData();
            var clock:AbstractClockView = new
             AnalogClock(_clockData);
```

```
            clock.x = 100;
            clock.y = 100;
            addChild(clock);
        }

    }
}
```

When you test this application, you'll see an analog clock appear displaying the current time.

Now let's modify the main class slightly so that it uses a timer to update the time property of the model after 2 seconds. Updating the model value will cause it to dispatch a change event which will, in turn, cause the view to redraw. The following code initially displays the clock with the current time, and then 2 seconds later it will display 5 o'clock:

```
package {

    import flash.display.Sprite;
    import flash.display.StageAlign;
    import flash.display.StageScaleMode;
    import com.peachpit.aas3wdp.mvcexample.data.ClockData;
    import com.peachpit.aas3wdp.mvcexample.clock.AbstractClockView;
    import com.peachpit.aas3wdp.mvcexample.clock.AnalogClock;
    import com.peachpit.aas3wdp.mvcexample.data.Time;
    import flash.utils.Timer;
    import flash.events.TimerEvent;

    public class ClockTest extends Sprite{

        private var _clockData:ClockData;

        public function ClockTest() {

            stage.align = StageAlign.TOP_LEFT;
            stage.scaleMode = StageScaleMode.NO_SCALE;

            _clockData = new ClockData();
            var clock:AbstractClockView = new
             AnalogClock(_clockData);
            clock.x = 100;
            clock.y = 100;
            addChild(clock);

            var timer:Timer = new Timer(2000, 1);
            timer.addEventListener(TimerEvent.TIMER, onTimer);
            timer.start();

        }

        private function onTimer(event:TimerEvent):void {
           _clockData.time = new Time(5, 0, 0);
        }

    }
}
```

Digital Clock View

Now that the analog clock view works, the next step is to build a digital clock view. The `DigitalClock` class, like the `AnalogClock` class, is a subclass of `AbstractClockView`. Define the class as follows:

```
package com.peachpit.aas3wdp.mvcexample.clock {
    import com.peachpit.aas3wdp.mvcexample.data.ClockData;
    import com.peachpit.aas3wdp.mvcexample.data.Time;
    import flash.display.Sprite;
    import flash.events.Event;
    import flash.text.TextField;
    import flash.text.TextFieldAutoSize;

    public class DigitalClock extends AbstractClockView {

        private var _frame:Sprite;
        private var _display:TextField;

        public function DigitalClock(data:ClockData) {

            // Call the super constructor, passing it the
            // data parameter.
            super(data);

            // Draw a 200 by 50 pixel rectangular frame.
            _frame = new Sprite();
            _frame.graphics.lineStyle(0, 0x000000, 1);
            _frame.graphics.drawRect(0, 0, 200, 50);
            addChild(_frame);

            // Add a text field.
            _display = new TextField();
            _display.width = 200;
            _display.height = 50;
            _display.autoSize = TextFieldAutoSize.RIGHT;
            _display.x = 195;
            _display.y = 5;
            addChild(_display);

            // Call draw() when the object is constructed.
            draw();
        }

        // Override the draw() method.
        override protected function draw(event:Event = null):void {
            var time:Time = _data.time;

            // Display the hour, minute, and second in the
            // text field. Use the zeroFill() method to ensure
            // that the minute and second values are always
            // two digits (e.g. 1 displays as 01.)
            _display.htmlText = "<font face='_typewriter'
            size='40'>" + time.hour + ":" +
            zeroFill(time.minute) + ":" + zeroFill(time.second)
            + "</font>";
        }
```

```
      private function zeroFill(value:Number):String {
        if(value > 9) {
          return value.toString();
        }
        else {
          return "0" + value;
        }
      }

    }
  }
```

You'll probably notice that DigitalClock is very similar to AnalogClock. The only difference is that it displays the value using a text field rather than a group of hands. Because DigitalClock extends AbstractClockView, it too automatically receives event notifications when the model changes.

Testing the Digital Clock

Because polymorphism is enabled for AnalogClock and DigitalClock on account of their common, inherited interface, you can substitute a DigitalClock for an AnalogClock very easily. To test the digital clock view, modify the main class by importing the DigitalClock class and using a DigitalClock constructor rather than an AnalogClock constructor, as shown here:

```
package {

    import flash.display.Sprite;
    import flash.display.StageAlign;
    import flash.display.StageScaleMode;
    import com.peachpit.aas3wdp.mvcexample.data.ClockData;
    import com.peachpit.aas3wdp.mvcexample.clock.AbstractClockView;
    import com.peachpit.aas3wdp.mvcexample.clock.AnalogClock;
    import com.peachpit.aas3wdp.mvcexample.clock.DigitalClock;
    import com.peachpit.aas3wdp.mvcexample.data.Time;
    import flash.utils.Timer;
    import flash.events.TimerEvent;

    public class ClockTest extends Sprite{

        private var _clockData:ClockData;

        public function ClockTest() {

            stage.align = StageAlign.TOP_LEFT;
            stage.scaleMode = StageScaleMode.NO_SCALE;

            _clockData = new ClockData();
            var clock:AbstractClockView =
             new DigitalClock(_clockData);
            clock.x = 100;
            clock.y = 100;
            addChild(clock);
```

(CODE CONTINUED)

```
            var timer:Timer = new Timer(2000, 1);
            timer.addEventListener(TimerEvent.TIMER, onTimer);
            timer.start();

        }

        private function onTimer(event:TimerEvent):void {
            _clockData.time = new Time(5, 0, 0);
        }

    }
}
```

Enabling Multiple Views for One Model

In this example, we have two views that we can use with one model type. We have demonstrated that we can use each view type with the same model, one at a time. Now we'll test that we can use both views simultaneously with the same model instance. To accomplish this goal, we'll modify the main class to create two clock views—one `AnalogClock` and one `DigitalClock`. Each will use the same `ClockData` object. This change requires just four new lines of code in the main class:

```
package {

    import flash.display.Sprite;
    import flash.display.StageAlign;
    import flash.display.StageScaleMode;
    import com.peachpit.aas3wdp.mvcexample.data.ClockData;
    import com.peachpit.aas3wdp.mvcexample.clock.AbstractClockView;
    import com.peachpit.aas3wdp.mvcexample.clock.AnalogClock;
    import com.peachpit.aas3wdp.mvcexample.clock.DigitalClock;
    import com.peachpit.aas3wdp.mvcexample.data.Time;
    import flash.utils.Timer;
    import flash.events.TimerEvent;

    public class ClockTest extends Sprite{

        private var _clockData:ClockData;

        public function ClockTest() {

            stage.align = StageAlign.TOP_LEFT;
            stage.scaleMode = StageScaleMode.NO_SCALE;

            _clockData = new ClockData();
            var clock:AbstractClockView =
             new DigitalClock(_clockData);
            clock.x = 100;
            clock.y = 100;
            addChild(clock);

            var clock2:AbstractClockView = new
             AnalogClock(_clockData);
            clock2.x = 200;
```

```
        clock2.y = 300;
        addChild(clock2);

        var timer:Timer = new Timer(2000, 1);
        timer.addEventListener(TimerEvent.TIMER, onTimer);
        timer.start();

    }

    private function onTimer(event:TimerEvent):void {
      _clockData.time = new Time(5, 0, 0);
    }

  }
}
```

Because both clock views use the same data model, they update at the same time.

Modifying Model Implementation

Because the view and the model use good encapsulation, we can modify the model implementation without breaking anything. To prove this, we'll make the following change to the Clock-Data class: enable a real-time feature whereby the model dispatches a change event every second.

The new ClockData class looks like this:

```
package com.peachpit.aas3wdp.mvcexample.data {

    import flash.events.EventDispatcher;
    import com.peachpit.aas3wdp.mvcexample.data.Time;
    import flash.utils.Timer;
    import flash.events.TimerEvent;
    import flash.events.Event;
    import flash.utils.getTimer;

    public class ClockData extends EventDispatcher {

        private var _time:Time;
        private var _timer:Timer;
        private var _realTime:Boolean;
        private var _startTime:uint;

        public function get time():Time {
            // Test if the _realTime property is true as well as
            // if the _time property is null.
            if(_realTime || _time == null) {
                var date:Date;
                // Only use a new Date object representing
                // the current time and date if the _time
                // property is null. Otherwise create a Date
                // object using the _time values and then
                // add to that the number of milliseconds
                // since the model was created.
                if(_time == null) {
```

(CODE CONTINUED)

```
                date = new Date();
            }
            else {
                date = new Date(null, null, null,
                _time.hour, _time.minute,
                _time.second);
                date.milliseconds = getTimer() —
                _startTime;
            }

            return new Time(date.hours, date.minutes,
             date.seconds);
        }
        else {
            return _time.clone();
        }
    }

    public function set time(value:Time):void {
        _time = value.clone();
        dispatchEvent(new Event(Event.CHANGE));
    }

    // Setting realTime starts and stops a timer that runs at 1
    // second intervals indefinitely.
    public function set realTime(value:Boolean):void {
        _realTime = value;
        if(value) {
            if(_timer == null) {
                _timer = new Timer(1000, 0);
                _timer.addEventListener(TimerEvent.TIMER, onTimer);
            }
            if(!_timer.running) {
                _timer.start();
            }
        }
        else {
            if(_timer.running) {
                _timer.stop();
            }
        }
    }

    public function ClockData() {
        _startTime = getTimer();
    }

    private function onTimer(event:TimerEvent):void {
        dispatchEvent(new Event(Event.CHANGE));
    }

    }
}
```

With these changes, you can now run the main class and you'll see exactly the same behavior as before. When you've verified that the application works as it did before, even with the changes to the model's implementation, you can now use the new functionality with a few changes to the main class. In this example, we'll delete the timer code from the main class (ClockTest), and we'll set the realTime property of the ClockData object so that the clocks display the current time as it updates in real time.

```
package {

    import flash.display.Sprite;
    import flash.display.StageAlign;
    import flash.display.StageScaleMode;
    import com.peachpit.aas3wdp.mvcexample.data.ClockData;
    import com.peachpit.aas3wdp.mvcexample.clock.AbstractClockView;
    import com.peachpit.aas3wdp.mvcexample.clock.AnalogClock;
    import com.peachpit.aas3wdp.mvcexample.clock.DigitalClock;
    import com.peachpit.aas3wdp.mvcexample.data.Time;

    public class ClockTest extends Sprite{

        private var _clockData:ClockData;

        public function ClockTest() {

            stage.align = StageAlign.TOP_LEFT;
            stage.scaleMode = StageScaleMode.NO_SCALE;

            _clockData = new ClockData();
            _clockData.realTime = true;

            var clock:AbstractClockView = new
             DigitalClock(_clockData);
            clock.x = 100;
            clock.y = 100;
            addChild(clock);

            var clock2:AbstractClockView = new
             AnalogClock(_clockData);
            clock2.x = 200;
            clock2.y = 300;
            addChild(clock2);

        }

    }
}
```

Adding A Controller

Up to this point we've only really seen models and views, but no controllers. Next we'll look at how to add a controller. A controller should be the way in which the system or user can change the view or model.

In our clock example we now have two views and one model. If we want to be able to control the views (toggle between views, for instance) or the model (setting the value) then we need to add a controller. In our example we'll create a controller called Clock. The Clock controller allows us to specify a model and one or more views. It then adds user interface controls that allow the user to set the model value and toggle between the views. The Clock class is written as follows:

```
package com.peachpit.aas3wdp.mvcexample.controllers {

    import flash.display.Sprite;
    import flash.text.TextField;
    import flash.text.TextFieldType;
    import flash.events.MouseEvent;
    import flash.events.Event;
    import com.peachpit.aas3wdp.mvcexample.data.Time;
    import com.peachpit.aas3wdp.mvcexample.data.ClockData;
    import com.peachpit.aas3wdp.mvcexample.clock.AbstractClockView;

    // Note that you'll need to include the AAS3WDP library to your
    // project's source path for this class.
    import com.peachpit.aas3wdp.controls.BasicButton;

    public class Clock extends Sprite {
        private var _hours:TextField;
        private var _minutes:TextField;
        private var _seconds:TextField;
        private var _clockData:ClockData;
        private var _viewIndex:int;
        private var _views:Array;
        private var _toggleView:BasicButton;

        // The controller has one model. It listens for updates to
        // the model.
        public function set data(value:ClockData):void {
            _clockData = value;
            _clockData.addEventListener(Event.CHANGE,
             onModelUpdate);
            onModelUpdate();
        }

        public function Clock() {

            // The controller can store references to one or
            // more views.
            _views = new Array();

            // Create three input text fields.
            _hours = createField();
            _minutes = createField();
            _seconds = createField();
            _minutes.x = 45;
            _seconds.x = 90;

            // Create a button that will allow the user to
            // toggle between views.
            _toggleView = new BasicButton("Toggle View");
            _toggleView.addEventListener(MouseEvent.CLICK,
```

```
            toggleView);
        addChild(_toggleView);
        _toggleView.x = 135;
    }

    // Add AbstractClockView instances to the _views array.
    public function addView(view:AbstractClockView):void {
        _views.push(view);

        // If this is the first view added then add it to
        // the display list by default.
        if(_views.length == 1) {
            addChild(view);
            _viewIndex = 0;
        }
        // Make sure the view appears just below the input
        // text fields.
        view.y = 40 — view.getBounds(view).top;
        view.x = -view.getBounds(view).left;
    }

    private function createField():TextField {
        var field:TextField = new TextField();
        field.width = 40;
        field.height = 22;
        field.border = true;
        field.background = true;
        field.restrict = "0-9";
        field.type = TextFieldType.INPUT;

        // Listen for focusOut events on each text field.
        field.addEventListener(FocusEvent.FOCUS_OUT,
         onFocusChange);
        addChild(field);
        return field;
    }

    // When the focus changes for a text field update the model
    // to correspond to the user input.
    private function onFocusChange(event:FocusEvent):void {
        if(event.target.length < 1) {
            event.target.text = 0;
        }
        var time:Time = new Time(uint(_hours.text), uint(_minutes.text),
 uint(_seconds.text));
        _clockData.time = time;
    }

    // Remove the current view, and add the next view in the
    // array.
    private function toggleView(event:MouseEvent):void {
        removeChild(_views[_viewIndex]);
        _viewIndex++;
        if(_viewIndex >= _views.length) {
            _viewIndex = 0;
        }
```

```
                addChild(_views[_viewIndex]);
        }

        // When the model changes update the text field values.
        private function onModelUpdate(event:Event = null):void {

            // Use if statements so that the text values don't
            // change if the user is currently changing the
            // value in a text field.
            if(stage != null) {
                if(stage.focus != _hours) {
                    _hours.text = _clockData.time.hour.toString();
                }
                if(stage.focus != _minutes) {
                    _minutes.text = _clockData.time.minute.toString();
                }
                if(stage.focus != _seconds) {
                    _seconds.text = _clockData.time.second.toString();
                }
            }
        }

    }
}
```

Now you can use a `Clock` instance as follows.

```
package {

    import flash.display.Sprite;
    import flash.display.StageAlign;
    import flash.display.StageScaleMode;
    import com.peachpit.aas3wdp.mvcexample.data.ClockData;
    import com.peachpit.aas3wdp.mvcexample.clock.AbstractClockView;
    import com.peachpit.aas3wdp.mvcexample.clock.AnalogClock;
    import com.peachpit.aas3wdp.mvcexample.clock.DigitalClock;
    import com.peachpit.aas3wdp.mvcexample.controllers.Clock;

    public class ClockTest extends Sprite{

        private var _clockData:ClockData;

        public function ClockTest() {

            stage.align = StageAlign.TOP_LEFT;
            stage.scaleMode = StageScaleMode.NO_SCALE;

            _clockData = new ClockData();
            _clockData.realTime = true;

            var clock:Clock = new Clock();
            clock.data = _clockData;
            addChild(clock);

            var view:AbstractClockView = new
             DigitalClock(_clockData);
```

(CODE CONTINUED)

```
            clock.addView(view);

            view = new AnalogClock(_clockData);
            clock.addView(view);

        }

    }

}
```

In this version the `Clock` instance is the controller by which the user can toggle between views and adjust the value of the model.

Summary

In this chapter, you've had an opportunity to learn about the basic concepts of the Model View Controller pattern .The basic principle of this pattern is to distinguish between the data and the presentation of that data. This approach enables greater flexibility and adaptability in a quite a few ways which were discussed throughout the chapter.

CHAPTER 4

Singleton Pattern

The Singleton design pattern is used to limit a class to one instance and provide global access to that instance. In many cases, you need to limit a class to only one instance. Common examples include classes that manage resources that are intrinsically singular such as selection focus, navigation history, and window depth. Consider the case of a class that manages the state of the user's cursor. Because there is only ever one cursor, you shouldn't have more than one instance of that class. Another example is a class that loads application settings from an XML file and provides access to those settings. You wouldn't want to waste resources by having two instances of that class or by loading the XML file more than once.

The dilemma in such cases is how to ensure that only one instance of a class exists and how to make that one instance globally accessible. The Singleton design pattern is a time-tested solution to this problem.

Essentially, three features make up a Singleton class:

- A private static property that holds the single instance of the class.

- A public static method that provides access to the single instance if it's created and creates the single instance if it hasn't been created yet.

- A way of restricting access to instantiating the class. This is usually achieved by making the constructor private. However, ActionScript 3.0 doesn't have private constructors. Later in this chapter, we'll examine an alternative way of restricting instantiation in ActionScript 3.0.

Object Instantiation

To create a new instance of a class, you use the `new` keyword followed by the class name. This statement calls the constructor of the class and returns a new instance, as in this example:

```
var myObject:MyClass = new MyClass();
```

This approach is almost undoubtedly a concept with which you are already familiar, but if our class uses this type of instantiation, we have no way of controlling its creation. For us to control the instantiation, we're going to use a static method called `getInstance()`. Because it is static, it can be invoked before an instance of the class exists. The following is an example of a class that uses this method:

```
public class MyClass {

   public function MyClass() {}

   public static function getInstance():MyClass {
      return new MyClass();
   }

}
```

Now we can create our instances of the class by using the static method, like this:

```
var myObject:MyClass = MyClass.getInstance();
```

Restricting Instantiation

As long as the instance is always accessed via the static `getInstance()` method, everything works according to plan. However, notice that there is nothing to prevent someone from constructing a second instance using the `new` keyword. In other languages this problem would be solved by making the constructor private, but private constructors aren't supported in ActionScript 3.0.

We could just leave the constructor public and put a big comment up at the top of the class telling other developers that this class should be instantiated only once. However, one of our goals in object-oriented programming should be to create a class that cannot be broken by improper implementation. We'll talk more about convention, as opposed to rules, later in this chapter.

So, we have a few other options at our disposal that allow us to limit instantiation. One feature of ActionScript 3.0 is that all parameters of a method are now required unless a default value is provided. This feature includes the constructor. Therefore, you can add a parameter to the constructor that is required and type it to something that is available only from inside the class.

NOTE

> This is not an absolute restriction since someone can get around this by passing null into the constructor. However, it is the best we can do without a true private constructor.

A second new feature of ActionScript 3.0 is the ability to add multiple class definitions to one file. You can access only one of the classes from outside the ActionScript file, and that is the class—inside the package definition—with the same name as the file name. But you can put other classes outside the package in the same file, and those classes are available only to the primary class. We'll use this feature to create a "private" class and make it our constructor parameter's type. It's actually easier than it sounds:

```
package {

    public class MyClass {

        public function MyClass(enforcer:SingletonEnforcer) {}

        public static function getInstance():MyClass {
            return new MyClass(new SingletonEnforcer());
        }

    }

}

class SingletonEnforcer {}
```

You can now create an instance of MyClass using the following code:

```
var myInstance:MyClass = MyClass.getInstance();
```

Note that our current implementation doesn't yet enforce a single instance of the class. Each time we call getInstance() our class will return a new instance. In the next section we'll look at how to ensure that there's only ever one instance.

Single Instance and Global Access

What can we do to enforce that the class is instantiated only once? Right now, the getInstance() method can be called multiple times just like a normal public constructor; and we also need to provide global access to this one instance. By modifying the getInstance() method slightly and adding a static property to hold our single instance, we'll knock out both of these requirements at once.

First let's add a private static property to the class that will hold our single instance. We need to make the property static so that it is available to our getInstance() method. Now when the static getInstance() method is called it creates an instance and stores it in the private static _instance property before returning the newly created instance. Here is how our class looks now:

```
package {

    public class MyClass {

        private static var _instance:MyClass;

        public function MyClass(enforcer:SingletonEnforcer) {}

        public static function getInstance():MyClass {
            MyClass._instance = new MyClass(new SingletonEnforcer());
            return MyClass._instance;
```

(CODE CONTINUED)

```
        }

    }

}

class SingletonEnforcer {}
```

Next, we're going to modify the getInstance() method so that it checks whether this single instance has already been created. If it has, then it returns that instance without calling the constructor again. Check out this modification:

```
package {

    public class MyClass {

        private static var _instance:MyClass;

        public function MyClass(enforcer:SingletonEnforcer) {}

        public static function getInstance():MyClass {
            if(MyClass._instance == null) {
                MyClass._instance = new MyClass(new SingletonEnforcer());
            }
            return MyClass._instance;
        }

    }

}

class SingletonEnforcer {}
```

CONVENTION VERSUS RULES

If you're new to design patterns, at first glance the Singleton pattern seems a bit like over engineering. You might be saying to yourself, "If I want only one instance of a class, then I'll create only one instance; if I need global access, then I'll stick it in some global variable." Although you could certainly do those two things—and they would probably work—they 'could pose problems in a team development environment. 'You may also have trouble with this approach if you're creating multiple versions of the application.

This underscores the importance of following structural rules rather than simple conventions. The idea of encapsulation in object-oriented programming is that a class should be self-contained. It should have well-documented inputs in the form of public methods and setters and outputs in the form of events. These inputs and outputs are commonly known as the API (Application Programming Interface). As we mentioned earlier, classes should function like a black box: nothing exposed in the API should permit improper implementation to "break it." In the case of our Singleton class, we should not allow another object to create more than one instance of the class. (See Chapter 1, "Designing Applications.")

Singleton Versus Static Members

After examining the structure of a Singleton class, you might ask the question, "Why not just make all the properties and methods of the class static? Why do we need to have an instance at all?" There are a few reasons why a Singleton is the better approach.

The first reason is inheritance. In ActionScript 3.0, you cannot inherit static properties or methods. Therefore, if all your class's functionality is in static methods, you cannot subclass it.

The second reason to use a Singleton pattern is so that you can refactor the class to allow more than one instance. A lesser-known design pattern called the Multiton is similar to the Singleton but allows for a managed number of instances. If you write your original class as a Singleton, you can refactor it to be a Multiton easily. For example, let's say version 1.0 of your application had a connection manager that managed a single connection to the server; but for version 2.0, it has been determined that you need to manage a pool of 10 connections to the server. This is where a Multiton could be used.

The third reason is that it can be a waste of resources to have all this logic initialized right away. Singletons use the concept of "lazy" instantiation, because the object is created only when the first call to getInstance() is made. Classes that use all static members do what is called "eager" instantiation. This is usually a waste of resources and can slow down the startup of your application.

Lastly, objects are just easier to manage. By using static methods instead of a single object your code is not created at a specific point in your application. This can cause some strange initialization issues that are difficult to debug. This is especially true if your Singleton class has a dependency on other objects in the application that might not be initialized. For this reason, consider using static members only if your class is 100% self-contained, with no dependencies on outside objects. Even then, your class is locked into this "self-contained" mode and isn't scalable anymore.

Building a Simple Singleton

Often a good example will go a long way when learning a design pattern. In the next few sections we'll look at an example using the Singleton pattern." In the first example, we simply create a generic Singleton and invoke it.

Creating the Singleton

We first need to create the Singleton class. Create it in the com.peachpit.aas3wdp.singletonexample package and name it Singleton. Notice that this class has all the standard elements of an Action-Script 3.0 Singleton class:

- A private static property, _instance, to hold the single instance of the class.

- A constructor with a parameter typed to a class, SingletonEnforcer, that is available only to the Singleton class. The SingletonEnforcer class definition is also required.

- A public static method, getInstance(), that provides access to the single instance and creates it if it does not exist.

The following code shows an example of standard singleton class. We'll us this to demonstrate how to build a singleton class.

```
package com.peachpit.aas3wdp.singletonexample {

   public class Singleton {

      static private var _instance:Singleton;

      public function Singleton(singletonEnforcer:SingletonEnforcer) {}

      public static function getInstance():Singleton {
         if(Singleton._instance == null) {
            Singleton._instance = new Singleton(new SingletonEnforcer());
         }
         return Singleton._instance;
      }

      public function doSomething():void {
         trace("SOMETHING!");
      }

   }

}

class SingletonEnforcer {}
```

As you can see, the doSomething() method is a public method that simply traces the text "SOMETHING!" to the console. While this example is very simple, it demonstrates the required elements of a class that follows the Singleton design pattern in ActionScript. The code in the next section demonstrates how to invoke a Singleton class.

NOTE

In order for trace statements to output information to the console you must debug the application rather than just run it.

Invoking the Singleton

Inside the main class, we're going to get the instance of the Singleton class and call a method on that object. We start by importing the Singleton class. Then inside the constructor, we call the Singleton's static getInstance() method and immediately call the doSomething() method on the returned instance. The doSomething() method simply traces "SOMETHING!" to the console.

```
package {

   import com.peachpit.aas3wdp.singletonexample.Singleton;
   import flash.display.Sprite;

   public class SimpleSingletonExample extends Sprite {
```

(CODE CONTINUED)
```
        public function SingletonExample() {
            Singleton.getInstance().doSomething();
        }
    }

}
```

Building a Settings Framework

In this next example we'll build a simple application that uses a Singleton class called `Settings` to hold global values.

The `Settings` class loads data from an XML file at runtime and provides access to its values. It's a simple concept, but it's very useful to be able to change these settings without recompiling the application.

Creating the XML Document

The XML document for this framework is simple. We have a `settings` root node that contains multiple `property` nodes. Each `property` node has an `id` and a `value` attribute. The `Settings` class does a lookup on the `id` attribute and returns the `value` attribute. The following is the XML document, titled config.xml, which we'll use in this example:

```
<?xml version="1.0" encoding="UTF-8"?>
<cs:settings xmlns:cs="http://www.dannypatterson.com/2006/ConfigSettings">
    <cs:property id="testOne" value="This is the first test value." />
    <cs:property id="testTwo" value="This is the second test value." />
</cs:settings>
```

Note that we added a namespace to this document to demonstrate how simple namespaces are to use inside E4X. For more information on XML namespaces, see Chapter 15, "E4X (XML)."

Creating the Settings Class

Now you'll need to create a new ActionScript class named `Settings` and put it in the `com.peachpit.aas3wdp.singletonexample` package. It has three main responsibilities:

- It follows the Singleton design pattern; therefore, it manages its creation and access the same way as the previous example.

- The `Settings` class also provides access to the values in the XML file through simple property access, like this:

  ```
  var myString:String = Settings.getInstance().testOne;
  ```

- Because testOne isn't a property of the Settings class, we have to allow the request to come in and capture it. To enable this functionality we need to make the class dynamic so that other classes can call undefined properties. To capture these undefined requests, we'll subclass the built-in flash.utils.Proxy class and override the getProperty() method.

EXTENDING PROXY

To gain the Proxy functionality we must subclass it and override the getProperty() method. This is a little tricky because the Proxy class' getProperty() method exists inside the flash_proxy namespace. For more on using the Proxy class, check out Chapter 6, "Proxy Pattern."

- Because this class loads an external XML file, it must have a method for loading that file and an event that is dispatched when the file has loaded successfully. To enable the class to dispatch events, we will use the built-in EventDispatcher class.

ADDING EVENTDISPATCHER FUNCTIONALITY THROUGH COMPOSITION

Because we have to subclass Proxy to use its functionality, and because ActionScript allows only for single inheritance, we must add the EventDispatcher functionality through composition by implementing the IEventDispatcher interface. For more on EventDispatcher and IEventDispatcher, see Chapter 13, "Working with Events."

```
package com.peachpit.aas3wdp.singletonexample {

    import flash.events.Event;
    import flash.events.EventDispatcher;
    import flash.events.IEventDispatcher;
    import flash.net.URLLoader;
    import flash.net.URLRequest;
    import flash.utils.Proxy;
    import flash.utils.flash_proxy;

    dynamic public class Settings extends Proxy implements IEventDispatcher {

        static private var _instance:Settings;
        private var _eventDispatcher:EventDispatcher;
        private var _data:XML;
        private var _isLoaded:Boolean;
        private var _urlLoader:URLLoader;
        static public const INIT:String = "init";

        public function get isLoaded():Boolean {
            return _isLoaded;
        }

        public function Settings(enforcer:SingletonEnforcer) {
            _eventDispatcher = new EventDispatcher();
            _isLoaded = false;
        }

        private function onXMLDataLoaded(event:Event):void {
            _data = XML(_urlLoader.data);
            _isLoaded = true;
            dispatchEvent(new Event(Settings.INIT, true, true));
        }

        public static function getInstance():Settings {
```

(CODE CONTINUED)

```
        if(Settings._instance == null) {
            Settings._instance = new Settings(new SingletonEnforcer());
        }
        return Settings._instance;
    }

    flash_proxy override function getProperty(name:*):* {
        var cs:Namespace = _data.namespace("cs");
        var qname:String = String(name);
        return _data.cs::property.(@id == qname).@value;
    }

    public function loadSettings(url:String):void {
        var urlRequest:URLRequest = new URLRequest(url);
        _urlLoader = new URLLoader();
        _urlLoader.addEventListener(Event.COMPLETE, onXMLDataLoaded);
        _urlLoader.load(urlRequest);
    }

    public function addEventListener(type:String, listener:Function, useCapture:
Boolean = false, priority:int = 0, weakRef:Boolean = false):void {
        _eventDispatcher.addEventListener(type, listener, useCapture, priority, weakRef);
    }

    public function dispatchEvent(event:Event):Boolean {
        return _eventDispatcher.dispatchEvent(event);
    }

    public function hasEventListener(type:String):Boolean {
        return _eventDispatcher.hasEventListener(type);
    }

    public function removeEventListener(type:String, listener:Function, useCapture:
Boolean = false):void {
        _eventDispatcher.removeEventListener(type, listener, useCapture);
    }

    public function willTrigger(type:String):Boolean {
        return _eventDispatcher.willTrigger(type);
    }

    }

}

class SingletonEnforcer {}
```

XML USAGE (E4X)

Inside the getProperty() method, we used the new E4X functionality to pull the data out of the XML object based on the name of the requested property. For more on E4X, check out Chapter 15, "E4X (XML)."

Invoking the Settings Class

Next, we'll need a main class for the application in order to utilize the Settings class. We'll call the main class SettingsExample, and define it as follows:

```
package {

    import com.peachpit.aas3wdp.singletonexample.Settings;
    import flash.events.Event;
    import flash.display.Sprite;

    public class SettingsExample extends Sprite {

        public function SettingsExample() {
            Settings.getInstance().loadSettings("config.xml");
            Settings.getInstance().addEventListener(Settings.INIT, onSettingsInit);
        }

        private function onSettingsInit(event:Event):void {
            trace(Settings.getInstance().testOne);
            trace(Settings.getInstance().testTwo);
        }

    }

}
```

This class is the start of the project. It retrieves the singleton instance of Settings, then it displays the values from the dynamic properties. In the constructor, we first get a reference to the single instance using the static getInstance() method. Then we call the loadSettings() method and add the Settings.INIT event listener.

Inside the onSettingsInit() event handler, we trace the value of testOne and testTwo from the Settings instance. These variables are not actually properties of the Settings class. You'll see later in this example that the Settings class uses a new feature of ActionScript 3.0 called Proxy to handle this request and return the value from the XML document.

Now you can debug the project. You should see the values of properties testOne and testTwo being displayed in the trace console.

Summary

The Singleton design pattern is a simple yet effective solution for restricting a class to one instance and providing a global access point to it. In this chapter, you learned how to implement this design pattern using ActionScript 3.0. You also learned the importance of the Singleton pattern over simply using static members.

CHAPTER 5

Factory and Template Method Patterns

When creating groups of related classes, it's important to maintain those relationships during object creation. One way to do this is with the Factory Method design pattern. The Factory Method pattern is a creational pattern and solves the problem of creating objects without specifying a concrete type. This is most often used in abstract classes that define a method for object creation. Subclasses can then override this method to define the specific object to be created.

The Factory Method is most often used in conjunction with another pattern called the Template Method. To better understand the Factory Method and provide more context for this solution, we'll also look at the Template Method in this chapter. Because the Factory Method uses and then builds on many of the same concepts, we'll look at the Template Method first.

Abstract Classes

Abstract classes play a major role in the Factory and Template Method patterns. Although ActionScript 3.0 doesn't natively support them, we can still use the concept of abstract classes and abstract methods. An *abstract class* is a class that is always extended and never instantiated directly. Its use is similar to that of an interface, but there is one major difference: An interface defines only the public method signatures, but an abstract class defines both the interface and the implementation.

An abstract class uses something called an *abstract method*, which has no functionality but serves only as a placeholder. In other languages such as C# and Java, you can define these abstract methods using the `abstract` keyword that tells subclasses they must override this method. Because ActionScript 3.0 does not have an `abstract` keyword, you might consider the convention of throwing an exception inside the abstract methods. Such an approach won't throw an error during compilation, but it will during runtime. The bottom line is that there is no sure way to enforce abstract methods in ActionScript 3.0.

You must know about two specific keywords when you're working with abstract classes in ActionScript 3.0. The first is the `override` keyword. Subclasses must use this keyword to override an abstract method defined in a base class. The method signature must also match exactly.

The other keyword is `final`. This term can be used by abstract classes that define methods its subclasses cannot override. We'll use the `final` keyword when we define Template Method patterns.

Template Method

A Template Method is defined in an abstract class that sets a general algorithm made up (at least partially) of abstract methods. The steps of that algorithm are defined when subclasses override the abstract methods. The structure of the algorithm is maintained in the Template Method.

Consider the following example in which we have an abstract class that defines the way games are initialized:

```
package com.peachpit.aas3wdp.factoryexample {

    public class AbstractGame {

        // Template Method
        public final function initialize():void {
            createField();
            createTeam("red");
            createTeam("blue");
            startGame();
        }

        public function createField():void {
            throw new Error("Abstract Method!");
        }

        public function createTeam(name:String):void {
            throw new Error("Abstract Method!");
        }

        public function startGame():void {
            throw new Error("Abstract Method!");
        }

    }

}
```

The `initialize()` method in the preceding example is the Template Method. It defines how the game is initialized by first calling the `createField()` method, then creating the teams with the `createTeam()` method calls, and finally calling the `startGame()` method. However, the methods it calls are not functional in this class. It's the responsibility of the subclass to define exactly how the field and teams are created and how the game is started.

Now we will create a `FootballGame` class that extends our `AbstractGame` class. This subclass overrides the abstract methods that are called from the `initialize()` Template Method in the abstract base class.

```
package com.peachpit.aas3wdp.factoryexample {

    public class FootballGame extends AbstractGame {

        public override function createField():void {
            trace("Create Football Field");
        }

        public override function createTeam(name:String):void {
            trace("Create Football Team Named " + name);
        }

        public override function startGame():void {
            trace("Start Football Game");
        }

    }

}
```

As you can see, our `FootballGame` class overrides the `createField()`, `createTeam()`, and `startGame()` methods to make them specific to football. However, the initialization algorithm is maintained. You can see how this same technique could also be used to build a `BaseballGame` or a `BastketballGame` class. We can run the example using the following client code:

```
package com.peachpit.aas3wdp.factoryexample {

    import com.peachpit.aas3wdp.factoryexample.FootballGame;
    import flash.display.Sprite;

    public class FactoryExample extends Sprite {

        public function FactoryExample() {
            // Create an instance of FootballGame
            var game:FootballGame = new FootballGame();
            // Call the template method defined in AbstractGame
            game.initialize();
        }

    }

}
```

The following shows the output from the preceding example. As you can see, the overridden methods in the subclass were called by the Template Method. The algorithm was maintained in the Template Method while the details were deferred to subclass methods.

```
Create Football Field
Create Football Team Named red
Create Football Team Named blue
Start Football Game
```

Factory Method

Without too much effort, we can now turn the preceding Template Method example into a Factory Method example. It's very common to implement Factory Methods in a Template Method.

In the preceding Template Method example, our createField() method doesn't return anything; it just traces out the phrase "Create Football Field." Let's update this so it creates and returns a field object. Because different games have different field types, we'll create an interface called IField that all the field classes will implement. Our interface will define a single method called drawField():

```
package com.peachpit.aas3wdp.factory {

  public interface IField {

    function drawField():void;

  }

}
```

Now we'll build a FootballField class that implements the IField interface. To keep our example focused, we won't actually draw a football field to the stage, but you can fill in the blanks. Here's the basic FootballField class definition:

```
package com.peachpit.aas3wdp.factoryexample {

  import com.peachpit.aas3wdp.factoryexample.IField;

  public class FootballField implements IField {

    public function drawField():void {
      trace("Drawing the Football Field");
    }

  }

}
```

The purpose of the Factory Method is to link up two or more separate but related class hierarchies. The first hierarchy is the AbstractGame class and its subclasses: FootballGame, BaseballGame, and BastketballGame. Our second class hierarchy is now the IField interface and the classes that implement it: FootballField, BaseballField, and BasketballField. The AbstractGame and IField objects are related, but the specific creation of these objects is determined by the game subclasses. **Figure 5.1** shows how our class hierarchies match up.

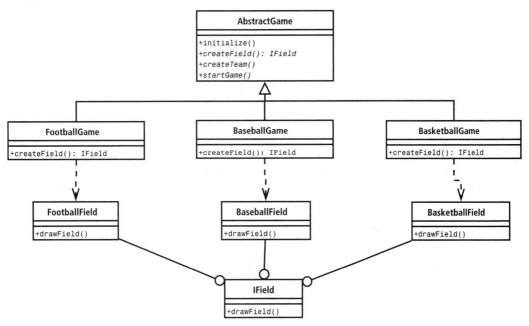

Figure 5.1
The hierarchy of classes in the Factory Method example.

Now we can refactor the `createField()` and `initialize()` methods of our `AbstractGame` class to reflect the existence of an `IField` object. Our `createField()` method is now a Factory Method that returns an object that implements the `IField interface`. The `initialize()` method can now go one step further and call the `drawField()` method on the `IField` object, as shown here:

```
package com.peachpit.aas3wdp.factoryexample {

    import com.peachpit.aas3wdp.factoryexample.IField;

    public class AbstractGame {

        // Template Method
        public final function initialize():void {
            var field:IField = createField();
            field.drawField();
            createTeam("red");
            createTeam("blue");
            startGame();
        }

        // Factory Method
        public function createField():IField {
            throw new Error("Abstract Method!");
        }

        public function createTeam(name:String):void {
```

(CODE CONTINUED)

```
            throw new Error("Abstract Method!");
        }

        public function startGame():void {
            throw new Error("Abstract Method!");
        }

    }

}
```

This abstract class and template algorithm are still completely anonymous and the specific objects created are in the hands of the subclass. Let's refactor the `FootballGame` class now to create and return a `FootballField` object:

```
package com.peachpit.aas3wdp.factory {

    import com.peachpit.aas3wdp.factory.FootballField;
    import com.peachpit.aas3wdp.factory.IField;

    public class FootballGame extends AbstractGame {

        public override function createField():IField {
            return new FootballField();
        }

        public override function createTeam(name:String):void {
            trace("Create Football Team Named " + name);
        }

        public override function startGame():void {
            trace("Start Football Game");
        }

    }

}
```

If we run this example, we'll get the following output:

```
Drawing the Football Field
Create Football Team Named red
Create Football Team Named blue
Start Football Game
```

A SIMPLE FACTORY

The Factory Method is often misunderstood. It's not uncommon to hear people mistakenly referring to their code as following the Factory Method pattern; after examining the code, we discover that the code isn't actually a Factory Method. Early in our careers, we'd make the same mistake: we'd write classes suc as the following and think it was a Factory Method:

```
package com.peachpit.aas3wdp.factoryexample {

    public class GameFactory {
```

(CODE CONTINUED)

```
        public static function createGame(gameType:String):IGame {
          switch(gameType) {
            case "football":
              return new FootballGame();
            case "baseball":
              return new BaseballGame();
            case "basketball":
            default:
              return new BasketballGame();
          }
        }

    }

  }
```

If you think this is a Factory Method, purge that bit of information from your head and keep reading because the Factory Method is much more. In fact, the preceding example isn't even a design pattern at all. It's commonly referred to as a Simple Factory or a Parameterized Factory Method. Not to say that it isn't useful; in fact, we use this technique in Chapter 12, "State Pattern," to set the state based on a name.

Summary

Abstract classes are a very important tool in object-oriented design. They are most commonly used in class libraries and frameworks because they are a solid way to factor out common behavior across subclasses.

The Template and Factory Method design patterns are handy when you're working with abstract classes. The Template Method allows you to create a common algorithm defined generally whose specific steps will later get defined by concrete subclasses. And the Factory Method allows you to trigger the creation of objects in an abstract class, but to defer the specific type to the subclass.

CHAPTER 6

Proxy Pattern

The Proxy pattern gives us a solution to a very common programming task. A *proxy* is a class that stands in for and provides access to another object. This other object isn't always an ActionScript object. It could be an image file, an XML file, a Flash Remoting service, or a Web service.

There are many reasons for wanting to use a proxy object, and each reason has its own type of proxy. One reason you might want to control access to an object is because it is a remote resource; in such a case, the proxy object can manage the communication to and from that object. This is called a Remote Proxy, and we'll discuss it later in this chapter. Another reason to use a proxy is to defer the full cost of the object's creation. This could be because the object takes a long time to create or because the object uses a lot of resources once its been created. This type of proxy is knows as a Virtual Proxy, and we'll discuss it in the next section.

There are many types of Proxy classes; however, the Remote and Virtual proxies are the two most common, and the two we will cover in this chapter.

The Proxy pattern is often confused with a couple other patterns that are very similar in functionality. Those patterns are the Adapter and Façade patterns. The main distinction of a Proxy pattern is that is has the exact same API or interface as the object it is standing in for while both the Façade and Adapter patterns modify the API. We'll briefly touch on these two related patterns towards the end of the chapter.

Virtual Proxy

The Virtual Proxy is used to proxy objects that are expensive to create or that aren't available for use right away. The Virtual Proxy can defer the creation or initialization of its subject until it is needed. Before and while the subject is being created, the Virtual Proxy stands in its place. After the creation is complete, it delegates requests directly to the subject.

Image Loader Example

One common example of a Virtual Proxy is an image loader. An image loader is an object that stands in for an external image while it's being loaded. It's important that this proxy object have the same API as the image object itself. This enables us to set the image's position and add effects to the image before it has completely loaded.

Flash Player 9 has a great example of an image loader Virtual Proxy built right into the player. It's called `Loader`, and it's found in the `flash.display` package. This class extends `DisplayObjectContainer`, so it has all the properties and methods necessary to add it to a display list, change its position, and even add effects.

In the following example, we'll use the `Loader` class to load an external image.

First create a new ActionScript project called **ImageProxyExample**.

Loading the Image

Inside the main class for this project, we will create and load the image. In the constructor of the `ImageProxyExample` class, we create the `Loader` object and load the remote image. Without waiting for the image to load, we add the `Loader` instance to the display list. We're able to do this because the `Loader` class is acting as a proxy to the real image.

```
package {

    import flash.display.Sprite;
    import flash.display.Loader;
    import flash.net.URLRequest;

    [SWF(backgroundColor="#FFFFFF", width=640, height=480)]
    public class ImageProxyExample extends Sprite {

        public function ImageProxyExample () {
            var image:Loader = new Loader();
            image.load(new URLRequest("http://www.communitymx.com/blog/images/dannyp.gif"));
            addChild(image);
        }

    }

}
```

NOTE

The SWF metatag allows us to set the background color, width, and height or the SWF in an ActionScript project. I'm using that in this example to better see the image placed on the display list.

Modifying the Image Before It's Loaded

If the Loader class weren't a proxy, we would have had to wait for the image to load before we could add it to the display list because only display objects can be added to the display list. In the next example, we modify the ImageProxyExample class by changing the image's position and adding effects, all before the real image ever loads:

```
package {

    import flash.display.Sprite;
    import flash.display.Loader;
    import flash.net.URLRequest;
    import flash.filters.GlowFilter;
    import flash.filters.BlurFilter;

    [SWF(backgroundColor="#FFFFFF", width=640, height=480)]
    public class ImageProxyExample extends Sprite {

        public function ImageProxyImp() {
            var image:Loader = new Loader();
            image.load(new URLRequest("http://www.communitymx.com/blog/images/dannyp.gif"));
            addChild(image);
            var glow:GlowFilter = new GlowFilter(0xff99ff, 2, 6, 6, 2, 1);
            var blur:BlurFilter = new BlurFilter(4, 4, 1);
            var filters:Array = new Array();
            filters.push(glow);
            filters.push(blur);
            image.filters = filters;
            image.x = 10;
            image.y = 10;
        }

    }

}
```

As you can see, a Virtual Proxy can make your code much easier to work with. Without the Loader acting as a proxy to the image, we would have to wait for the image to be successfully loaded before we could add it to the display list and add effects.

It's important to note here that although the Loader class does stand in for the loaded image, its not a pure form of a virtual proxy. The Loader class doesn't actually proxy modifications to the image, but instead applies the modifications to itself. The image gets those modifications because it is a child of the Loader class. In the next example, we'll show a true proxy that passes its requests directly to the subject.

Lazy Serialization Example

The other use of a Virtual Proxy is to stand in place of an object that is expensive to create. A great example of an expensive operation is serialization. Consider an object that models an XML element; we have two options for serialization. First, we could pass the data into the constructor of the model object and parse the values right away into the properties of the object.

This approach is known as "eager" serialization and with large, complex objects it can be very expensive. Our second option is called "lazy" serialization, in which we serialize the properties of the object on demand. This second option eliminates unnecessary serialization to unused properties and it spreads the serialization process out instead of doing it all up front. **Figure 6.1** illustrates this process.

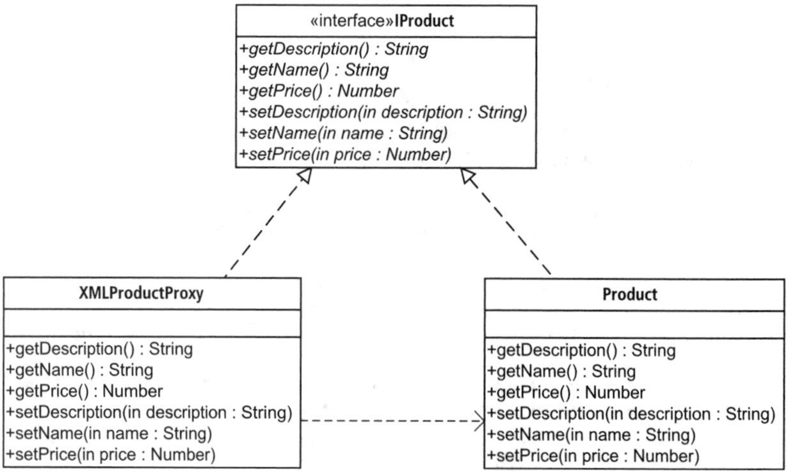

Figure 6.1

An example of lazy serialization.

To get started, create a new ActionScript project called **SerializationProxyExample**.

Creating the Product Interface

For this example, both our "real" Product class and our "proxy" Product class implement the same interface. This interface defines the methods that both classes need to implement and allows us to treat the two classes the same. The interface is named IProduct and defines the getTitle(), getPrice(), setTitle(), and setPrice() methods:

```
package com.peachpit.aas3wdp.proxyexample {

    public interface IProduct {

        function getPrice():Number;

        function getTitle():String;

        function setPrice(price:Number):void;

        function setTitle(title:String):void;

    }

}
```

Creating the Product Class

The Product class is the "real" class behind our proxy. This class simply holds the values for the product's title and price properties and has methods for getting and setting those values:

```
package com.peachpit.aas3wdp.proxyexample {

    import com.peachpit.aas3wdp.proxyexample.IProduct;

    public class Product implements IProduct {

        private var _price:Number;
        private var _title:String;

        public function Product() {}

        public function getPrice():Number {
            return _price;
        }

        public function getTitle():String {
            return title;
        }

        public function setPrice(_price:Number):void {
            this._price = _price;
        }

        public function setTitle(_title:String):void {
            this._title = _title;
        }

    }

}
```

Creating the Product Proxy Class

The XMLProductProxy class stands in for the Product class to manage the serialization on demand. The proxy uses composition to inherit all the methods of the Product class. When a request is made to getPrice(), for example, the proxy first checks to see whether its instance of the Product class has a value for price. If it does, that value is returned; if not, the proxy grabs the data out of the XML object and sets the value on the "real" product, pbject. This is how serialization occurs only when a method is invoked. Then the correct value is returned. By deferring the serialization to the request, we minimize the amount of serialization that happens up front.

```
package com.peachpit.aas3wdp.proxyexample {

    import com.peachpit.aas3wdp.proxyexample.IProduct;
    import com.peachpit.aas3wdp.proxyexample.Product;

    public class XMLProductProxy implements IProduct {
```

(CODE CONTINUED)

```
        private var _data:XML;
        private var _product:Product;


        public function XMLProductProxy(_data:XML) {
           this._data = _data;
           product = new Product();
        }


        public function getPrice():Number {
           if(isNaN(_product.getPrice())) {
              _product.setPrice(Number(_data.price.toString()));
           }
           return _product.getPrice();
        }

        public function getTitle():String {
           if(_product.getTitle() == null) {
              _product.setTitle(_data.title.toString());
           }
           return _product.getTitle();
        }

        public function setPrice(price:Number):void {
           _data.price = price;
           _product.setPrice(price);
        }

        public function setTitle(title:String):void {
           _data.title = title;
           _product.setTitle(title);
        }

     }

  }
```

Using the Proxy

Using the proxy we just created is simple. First we create a sample XML object structured to work with our proxy class. Then we create a new instance of the XMLProductProxy class and pass the sample XML object to the constructor. Now, when we call the getTitle() or getPrice() method on the proxy, it returns the value from the XML object. Subsequent calls to those same methods will return the values from the product object and no serialization is required.

```
    package {

       import com.peachpit.aas3wdp.proxypattern.IProduct;
       import com.peachpit.aas3wdp.proxypattern.XMLProductProxy;
       import flash.display.Sprite;

       public class SerializationProxyExample extends Sprite {
```

(CODE CONTINUED)

```
        public function SerializationProxyExample () {
          var data:XML = <product>
            <title>Widget</title>
            <price>19.95</price>
          </product>;

          var product:IProduct = new XMLProductProxy(data);
          trace(product.getTitle() + " -- $" + product.getPrice());
        }

    }

  }
```

Even though this is a simple example, the advantages of lazy serialization become clear when you introduce a complex data structure with multiple levels of objects. In such a case, lazy serialization can help make your application run smoother by reducing the amount of serialization that happens up front in an application and by eliminating serialization for items that are never requested.

Remote Proxy

The Remote Proxy also stands in for an object, but in this case the subject is remote. This could be a separate SWF file, an XML file, a Flash Remoting service, a SOAP or REST service, or any number of other type of services. The Remote Proxy acts as a local representative to this remote object. It has the same public methods as the remote resource and delegates requests to that resource. It also handles the communication with the remote resource.

Flickr Search Proxy Example

Flickr (www.flickr.com) is a popular online photo-sharing site. In this example, we're going to write a simple Remote Proxy to Flickr's search API. The proxy will implement a search method and handle the communication with the Flickr API. It will then broadcast an Event.COMPLETE or an ErrorEvent.ERROR event with the result.

NOTE

> The Flickr examples in this chapter require that you apply for a key to access the Flickr API. In the examples, you'll need to replace the text <ADD_YOUR_KEY_HERE> with your Flickr API key. You can apply for anAPI key at the following URL: http://www.flickr.com/services/api/misc.api_keys.html.

First, create a new ActionScript project called **RemoteProxyExample**.

Creating the Search Proxy

The PhotoSearchProxy class takes local requests using its search method and relays them to the remote Flickr API. Flickr offers a few different flavors of its API. For our example, we're using

the REST API. This API is just a simple HTTP GET request that returns an XML result.
The parameters are sent in the query string of the request.

```
package com.peachpit.aas3wdp.proxypattern {

    import flash.events.DataEvent;
    import flash.events.Event;
    import flash.events.EventDispatcher;
    import flash.net.URLLoader;
    import flash.net.URLRequest;

    public class PhotoSearchProxy extends EventDispatcher {

        private static const API_KEY:String = "<ADD_YOUR_KEY_HERE>";
        private static const FLICKR_URL:String = " http://api.flickr.com/services/rest/";

        public function PhotoSearchProxy() {}

        private function onComplete(event:Event):void {
            dispatchEvent(new DataEvent(Event.COMPLETE, false, false,
                            XML(event.target.data)));
        }

        public function search(userId:String, tags:String):void {
            var loader:URLLoader = new URLLoader();
            var request:URLRequest = new URLRequest(PhotoSearchProxy.FLICKR_URL +
                "?method=flickr.photos.search&user_id=" + userId + "&tags=" + tags +
                "&api_key=" + PhotoSearchProxy.API_KEY);
            loader.addEventListener(Event.COMPLETE, onComplete);
            loader.load(request);
        }

    }

}
```

Using the Search Proxy

To test the remote search proxy, we just create a new instance of the proxy (PhotoSearchProxy),
register the complete and error events, and make a call to the search() method, like this:

```
package {

    import com.peachpit.aas3wdp.proxypattern. PhotoSearchProxy;
    import flash.display.Sprite;
    import flash.events.DataEvent;
    import flash.events.Event;

    public class RemoteProxyExample extends Sprite {

        public function RemoteProxyEmaple() {
            var flickr:PhotoSearchProxy = new PhotoSearchProxy();
            flickr.addEventListener(Event.COMPLETE, onComplete);
            flickr.search("", "yellow");
        }
```

```
        private function onComplete(event:DataEvent):void {
            trace(event.data);
        }
    }

}
```

When you debug this example in Flex Builder, you'll see the XML result from the Flickr REST request output to the debug console.

The flash.utils.Proxy

In ActionScript 1 and 2, there was a method in the built-in `Object` class called `__resolve`. By overriding this method, you could capture any call made on that object that was undefined, including both properties and methods. The most common implementation of this feature was the Remoting and Web Service frameworks that used `__resolve` to proxy operations on remote methods.

This feature has grown up a bit in ActionScript 3.0 and is now encapsulated in the `flash.utils.Proxy` class. This class is never used directly, but is instead extended and its methods overridden. In Chapter 4, "Singleton Pattern," we used the `Proxy` class to capture calls to undefined properties and instead return a value from an XML configuration file. This was achieved by overriding the `getProperty()` method. To capture calls to undefined methods, we need to override the `callProperty()` method. In the next example, we will capture the calls to undefined methods to proxy those calls to the remote Flickr API. This will allow us to create a more flexible proxy.

NOTE

This chapter isn't a reference about the built-in Proxy class. This example illustrates the relationship of the Proxy class and the Proxy pattern, not a comprehensive description of how to use the Proxy class.

We just created a remote proxy example that calls a remote search method in the Flickr API, but what if we want to implement all the photo operations available in the Flickr API? We could systematically add each method to the `PhotoSearchProxy` class. This would be perfectly acceptable. But if we didn't know all the remote operations, or Flickr was continuously adding new operations, the `PhotoSearchProxy` class would fall short The solution is to use the built-in `flash.utils.Proxy` class.

Creating the Remote Photo Proxy

By extending the built-in `Proxy` class, we can catch calls to undefined methods and relay them to the remote Flickr API. This is a fairly simple process:

1. We must make our class dynamic so that a call to an undefined method is allowed.

2. The class needs to extend `flash.utils.Proxy` and override the `callProperty()` method. Each time a call to an undefined method is made on our class, we can catch it in `callProperty()`.

3. We must implement the `IEventDispatcher` interface and add the `EventDispatcher` functionality through composition. In our first Remote Proxy example, we extended `EventDispatcher`, but we can't do that this time because we're extending `Proxy` and multiple inheritance is not permitted in ActionScript 3.0.

There is one minor catch: The call to Flickr requires us to format the method parameters in a query string with name/value pairs. However, ActionScript doesn't have named parameters at runtime, so we need to find out what every parameter's name is. Fortunately, the Flickr API has a reflection method — `flickr.reflection.getMethodInfo` — that allows us to get all the parameters for a given method in the API. So when a call to an undefined method is made, we can save the parameters and extract the method name. Then we can make a reflection call based on the method name. When the reflection call is returned, we can match the saved parameters with their names from the reflection result to generate the query string needed to make the original operation. Here's how that logic works:

```
package com.peachpit.aas3wdp.proxypattern {

    import flash.events.DataEvent;
    import flash.events.Event;
    import flash.events.EventDispatcher;
    import flash.events.IEventDispatcher;
    import flash.net.URLLoader;
    import flash.net.URLRequest;
    import flash.utils.flash_proxy;
    import flash.utils.Proxy;

    dynamic public class PhotoProxy extends Proxy implements IEventDispatcher {

        private static const API_KEY:String = "<ADD_YOUR_KEY_HERE>";
        private static const FLICKR_URL:String = " http://api.flickr.com/services/rest/";
        private var eventDispatcher:EventDispatcher;
        private var pendingArgs:Array;

        public function PhotoProxy() {
            eventDispatcher = new EventDispatcher();
        }

        // The following event handler is called when the
        // reflection call is made to the Flickr API. The results
        // of this call tell us what to name the original request's
        // parameters and allows us to build a query string with
        // name/value pairs
        private function onReflectionComplete(event:Event):void {
            var queryString:String = "";
            var reflection:XML = XML(event.target.data);
            var methodArguments:XMLList = reflection.arguments.argument;
            for(var i:Number = 0; i < pendingArgs.length; i++) {
                if(pendingArgs[i] != null) {
                    queryString += "&" + methodArguments[i].@name.toString() + "=" +
                    pendingArgs[i];
                }
            }
            var loader:URLLoader = new URLLoader();
```

```
            var request:URLRequest = new URLRequest(PhotoProxy.FLICKR_URL + "?method=" +
                reflection.method.@name.toString() + queryString);
            loader.addEventListener(Event.COMPLETE, onComplete);
            loader.load(request);
        }

        // This event handler is called when the real result is
        // received from the Flickr API. It simply broadcasts this
        // data as a DataEvent event.
        private function onComplete(event:Event):void {
            dispatchEvent(new DataEvent(Event.COMPLETE, false, false,
            XML(event.target.data)));
        }

        // This is the method that captures the request. It is a
        // part of the flash.utils.Proxy class.
        flash_proxy override function callProperty(methodName:*, ...args):* {
            pendingArgs = args;
            pendingArgs.unshift(PhotoProxy.API_KEY);
            var loader:URLLoader = new URLLoader();
            var request:URLRequest = new URLRequest(PhotoProxy.FLICKR_URL +
                "?method=flickr.reflection.getMethodInfo&method_name=flickr.photos." +
                methodName.toString() + "&api_key=" + PhotoProxy.API_KEY);
            loader.addEventListener(Event.COMPLETE, onReflectionComplete);
            loader.load(request);
            return methodName.toString();
        }

        public function addEventListener(type:String, listener:Function,
            useCapture:Boolean = false, priority:int = 0, weakRef:Boolean = false):void {
            eventDispatcher.addEventListener(type, listener, useCapture, priority, weakRef);
        }

        public function dispatchEvent(event:Event):Boolean {
            return eventDispatcher.dispatchEvent(event);
        }

        public function hasEventListener(type:String):Boolean {
            return eventDispatcher.hasEventListener(type);
        }

        public function removeEventListener(type:String, listener:Function,
            useCapture:Boolean = false):void {
            eventDispatcher.removeEventListener(type, listener, useCapture);
        }

        public function willTrigger(type:String):Boolean {
            return eventDispatcher.willTrigger(type);
        }

    }

}
```

Using the Photo Proxy

To use this photo proxy, we need to slightly modify the main class from the first remote proxy example. The only change is the reference to the `PhotoProxy` class in place of the `PhotoSearchProxy` class. Also, to show that all the photo operations are now available through this proxy, we will now call the getRecent() operation.

```
package {

    import com.peachpit.aas3wdp.proxypattern.FlickrResultEvent;
    import com.peachpit.aas3wdp.proxypattern.PhotoProxy;
    import flash.display.Sprite;
    import flash.events.Event;
    import flash.events.DataEvent;

    public class RemoteProxyExample extends Sprite {

        public function RemoteProxyExample() {
            var flickr:PhotoProxy = new PhotoProxy();
            flickr.addEventListener(Event.COMPLETE, onComplete);
            flickr.getRecent();
        }

        private function onComplete(event:DataEvent):void {
            trace(event.data);
        }
    }

}
```

Adapter and Façade Patterns

The Adapter and Façade patterns are very similar to the Proxy pattern. The main difference is that a `Proxy` class has the same public methods (usually by implementing the same interface) as the object it represents. The Adapter and Façade patterns don't necessarily have the same methods as the object (or objects) they represent. Although the Adapter and Façade patterns are almost identical, the difference is that an Adapter's purpose is to convert an object's API, whereas the Façade's purpose is to simplify.

Summary

In this chapter, we examined the Proxy pattern and its many uses. The two flavors of Proxy pattern we looked at are the Virtual and Remote Proxy patterns. We also went through several examples to fully understand the Proxy pattern:

- We used the built-in `flash.display.Loader` class to proxy the loading of an image.

- We created a Virtual Proxy to defer serialization of XML to a model object.

- We built a simple Remote Proxy for handling Flickr searches.

CHAPTER 7

Iterator Pattern

Nearly every application uses collections. A collection is simply a group of organized data. ActionScript has lots of collections including standard types such as arrays and associative arrays as well as more sophisticated collections such as multidimensional arrays and custom collection data types. When working with collections, you will naturally need to access the elements of that collection. The Iterator pattern described in this chapter does all that while avoiding some of the pitfalls that other approaches to data access might present.

Understanding the Problems with Iteration

For the purposes of this early discussion of iterating over collection data, we'll use the following class to illustrate points. The customized UIntCollection class is essentially a glorified array. However, although an array can store any sort of data, the UIntCollection stores only data of type uint.

```
package com.peachpit.aas3wdp.collections {
  public class UIntCollection {
    private var _data:Array;

    public function UIntCollection() {
      _data = new Array();
    }

    public function addElement(value:uint):void {
      _data.push(value);
    }

  }
}
```

Iterating over collection data presents several common dilemmas. One dilemma deals with how an object allows access to the collection. One option is to simply expose the collection.

For example, if a class has an `array` property, it can expose the array using a getter method. Adding the following getter method to the `UIntCollection` class does just that:

```
public function get data():Array {
    return _data;
}
```

The preceding solution enables you to iterate through the collection using a `for` statement, as follows:

```
var collection:UIntCollection = new UIntCollection ();
collection.addElement(1);
collection.addElement(2);
var i:uint;
for(i = 0; i < collection.data.length; i++) {
    // Code that uses collection data.
    trace(collection.data[i]);
}
```

There are two major related flaws with the preceding solution. The first is that exposing the array directly breaks encapsulation in a fundamental way. The intention of exposing the collection by way of a getter method is to enable iteration over the collection elements. However, as a consequence, it's also possible to alter the collection without the object knowing anything about it. For example, consider the following:

```
var collection:UIntCollection = new UIntCollection ();
collection.data[0] = "one";
```

In this example, you can see that a value is assigned to the data collection without the object being notified. Furthermore, the example assigns a string value to the collection element even though the `UIntCollection` class expects that the data collection contains only unsigned integers.

NOTE

> ActionScript does not currently support typed arrays, which is why the preceding example allows us to assign a string to an element of the array. In a language with typed arrays, you would have to declare an array of a particular type (for example, *uint*).

The second flaw in the preceding solution is that it exposes not only the data, but also the structure of the data. If you want to iterate over the elements of a collection, there's no reason you have to know the structure of the collection to accomplish that. In fact, having to know the structure is a hindrance because it requires different ways to iterate over different structures.

A second dilemma with iterating over collection data deals with the interface. In the preceding example, we noted that exposing collection data directly is not a good idea because it could have unexpected consequences. As a solution, it might seem like a good idea to define an API for the collection class that enables you to iterate over the collection data. For example, the following addition to the `UIntCollection` class enables you to loop through the elements of the collection while maintaining good encapsulation:

```
package com.peachpit.aas3wdp.collections {
  public class UIntCollection {
    private var _data:Array;
    private var _index:uint;

    public function UIntCollection() {
      _data = new Array();
      _index = 0;
    }

    public function addElement(value:uint):void {
      _data.push(value);
    }

    public function reset():void {
      _index = 0;
    }

    public function hasNext():Boolean {
      return _index < _data.length;
    }

    public function next():uint {
      return uint(_data[_index++]);
    }

  }
}
```

The downside with the preceding API is that it makes the collection responsible for iterating over the data. There are at least two major flaws with that: One flaw is that each collection object maintains its own cursor (_index) so that you cannot iterate over the collection object's data more than once simultaneously. The second flaw is that the collection class has to define every possible way to iterate over the data. The preceding example assumes that you always want to iterate over the data in a forward direction, one element at a time, in the order that elements appear in the array. If you want to add methods for iterating over the collection in ascending value order or skipping every other element, you must add a lot of responsibilities to the collection class itself.

Understanding Iterator Elements

The Iterator pattern is a solution that enables you to iterate over a collection's elements while maintaining good encapsulation and not having to expose the structure of the data. The Iterator pattern offloads the iteration responsibilities to a new object, and as a consequence, the collection class remains simple, and you can iterate over the collection more than once simultaneously.

The Iterator pattern consists of the following elements:

- Iterator interface: The interface for iterating over the collection data
- Concrete iterator: The implementation of the iterator interface

- Collection interface: The interface that defines how to retrieve an iterator

- Concrete collection: The implementation of the collection interface

The Iterator Interface

To define an iterator interface, you have to determine how much you want the iterator to be able to do. Initially it may seem important to define an interface that allows for moving forward or backward through the collection data. However, in practice, you generally don't need the ability to move both forward and backward through the collection data. Rather, you generally want to move through the data in only one direction, one element at a time. The ability to reset an iterator back to the start is also useful. The following interface accomplishes these goals, and it is the one that we use throughout this book.

```
package com.peachpit.aas3wdp.iterators {
    public interface IIterator {

        function reset():void;
        function next():Object;
        function hasNext():Boolean;

    }
}
```

The preceding interface allows you to iterate over a collection, one element at a time. The reset() method simply moves the cursor back to the start of the collection data. The next() method returns the next element and advances the cursor. The hasNext() method returns true if there is a next element and false if there is no next element. And the current() method returns the current element without advancing the cursor.

NOTE

It's important to understand that the IIterator interface is merely an interface. It does not dictate implementation. Although we might be accustomed to thinking of the word *next* as meaning moving forward, the *next()* method of an implementing class can just as easily move backward through a collection. For that matter an implementing class could skip every other element or even return random elements. The interface simply specifies what methods an implementing class must define.

The Concrete Iterator

The interface simply determines what methods the concrete iterator must implement. The concrete iterator defines the actual functionality. Perhaps one of the most common types of iterators for ActionScript is an iterator that can iterate over an array one element at a time starting with index 0. The following ArrayIterator definition accomplishes just that:

```
package com.peachpit.aas3wdp.iterators {
    public class ArrayIterator implements IIterator {

        private var _index:uint = 0;
```

```
      private var _collection:Array;

      public function ArrayIterator(collection:Array) {
        _collection = collection;
        _index = 0;
      }

      public function hasNext():Boolean {
        return _index < _collection.length;
      }

      public function next():Object {
        return _collection[_index++];
      }

      public function reset():void {
        _index = 0;
      }

    }
  }
```

Of course, you can define many types of iterators depending on the collection data structures and the way in which you want to iterate over the data. The preceding example iterates over an array one element at a time with increasing indices. You could also define an iterator that returns the elements in reverse order, like this:

```
package com.peachpit.aas3wdp.iterators {
  public class ArrayReverseIterator implements IIterator {

    private var _index:uint = 0;
    private var _collection:Array;

    public function ArrayIterator(collection:Array) {
      _collection = collection;
      _index = _collection.length - 1;
    }

    public function hasNext():Boolean {
      return _index >= 0;
    }

    public function next():Object {
      return _collection[_index--];
    }

    public function reset():void {
      _index = _collection.length - 1;
    }

  }
}
```

Obviously, these are just two of the many types of iterators. Every iterator can define its own unique implementation. What is critical is that every iterator implements the same interface.

The different implementations of the IIterator interface might allow access to different types of collections (associative arrays, for example). However, even if the collections are different, the iterator interface is the same, meaning you can access the data in the same way.

The Collection Interface

The collection interface defines the way in which you can access the iterator for a collection. The simplest interface is as follows:

```
package com.peachpit.aas3wdp.collections {
    public interface ICollection {
        function iterator():IIterator;
    }
}
```

However, consider that you might want to enable many types of iterators for a collection. For example, you might want to allow a collection to return an iterator that advances one element at a time forward through the collection, or you might want to return an iterator that skips every other element in ascending order. For that reason, it is advantageous to define the interface as follows:

```
package com.peachpit.aas3wdp.collections {
    public interface ICollection {
        function iterator(type:String = null):IIterator;
    }
}
```

The implementing collection class can then return a different iterator type depending on the parameter passed to the method. The UIntCollection example in the next section illustrates this.

The Concrete Collection

The concrete collection class implements the collection interface. The following example rewrites the UIntCollection class so that it implements ICollection:

```
package com.peachpit.aas3wdp.collections {
    import com.peachpit.aas3wdp.IIterator;
    import com.peachpit.aas3wdp.ArrayIterator;
    public class UIntCollection implements ICollection {
        private var _data:Array;

        public function UIntCollection() {
            _data = new Array();
        }

        public function addElement(value:uint):void {
            _data.push(value);
        }

        public function iterator(type:String = null):IIterator {
            return new ArrayIterator(_data);
        }

    }
}
```

The preceding implementation returns only one type of iterator. However, if appropriate, you could enable several types of iterators, and the iterator that is returned would depend on the parameter value, as in the following example:

```
public function iterator(type:String = null):IIterator {
   if(type == "ArrayReverseIterator") {
      return new ArrayReverseIterator(_data);
   }
   else {
      new ArrayIterator(_data);
   }
}
```

In this example the user can create one UIntCollection object, and from the same interface she can request several different types of iterators.

```
var collection:UIntCollection = new UIntCollection();
collection.addElement(1);
collection.addElement(20);
collection.addElement(5);
collection.addElement(15);
var iteratorAscending:IIterator = collection.iterator();
var iteratorDescending:IIterator = collection.iterator("ArrayReverseIterator");
```

Using Iterators

After you've defined iterators and collections, you can use the iterators as in the following example, which adds four elements to a UIntCollection object and then uses an iterator to access that data:

```
var collection:UIntCollection = new UIntCollection();
collection.addElement(1);
collection.addElement(20);
collection.addElement(5);
collection.addElement(15);
var iterator:IIterator = collection.iterator();
while(iterator.hasNext()) {
   trace(iterator.next());
}
```

The preceding example uses the iterator to loop through each of the elements of the collection and write it to the debug console. Notice that because the iterator interface is identical for all iterator types, it doesn't matter what concrete type the iterator() method returns. For example, the preceding code would continue to function correctly if you specified ArrayReverseIterator as the parameter for iterator(), thus returning an ArrayReverseIterator instead of an ArrayIterator. The only difference would be the output—which would return the collection values in reverse order.

Consider how different this approach is from using the array directly. When you allow direct access to the array, not only do you break encapsulation, you also create code that is specific to the implementation. For example, if you wanted to use a for statement to loop through the elements of an array directly, you would have to change the for statement expressions when you wanted to change how you loop through the array. But when you use the iterators, you don't have to make such changes because the implementation is within the iterator itself.

Using Null Iterators

One special iterator type is the null iterator. The null iterator enables you to build classes that adhere to an interface (they are iterable) but that don't actually have any collection data. The classic case for null iterators is the leaf element of a composite object (as discussed in Chapter 8, "Composite Pattern"). In such cases, it's necessary that the leaf elements (those containing no collection data) and the composite elements (those that do contain collection data) implement the same interface and be treated in the same way. For recursive traversal purposes, it's necessary that the interface provide access to an iterator for *both* composite and leaf elements. One option is to return null for the leaf element iterator. However, doing so presents a special case that you must detect—namely, you must add if statements to test whether the iterator is null or not before calling the methods such as hasNext() and next(). A more elegant solution is to use a special type of iterator that always returns false for hasNext() and returns null for next(). That special-case iterator is a null iterator as defined in the following code:

```
package com.peachpit.aas3wdp.iterators {
   public class NullIterator implements IIterator {

      public function NullIterator() {}

      public function hasNext():Boolean {
         return false;
      }

      public function next():Object {
         return null;
      }

      public function reset():void {
      }

   }
}
```

We'll see an example of how to use this iterator type in the next chapter.

Summary

The Iterator pattern enables client code to read a collection's data without exposing the structure of the data or making the data inadvertently writable. The Iterator pattern is a common pattern that provides a standard interface for reading collection data.

Although the Iterator pattern is simple, it is very useful. In fact, it is the pattern's simplicity that makes it so useful. Because the pattern standardizes the way to access data from collections, it allows you to create interfaces that interact with the IIterator interface rather than with any specific implementation. That means that your code is more flexible and adaptable.

Composite Pattern

The Composite pattern enables you to elegantly deal with recursive or hierarchical data structures. There are many examples of hierarchical data structures, making the Composite pattern very useful. A common example of such a data structure is one that you encounter every time you use a computer: the file system. The file system consists of directories and files. Every directory potentially has contents. The contents of a directory might be files, but they also might be directories. In this way, the file system of a computer is organized in a recursive structure. If you want to represent such a data structure programmatically, you can use the Composite pattern.

The Composite pattern has the following elements:

- Element interface: An interface for all participating elements.

- Leaf: A class representing terminating elements in the data structure. In the file system example, files are leaf elements because they don't have child elements. Leaf classes must implement the element interface.

- Composite: A class for the collections in the data structure. In the file system example, directories are composite elements. Composite classes must implement the element interface.

Understanding the Element Interface

All elements within the Composite pattern, whether leaves or composites, should be essentially interchangeable. This means that they must all implement a common interface. It's impossible to determine what the exact interface ought to look like for every use of the Composite pattern. However, at a minimum, it will likely look much like a collection. The following is an example of what a basic element interface might look like:

```
package {
  public interface IElement {
     function iterator():IIterator;
     function addItem(item: IElement):void;
     function removeItem(item: IElement):void;
     function getParent():IElement;
     function setParent(parent: IElement):void;
  }
}
```

NOTE

The preceding interface uses the IIterator interface as discussed in Chapter 7, "Iterator Pattern." This chapter makes use of the Iterator pattern; if you have not yet read Chapter 7, you might want to consider reading that chapter before continuing with this one.

Note that this basic element interface example specifies IElement as the type for the addItem(), removeItem(), and setParent() methods. In theory, this means that any class that implements the IElement interface can be added to any other object that implements the same interface. This is what enables all elements in the Composite pattern to look identical. Of course, the implementation will be different for leaf and composite elements. A leaf element cannot actually contain other elements, but it must implement the same interface for the pattern to work.

In a practical example, the element interface will probably have more methods than are included in the IElement example. Throughout this chapter, we'll be looking at a file system example. The following IFileSystemItem interface is the element interface we will use for the file system example:

```
package com.peachpit.aas3wdp.compositeexample.data {

   // You'll need to ensure that IIterator from Chapter 7 is in your
   // classpath.
   import com.peachpit.aas3wdp.iterators.IIterator;

public interface IFileSystemItem {
   function iterator():IIterator;
   function addItem(item:IFileSystemItem):void;
   function removeItem(item:IFileSystemItem):void;
   function getName():String;
   function setName(name:String):void;
   function getParent():IFileSystemItem;
   function setParent(parent:IFileSystemItem):void;
  }
}
```

For this example, it's also useful to create a simple implementation in the form of an abstract class we'll call FileSystemItem. Although an abstract class is not a requirement in this case, we're using one because that way each of the concrete classes can inherit a common implementation rather than having redundant code in each of the classes. All our code still references the interface rather than the abstract class to maintain maximum adaptability. The abstract class looks like the following:

```
package com.peachpit.aas3wdp.compositeexample.data {
  import com.peachpit.aas3wdp.iterators.IIterator;

  public class FileSystemItem implements IFileSystemItem {
    protected var _parent:IFileSystemItem;
    protected var _name:String;

    public function FileSystemItem() {
    }

    public function iterator():IIterator {
      return null;
    }

    public function addItem(item:IFileSystemItem):void {

    }

    public function removeItem(item:IFileSystemItem):void {

    }

    public function getName():String {
      return _name;
    }

    public function setName(name:String):void {
      _name = name;
    }

    public function getParent():IFileSystemItem {
      return _parent;
    }

    public function setParent(parent:IFileSystemItem):void {
      _parent = parent;
    }
  }
}
```

In this case, we're using an abstract class (`FileSystemItem`) because it provides some basic implementation that concrete leaf and composite subclasses can inherit. This way the, `File` and `Directory` subclasses don't have to each implement getName(),setName(), getParent(), and setParent().

NOTE

The preceding interface and abstract class might seem strange because they require all concrete classes to implement methods that may or may not appear directly related to all types. For example, leaf elements might not appear to need *addItem()*, *removeItem()*, and *iterator()* methods. Although it's true that, in most cases, it is inadvisable for an interface to require a concrete type to implement methods that don't apply to all types, in the case of the Composite pattern it is essential to the pattern that composite and leaf elements appear to be identical. Therefore the leaf elements must implement *addItem()*, *removeItem()*, and *iterator()*.

Understanding Leaf Elements

Leaf elements are the terminating elements in the Composite pattern. Leaf elements can be placed in composite elements, but composite elements cannot be placed in leaf elements. In terms of our file system example, files are leaf elements—you can place files in directories, but you cannot place directories in files.

Leaf elements must implement the same interface as composite elements for the pattern to work. This approach might seem odd at first because the element interface always allows for adding and removing elements, yet a leaf element cannot contain elements. In the Composite pattern, the leaf element does include the methods to add, remove, and access elements to satisfy the requirements of the interface, yet the implementation does not allow you to actually add, remove, or access elements. The following is the implementation for a File class as part of our file system example. Notice that it inherits from the abstract FileSystemItem class so that it doesn't need to implement most of the required methods (it inherits the implementations from its superclass). In particular, it doesn't have to override addItem() or removeItem() because the superclass implementations do nothing, which is exactly what we want the leaf class implementation to do. Although the File class does not need to override iterator(), to simplify working with File objects in the Composite pattern, we'll override iterator() so that it returns a NullIterator instance, as shown here:

```
package com.peachpit.aas3wdp.compositeexample.data {
    import com.peachpit.aas3wdp.iterators.IIterator;
    import com.peachpit.aas3wdp.iterators.NullIterator;

    public class File extends FileSystemItem {

        public function File() {

        }

        override public function iterator():IIterator {
            return new NullIterator();
        }

    }
}
```

We talked about the NullIterator type in Chapter 7. Although the File implementation of iterator() could simply return null, it's slightly more elegant to return a NullIterator object. The reason is that if iterator() returns null, you might have to test for null values when using File objects. Yet if the method returns a NullIterator object, you can use the return value interchangeably with the return value from a composite object. Because a NullIterator object always returns false for hasNext(), it should allow a leaf object to work just like a composite object without ever actually iterating over child elements.

Understanding Composite Elements

Composite elements also implement the element interface, but unlike leaf elements, you can add child elements to composites. In our file system example, directories are composite elements.

The following is a Directory class that represents a file system directory in our file system example. Notice that the class extends the abstract FileSystemItem class. Because the abstract class defers the implementation of iterator(), addItem(), and removeItem() to subclasses, the Directory class must override these methods.

```
package com.peachpit.aas3wdp.compositeexample.data {
    import com.peachpit.aas3wdp.iterators.IIterator;
    import com.peachpit.aas3wdp.iterators.ArrayIterator;

    public class Directory extends FileSystemItem {

        // The array of child elements
        private var _items:Array;

        public function Directory() {
            _items = new Array();
        }

        override public function addItem(item:IFileSystemItem):void {
            _items.push(item);
        }

        override public function removeItem(item:IFileSystemItem):void {
            var i:uint;
            // Loop through all the child elements.
            for(i = 0; i < _items.length; i++) {
                // If one of the elements matches the
                // parameter remove it from the array.
                if(_items[i] == item) {
                    _items.splice(i, 1);
                    break;
                }
            }
        }

        override public function iterator():IIterator {
            // See the "Iterator Pattern" chapter for details on     // ArrayIterator
            return new ArrayIterator(_items);
        }
    }
}
```

The Directory class implementation is fairly simple. It must override addItem() to append the element to the _items array. The class overrides removeItem() to remove the specified item by looping through all the elements of the _items array until it finds the matching element. And the class overrides iterator() to return an ArrayIterator instance.

Building a File System Example

The Composite pattern is simple in terms of its implementation, but its usage might be a little unclear as of yet. We've already discussed the details of how it works, but an example usually helps illustrate the concepts. In this example, we'll build a simple application that uses the file-system metaphor to show how the Composite pattern works.

This example uses the IFileSystemItem interface as well as the FileSystemItem, File, and Directory classes discussed earlier in this chapter. In addition, we'll create a FileSystemItemView class and a main class (CompositeExample). The application will load data from an XML file and use that data to allow the user to browse a graphical representation of a file system. The directories are represented by folder icons, and files are represented by white rectangles. The user can click a directory to browse the contents of the directory.

For the purposes of this example, we'll read the data from an XML file called fileSystem.xml with the following content:

```
<fileSystem>
    <fileSystemItem type="Directory" name="Program Files" bytes="1024">
        <fileSystemItem type="Directory" name="Adobe Illustrator">
            <fileSystemItem type="File" name="Illustrator.exe" />
        </fileSystemItem>
    </fileSystemItem>
    <fileSystemItem type="Directory" name="My Documents">
        <fileSystemItem type="File" name="Document.txt" />
        <fileSystemItem type="File" name="Image.jpg" />
    </fileSystemItem>
</fileSystem>
```

You can see that the root node is <fileSystem>, and contained within that are nested <fileSystemItem> tags. Each <fileSystemItem> tag is of type Directory or File. Directory nodes can contain nested elements whereas File nodes cannot. Each element has a name attribute as well. We'll load this XML file into the application and parse it into our composite structure.

Next we'll need a class that is a view for the File and Directory classes. The FileSystemItemView constructor accepts a parameter of type IFileSystemItem and then draws the correct icon and adds a label. Note that FileSystemItemView extends Sprite because it needs to be a display object.

```
package com.peachpit.aas3wdp.compositeexample.views {
    import flash.display.Sprite;
    import flash.text.TextField;
    import flash.text.TextFieldAutoSize;
    import flash.filters.BevelFilter;
    import com.peachpit.aas3wdp.compositeexample.data.Directory;
    import com.peachpit.aas3wdp.compositeexample.data.IFileSystemItem;

    public class FileSystemItemView extends Sprite {

        // The file or directory to display.
        private var _item:IFileSystemItem;

        // The icon for the item - either a white rectangle or
```

```
            // a folder icon
            private var _icon:Sprite;

            // The name of the item
            private var _label:TextField;

            // Return a reference to the file or directory
            public function get data():IFileSystemItem {
               return _item;
            }

            public function FileSystemItemView(item:IFileSystemItem) {
               _item = item;
               _icon = new Sprite();
               // Test if the item is a Directory or File. Draw the
               // appropriate icon for the item type
               if(item is Directory) {
                  _icon.graphics.lineStyle();
                  _icon.graphics.beginFill(0xFFFF00);
                  _icon.graphics.drawRect(0, 10, 50, 30);
                  _icon.graphics.endFill();
                  _icon.graphics.beginFill(0xFFFF00);
                  _icon.graphics.drawRoundRect(0, 0, 25, 15, 5, 5);
                  _icon.graphics.endFill();
                  _icon.filters = [new BevelFilter()];
               }
               else {
                  _icon.graphics.lineStyle(0, 0x000000, 1);
                  _icon.graphics.beginFill(0xFFFFFF);
                  _icon.graphics.drawRect(0, 0, 40, 50);
                  _icon.graphics.endFill();
               }
               addChild(_icon);

               // Add a label text field
               _label = new TextField();
               _label.text = _item.getName();
               _label.autoSize = TextFieldAutoSize.LEFT;
               _label.x = 50;
               addChild(_label);
            }

            // This method allows you to override the label text
            // value for special cases such as parent directories
            // where you want to display a specific label rather than
            // the name of the item
            public function overrideLabel(label:String):void {
               _label.text = label;
            }

      }
   }
```

Next we need to define a main class. In this example, the main class is called `CompositeExample`. The main class loads the XML file, parses it into the composite structure, and displays the contents of the top-level directory. When the user clicks a directory, the main class dispatches an event that updates the view.

```
package {
    import flash.display.Sprite;
    import flash.net.URLLoader;
    import flash.net.URLRequest;
    import flash.events.Event;
    import flash.events.MouseEvent;
    import com.peachpit.aas3wdp.compositeexample.data.Directory;
    import com.peachpit.aas3wdp.compositeexample.data.File;
    import com.peachpit.aas3wdp.compositeexample.data.FileSystemItem;
    import com.peachpit.aas3wdp.iterators.IIterator;
    import com.peachpit.aas3wdp.compositeexample.views.FileSystemItemView;
    import com.peachpit.aas3wdp.compositeexample.data.IFileSystemItem;

    public class CompositeExample extends Sprite {

        // The top-level directory which contains all the
        // child elements
        private var _fileSystem:Directory;

        // An array of all the views currently displayed
        private var _itemViews:Array;

        public function CompositeExample() {

            // Load the XML
            var loader:URLLoader = new URLLoader();
            loader.addEventListener(Event.COMPLETE, onLoadXML);
            loader.load(new URLRequest("fileSystem.xml"));

            // Construct the top-level directory. Set the name,
            // and set the parent to null. Setting the parent to
            // null will indicate that there are no parent
            // composite objects for this directory.
            _fileSystem = new Directory();
            _fileSystem.setName("File System");
            _fileSystem.setParent(null);

            _itemViews = new Array();
        }

        // When the XML loads parse the XML into the composite
        // structure. The parseXmlToFileSystem() method accepts an
        // XMLList parameter and a Directory parameter. It parses
        // all the XMLList children into elements within the
        // directory.
        private function onLoadXML(event:Event):void {
            XML.ignoreWhitespace = true;
            var xml:XML = new XML(event.target.data);
            parseXmlToFileSystem(xml.children(), _fileSystem);

            // Display the contents of the top-level directory
```

```
            updateView(_fileSystem);
    }

    private function updateView(directory:Directory):void {
        var i:uint;
        // Loop through all the currently-displayed item
        // views, and remove them.
        for(i = 0; i < _itemViews.length; i++) {
            removeChild(_itemViews[i]);
            delete _itemViews[i];
        }
        _itemViews = new Array();

        // Retrieve the iterator for the current directory
        var iterator:IIterator = directory.iterator();
        var itemY:Number = 0;
        var item:IFileSystemItem;
        var view:FileSystemItemView;

        // If the directory has a parent, then add a view for
        // the parent directory and override the label so
        // it simply says Parent Directory. Add a click
        // event listener so when the user clicks, it changes
        // to the parent directory
        if(directory.getParent() != null) {
            view = new FileSystemItemView(directory.getParent());
            view.overrideLabel("Parent Directory");
            view.addEventListener(MouseEvent.CLICK, onClick);
            addChild(view);
            _itemViews.push(view);
            itemY += view.height + 5;
        }

        // Loop through all the items in the directory. Add
        // a view for each item. If the item is a directory,
        // add a click event listener.
        while(iterator.hasNext()) {
            item = IFileSystemItem(iterator.next());
            view = new FileSystemItemView(item);
            view.y = itemY;
            itemY += view.height + 5;
            if(item is Directory) {
                view.addEventListener(MouseEvent.CLICK, onClick);
            }
            addChild(view);
            _itemViews.push(view);
        }
    }

    private function parseXmlToFileSystem(xml:XMLList, directory:Directory):void {
        var i:uint;
        var item:FileSystemItem;
        // Loop through all the children of the XMLList.
        // If the item is a directory, then make a new
        // directory and call parseXmlToFileSystem()
        // recursively to populate the directory. Otherwise
```

(CODE CONTINUED)

```
            // construct a file.
            for(i = 0; i < xml.length(); i++) {
               if(xml[i].@type == "Directory") {
                  item = new Directory();
                  parseXmlToFileSystem(xml[i].children(), Directory(item));
               }
               else {
                  item = new File();
               }
               item.setParent(directory);
               item.setName(xml[i].@name);
               directory.addItem(item);
            }
         }

         // When the user clicks an item view, update the view to the
         // contents of the directory that the user clicked.
         private function onClick(event:MouseEvent):void {
            updateView(Directory(event.currentTarget.data));
         }
      }
   }
}
```

When you run the application, you ought to see two folders initially: ProgramFiles and MyDocuments. If you click one of the folders, the view updates to display the contents of the directory as well as a folder icon with a ParentDirectory label. An example of the application is shown in Figure 8.1.

Figure 8.1

The sample application.

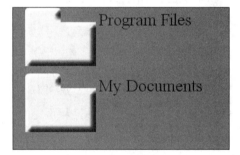

Summary

The Composite pattern is an important pattern for creating hierarchical structures in which you want to be able to treat all the elements in the same way. This chapter uses a file system example composed of files and directories to illustrate one case in which the Composite pattern can be useful. In this example, files and directories implement the same interface, which is a key feature of the Composite pattern. By implementing the same interface, you can treat files and directories in exactly the same way, and you can store either a file or a directory as a child of a directory.

CHAPTER **9**

Decorator Pattern

The Decorator pattern enables you to apply new behavior to an object at runtime. Traditionally, many developers learn to add behavior by using inheritance rather than composition. This means that if you want to add a move() method to an existing Widget class, you'd extend Widget to define a new MovableWidget class. Or, if you want to redefine the move() method of MovableWidget so that it moves only until its fuel is used up, you could extend MovableWidget to define FuelableMovableWidget. However, inheritance has two major drawbacks in such cases:

- You cannot change an object's behavior at runtime. For example, a Widget is always a Widget. It isn't possible to convert a Widget to a MovableWidget or a FuelableMovableWidget when traditional inheritance is used.

- As more permutations become available, the number of classes required becomes unwieldy. For example, if you want to extend a Widget class so that it is scalable, you might define a ScalableWidget subclass. If you want to extend the class so that it is rotatable, you might define a RotatableWidget subclass. To make a movable widget, you might define a MovableWidget subclass. However, what if you want to combine some of the behaviors? Using inheritance, you'd have to define ScalableRotatableWidget, ScalableMovableWidget, RotatableMovableWidget, and ScalableRotatableMovableWidget. Each new behavior increases the number of required classes in a factorial fashion such that after just a few behaviors, the number of classes is unmanageable.

The solution to these inheritance drawbacks is the Decorator pattern. The Decorator pattern uses composition rather than inheritance to add new behavior to an object. This means that it's possible to add behavior and change behavior at runtime. Additionally, because the Decorator pattern uses composition, it's often possible to chain together several new behaviors in a manageable fashion.

It is often useful to visualize how a pattern works. Imagine that the Decorator pattern is like a set of Russian dolls—the type of dolls that stack inside one another. Obviously, this analogy is limited, but it does illustrate the basic nesting relationship between decorator and decorated objects. The Decorator pattern starts with a base object that can be decorated. This decorated object is analogous to the innermost Russian doll. The decorator objects use composition to add behavior to the decorated object. The decorator objects are analogous to the larger Russian dolls within which you place the smaller dolls. After you stack a Russian doll in the next larger doll, you can then stack that doll in the *next* larger doll. So too with the Decorator pattern; you can often use a decorator to add yet more behavior to another decorator—thus treating the decorator like a decorated object. We'll look at these types and their relationships in more detail throughout the chapter.

Understanding the Decorator Pattern

The basic idea of the Decorator pattern is that new types of objects (decorators) can add new behavior or change existing behavior of a decorated object. The decorators and the decorated object must implement the same interface. That way, the decorator and decorated objects can be used interchangeably.

The Decorator pattern consists of the following elements:

- Decorator/decorated interface
- Concrete decorated class
- Abstract decorator class
- Concrete decorator class(s)

The following sections look at these elements in more detail.

Decorator/Decorated Interface

Everything about the Decorator pattern hinges on the decorator objects and the decorated objects implementing the same interface. This way, they can be treated in exactly the same way and used interchangeably. The exact interface depends entirely on the required behavior of the objects. There is no universal interface for all decorator and decorated objects. For the purpose of a simple example, consider the following interface. In the next few sections, we'll show how to implement this interface using the Decorator pattern.

```
package com.peachpit.aas3wdp.decorator {
    public interface IWidget {
        function getDescription():String;
        function run():void;
    }
}
```

TIP

> The distinction between decorator and decorated objects might not be immediately clear. Decorators are objects that use composition to add to or modify the behavior of another object at runtime. The object to which the behavior is added or modified is the decorated object. Because decorator objects themselves can be decorated by other decorators, it's essential that both types of objects implement the same interface.

Concrete Decorated Class

The concrete decorated class is the basic type that implements the interface. Continuing the example from the preceding section, the following Widget class implements IWidget as the basic decorated type:

```
package com.peachpit.aas3wdp.decorator {
   public class Widget implements IWidget {
      public function Widget() {}

      public function getDescription():String {
         return "Widget";
      }

      public function run():void {
         trace("running");
      }
   }
}
```

This simple decorated type is the basis of the pattern (like the innermost Russian doll). The base decorated type is the foundation on which all other decorators are applied. This example is purposefully simple. It merely implements the two methods required by the interface (IWidget).

Abstract Decorator Class

Technically, all that is required of a decorator is that it implements the same interface as the decorated type. However, practically speaking, most decorators inherit from an abstract decorator class that implements some of the basic functionality such as compositing the decorated object and passing through the method calls. The following example illustrates a basic abstract decorator class for the widget example:

```
package com.peachpit.aas3wdp.decorator {
   public class AbstractWidgetDecorator implements IWidget {

      protected var decorated:IWidget;

      public function AbstractWidgetDecorator(decoratedWidget:IWidget) {
         decorated = decoratedWidget;
      }

      public function getDescription():String {
         return _decorated.getDescription();
```

```
        }

        public function run():void {
            _decorated.run();
        }
    }
}
```

The AbstractWidgetDecorator class must implement the IWidget interface because it is the same interface implemented by the decorated type (Widget). This is the basis of the Decorator pattern—that both the decorator and the decorated types implement the same interface.

Note that the constructor accepts a parameter of type IWidget. This parameter is the object that the decorator will decorate. Although there's no requirement that you pass the decorated object through the constructor (you could use a different method to accomplish this), it is the convention. It's important that the decorated type is set to the interface rather than a concrete (or abstract) type in order to fully support polymorphism. This approach allows the decorator to decorate not only a concrete decorated type, but also other decorators.

It's also important to note that in this example the decorated property is set as protected. By setting the property as protected, it is accessible to subclasses of AbstractWidgetDecorator.

The actual implementation of the methods may vary in every case. In this particular example, each of the methods simply passes through the request to the decorated object. However, it is useful to have an abstract class in many cases to ensure that the core, common behavior is inheritable.

Concrete Decorator Class(es)

The concrete decorator(s) must implement the same interface as the decorated object type. Normally, this is accomplished by extending the abstract decorator class. The decorator class can do the following.

- *Modify existing behavior.* Decorators often proxy requests to decorated methods. Although it's possible for a decorator to simply pass through requests to the decorated object exactly as they were made, a decorator can also pre-process or post-process. Decorators can also handle the entire request at the decorator level without ever forwarding the request to the decorated object.

- *Add new behavior.* Decorators must implement the interface, but they can also add new methods. This is an option and not a requirement. Adding new behavior can be advantageous because you can add functionality to an object at runtime. However, adding methods means that you cannot effectively chain decorators as is discussed later in this chapter.

The following code illustrates a concrete decorator for the widget example:

```
package com.peachpit.aas3wdp.decorator {
    public class DigitalWidget extends AbstractWidgetDecorator {
        public function DigitalWidget(decorated:IWidget) {
            super(decorated);
        }

        override public function getDescription():String {
            var description:String = _decorated.getDescription();
            return "digital " + description;
        }
    }
}
```

This example declares `DigitalWidget` to extend `AbstractWidgetDecorator`. Note that the constructor accepts a parameter of type `IWidget`, meaning that it could be either a concrete decorated type (`Widget`) or another decorator type. The constructor in this example simply passes along the parameter to the constructor of the superclass.

This example inherits the default implementation for the `run()` method, but it overrides `getDescription()`. The `getDescription()` method returns the description from the decorated object prepended with the word `digital`.

Building Reader Decorators

So far, you've had the chance to read about the theory of the Decorator pattern with an extremely simple example. In this section, you'll have the chance to see a slightly more sophisticated and practical example that makes use of the Decorator pattern. We'll build a group of classes that work together for reading text data in many different ways.

The reader example starts with a concrete decorated type that takes a string value and reads it one character at a time. Then, we'll add decorators that can read from the string by the word and by the line. We'll then add additional decorated and decorator types to demonstrate how they can be used interchangeably.

Creating the Decorator/Decorated Interface

To implement the Decorator pattern, we first need an interface. For this example, we'll define an interface called `com.peachpit.aas3wdp.decoratorexample.io.IReader`. All reader decorated and decorator classes must implement this interface. For our example, we'll require that all reader types should be capable of dispatching events. For this reason `IReader` extends `flash.events.IEventDispatcher`.

Here's our interface:

```
package com.peachpit.aas3wdp.decoratorexample.io {

    import flash.events.IEventDispatcher;
```

(CODE CONTINUED)

```
    public interface IReader extends IEventDispatcher {

        function read():String;
        function readArray(offset:uint = 0, length:uint = 0):Array;
        function readString():String;
        function hasNext():Boolean;
        function isReady():Boolean;
        function reset():void;
    }
}
```

As we've already mentioned, our IReader interface extends IEventDispatcher, which means any implementing class must implement all of the IEventDispatcher methods in addition to the methods required by IReader. The IEventDispatcher interface requires the following methods: addEventListener(), removeEventListener(), dispatchEvent(), hasEventListener(), and willTrigger(). As you'll see in the next section, the simplest way to implement the interface in most cases is simply to extend EventDispatcher.

The IReader interface also requires a handful of methods. The read(), readArray(), and readString() methods each provide a mechanism for accessing an element or elements of text. The actual implementations will differ in concrete classes, but the idea remains the same: read() returns the next element in much the same way an iterator returns the next element. The readArray() method returns an array of elements. The readString() method returns the original value. The isReady() method returns a Boolean indicating whether or not the reader is ready for reading. The hasNext() method returns a Boolean indicating whether or not there are additional elements. The reset() method resets the reader to the first element.

Defining an Abstract Reader Class

As we've already seen, all implementing classes of IReader must implement quite a few methods—both those from IEventDispatcher and from IReader. In many of the reader classes, the implemented methods look very similar. For that reason, we can simplify those classes by first defining an abstract class. In this case, we'll define com.peachpit.aas3wdp.decoratorexample.io.AbstractReader as an abstract class implementing the IReader interface. Because the IReader interface extends IEventDispatcher, you can either implement all the required methods or extend a class that already implements those methods. In this case, Reader extends EventDispatcher, a class that is part of the Flash Player API.

```
    package com.peachpit.aas3wdp.decoratorexample.io {

        import flash.events.Event;
        import flash.events.EventDispatcher;

        public class AbstractReader extends EventDispatcher implements IReader {

            protected var index:uint = 0;

            public function Reader() {
            }
```

(CODE CONTINUED)

```
      public function hasNext():Boolean {
         return false;
      }

      public function reset():void {
         index = 0;
      }

      public function isReady():Boolean {
         return true;
      }

      public function read():String {
         return null;
      }

      public function readArray(offset:uint = 0, length:uint = 0):Array {
         return null;
      }

      public function readString():String {
         return null;
      }

   }
}
```

The preceding code is fairly basic. Most of the methods simply return default values. The only actual implementation is the declaration of index and the definition of the reset() method.

Defining the Concrete Decorated Class

In this example, we'll build two concrete decorated types. The first StringReader, is the first concrete decorated class and is the simpler of the two.

```
package com.peachpit.aas3wdp.decoratorexample.io {

   public class StringReader extends AbstractReader {

      private var _content:String;

      public function StringReader(content:String) {
         _content = content;
      }

      // The read() method uses the String class method charAt()
      // to return one character at a time, incrementing _index
      // each time the method is called.
      override public function read():String {
         return _content.charAt(_index++);
      }

      override public function readArray(offset:uint = 0, length:uint = 0):Array {
         // If length is null then use the length of the
         // string.
```

(CODE CONTINUED)

```
            if(length == 0) {
               length = _content.length - offset;
            }
            var array:Array = new Array();

            // Add one character at a time to the array.
            for(var i:uint = offset; i < length; i++) {
               array.push(_content.charAt(i));
            }
            return array;
         }

         override public function readString():String {
            return _content;
         }

         override public function hasNext():Boolean {
            return _index < _content.length;
         }

      }
   }
```

The StringReader class accepts one parameter in the constructor. It stores that value in a private property. It then defines the read() and readArray() methods to return one character at a time from that value. Here's a simple example of how you could use the StringReader:

```
var reader:IReader = new StringReader("abcdefg");
while(reader.hasNext()) {
 trace(reader.read());
}
```

This example writes the characters *a*, *b*, *c*, *d*, *e*, *f*, and *g* one at a time to the console.

Creating the Abstract Decorator Class

Now that we've defined a concrete decorated type, we can look at creating decorators for it. To simplify the decorators, we'll create an abstract decorator called com.peachpit.aas3wdp. decoratorexample.io.AbstractReaderDecorator. The AbstractReaderDecorator class extends AbstractReader just like the StringReader class does (all the decorated and decorator classes must implement the same interface). Note that we need to override several of the methods so that they delegate requests to the decorated instance, _content.

```
package com.peachpit.aas3wdp.decoratorexample.io {

   import com.peachpit.aas3wdp.decoratorexample.io.IReader;
   import com.peachpit.aas3wdp.decoratorexample.io.Reader;

   public class AbstractReaderDecorator extends AbstractReader {

      private var _content:IReader;

      // The constructor accepts a parameter of type IReader
```

```
      // that will be the decorated object.
      public function ReaderDecorator(reader:IReader) {
        _content = reader;
      }

      override public function read():String {
        return _content.read();
      }

      override public function readArray(offset:uint = 0, length:uint = 0):Array {
        return _content.readArray(offset, length);
      }

      override public function readString():String {
        return _content.readString();
      }

    }
  }
```

The abstract decorator class is quite simple. It just delegates requests. Next we'll look at creating concrete decorators.

Defining the First Concrete Decorator Class

Next, we define the first of the concrete decorator classes, WordReader. Notice that this class extends the abstract decorator class, AbstractReaderDecorator.

```
package com.peachpit.aas3wdp.decoratorexample.io {

  import com.peachpit.aas3wdp.decoratorexample.io.IReader;
  import com.peachpit.aas3wdp.decoratorexample.io.ReaderDecorator;

  public class WordReader extends ReaderDecorator {

    private var _words:Array;

    public function WordReader(reader:IReader) {
      // Call the superclass constructor, passing the
      // parameter along so that the _content property is
      // set.
      super(reader);

      // Define a regular expression to find words.
      var expression:RegExp = /[a-z]+/ig;

      // Retrieve all the words from the decorated content
      // by calling readString() and using the match()
      // method with the regular expression. Note that
      // readString() is implemented in the abstract
      // ReaderDecorator class.
      _words = readString().match(expression);
    }

    // Override read() so it returns the next word from the
```

```
                // _words array.
                override public function read():String {
                    var word:String = _words[_index++];
                    return word;
                }

                // Override readArray() so it returns a new array
                // containing part of the _words array.
                override public function readArray(offset:uint = 0, length:uint = 0):Array {
                    return _words.slice(offset, length);
                }


                override public function hasNext():Boolean {
                    return _index < _words.length;
                }


            }
        }
```

This decorator allows you to wrap any other object that implements the `IReader` interface, and it changes the functionality while keeping the same interface. For example, the following code illustrates this operation:

```
var reader:IReader = new StringReader("one two three four");
// First display each character one at a time.
while(reader.hasNext()) {
    trace(reader.read());
}
reader = new WordReader(reader);
// Next display one word at a time.
while(reader.hasNext()) {
    trace(reader.read());
}
```

Testing the Decorator

Next, we'll define a main class to test the example.

```
package {

    import flash.display.Sprite;
    import com.peachpit.aas3wdp.decoratorexample.io.IReader;
    import com.peachpit.aas3wdp.decoratorexample.io.StringReader;
    import com.peachpit.aas3wdp.decoratorexample.io.WordReader;

    public  class ReaderDecoratorExample extends Sprite {

        public function ReaderDecoratorExample() {
            var stringReader:StringReader = new StringReader("Lorem ipsum\ndolor sit amet");
            var wordReader:WordReader = new WordReader(stringReader);
            traceReader(stringReader);
            traceReader(wordReader);
        }
```

(CODE CONTINUED)

```
      public function traceReader(reader:IReader):void {
        while(reader.hasNext()) {
          trace(reader.read());
        }
      }

    }

  }
```

Debug the application, and you'll see that the first call to `traceReader()` displays each of the characters of the string from the `StringReader` object. The second call to `traceReader()` displays each word using the `WordReader` object. Because `traceReader()` is defined to accept an `IReader` parameter, either `StringReader` (decorated) or `WordReader` (decorator) will work. Each object implements the same interface, but they have different behaviors.

Defining an Additional Concrete Decorator Class

One of the advantages of the Decorator pattern is that you can create many decorators. Because each decorator can decorate any other decorator, there is no real limit to how many decorators you can use. To illustrate this truth, we'll next add a new decorator class called `com.peachpit.aas3wdp.decoratorexample.io.LineReader`. As the name implies, `LineReader` reads the content one line at a time.

```
package com.peachpit.aas3wdp.decoratorexample.io {

  import com.peachpit.aas3wdp.decoratorexample.io.IReader;
  import com.peachpit.aas3wdp.decoratorexample.io.ReaderDecorator;

  public class LineReader extends AbstractReaderDecorator {

    private var _lines:Array;

    public function LineReader(reader:IReader) {
      super(reader);
      var expression:RegExp = /[\n\r\f]/g;
      _lines = readString().split(expression);
    }

    override public function read():String {
      var line:String = _lines[_index++];
      return line;
    }

    override public function readArray(offset:uint = 0, length:uint = 0):Array {
      return _lines.concat();
    }

    override public function hasNext():Boolean {
      return _index < _lines.length;
    }

  }
}
```

The LineReader class inherits from AbstractReaderDecorator. It accepts any reader type as a parameter to the constructor, and it uses that parameter as the content which it then parses into an array of lines.

With the addition of the LinerReader, we can next verify that it works by making a few edits to the main class as follows:

```
package {

    import flash.display.Sprite;
    import com.peachpit.aas3wdp.decoratorexample.io.IReader;
    import com.peachpit.aas3wdp.decoratorexample.io.StringReader;
    import com.peachpit.aas3wdp.decoratorexample.io.WordReader;
    import com.peachpit.aas3wdp.decoratorexample.io.LineReader;

    public  class ReaderDecoratorExample extends Sprite {

        public function DecoratorExample() {
            var stringReader:StringReader = new StringReader("Lorem ipsum\ndolor sit amet");
            var wordReader:WordReader = new WordReader(stringReader);
            var lineReader:LineReader = new LineReader(stringReader);
            traceReader(stringReader);
            traceReader(wordReader);
            traceReader(lineReader);
        }

        public function traceReader(reader:IReader):void {
            while(reader.hasNext()) {
                trace(reader.read());
            }
        }

    }

}
```

When you debug the application, you'll see that this time the third call to traceReader() outputs each line of text. Because the original text has a newline character (\n), the output displays on two lines.

Defining a New Decorated Type

Now that we have a decorated type in place, we've already seen that we can add as many decorators as we want. However, we can also add more decorated types. All that's required is that the new decorated type implements the same interface as all the existing decorated types and decorators. To illustrate this point, we'll next define a new decorated type, com.peachpit.aas3wdp. decoratorexample.io.FileReader. The FileReader class allows you to load the contents of a file. By default, it reads one character at a time similar to the StringReader.

```
package com.peachpit.aas3wdp.decoratorexample.io {

    import flash.net.URLLoader;
```

```
import flash.net.URLRequest;
import flash.events.Event;

public class FileReader extends AbstractReader {

    private var _content:String;
    private var _file:URLLoader;
    private var _canRead:Boolean = false;

    public function FileReader(file:String) {
        // Use a URLLoader object to load the text from a
        // file specified by the parameter.
        _file = new URLLoader();
        var request:URLRequest = new URLRequest(file);
        _file.load(request);

        // Call onData() when the content loads.
        _file.addEventListener(Event.COMPLETE, onData);
    }

    private function onData(event:Event):void {

        // Set the content to the data loaded from the file.
        _content = String(_file.data);

        // The object is read for reading.
        _canRead = true;

        // Dispatch an event notifying listeners that the
        // object is ready.
        dispatchEvent(new Event(Event.COMPLETE));
    }

    override public function isReady():Boolean {
        return _canRead;
    }

    override public function read():String {
        return _content.charAt(_index++);
    }

    override public function readString():String {
        return _content;
    }

    override public function hasNext():Boolean {
        return _index < _content.length;
    }

    }
}
```

This class loads text from a URL. Because the data loads asynchronously, the isReady()
method returns false until the data has been loaded. Otherwise, it functions very similarly to
the StringReader class.

With the addition of this new decorated type, we can test it by redefining the main class to use a `FileReader` instance instead of a `StringReader` instance. Because `FileReader` is asynchronous, we'll listen for a `COMPLETE` event, decorate the object with a `WordReader` object, and then call `traceReader()`.

NOTE

For this example to work, you'll need a text file called data.txt. You can save a text file in the same directory to which you deploy the .swf from this example. In the text file, you can add text such as the string passed to the *StringReader* constructor in the earlier example.

```
package {

    import flash.display.Sprite;
    import com.peachpit.aas3wdp.decoratorexample.io.IReader;
    import com.peachpit.aas3wdp.decoratorexample.io.FileReader;
    import com.peachpit.aas3wdp.decoratorexample.io.WordReader;
    import flash.events.Event;

    public  class ReaderDecoratorExample extends Sprite {

        public function ReaderDecoratorExample() {
            var fileReader:FileReader = new FileReader("data.txt");
            fileReader.addEventListener(Event.COMPLETE, onFile);
        }

        private function onFile(event:Event):void {
            var wordReader:WordReader = new WordReader(FileReader(event.target));
            traceReader(wordReader);
        }

        public function traceReader(reader:IReader):void {
            while(reader.hasNext()) {
                trace(reader.read());
            }
        }

    }

}
```

This code illustrates that the same decorator we used in conjunction with a `StringReader` object can be used with a FileReader object as well.

Decorating Decorators

To illustrate that decorators can potentially decorate decorators, we'll define a new decorator class called `com.peachpit.aas3wdp.decoratorexample.io.SortedReader`. `SortedReader` allows you to access the contents of a decorated reader in a sorted order.

```
package com.peachpit.aas3wdp.decoratorexample.io {

    public class SortedReader extends AbstractReaderDecorator {
```

```
        private var _content:Array;

        public function SortedReader(reader:IReader) {
          super(reader);

          // Read all the content from the decorated reader as
          // an array. Then sort that content.
          _content = reader.readArray().concat();
          _content.sort();
        }

        override public function read():String {
          return _content[_index++];
        }

        override public function readArray(offset:uint = 0, length:uint = 0):Array {
          var data:Array = new Array();
          for(var i:uint = offset; i < length; i++) {
            data.push(_content[i]);
          }
          return data;
        }

        override public function hasNext():Boolean {
          return _index < _content.length;
        }

      }
    }
```

We can see how this new decorator works by editing the main class as follows:

```
package {

    import flash.display.Sprite;
    import com.peachpit.aas3wdp.decoratorexample.io.IReader;
    import com.peachpit.aas3wdp.decoratorexample.io.FileReader;
    import com.peachpit.aas3wdp.decoratorexample.io.WordReader;
    import com.peachpit.aas3wdp.decoratorexample.io.SortedReader;
    import flash.events.Event;

    public  class ReaderDecoratorExample extends Sprite {

        public function DecoratorExample2() {
            var fileReader:FileReader = new FileReader("data.txt");
            fileReader.addEventListener(Event.COMPLETE, onFile);
        }

        private function onFile(event:Event):void {
            var wordReader:WordReader = new WordReader(FileReader(event.target));
            var sortedReader:SortedReader = new SortedReader(wordReader);
            traceReader(sortedReader);
        }

        public function traceReader(reader:IReader):void {
            while(reader.hasNext()) {
```

```
                trace(reader.read());
            }
        }

    }

}
```

When you test the application this time, all the words are traced in alphabetical order.

The `SortedReader` decorator can decorate any object that implements the `IReader` interface. That means you can use a `SortedReader` instance to decorate a `WordReader` instance as was done in this example, but you can also use it to decorate a `LineReader` or any other object that implements `IReader`.

Building Visual and Commutative Decorators

The preceding example gave you a chance to use the Decorator pattern in a fairly simple example. For the most part, the decorators in the preceding example were not chainable; that is, you couldn't meaningfully composite a `WordReader` within a `LineReader` object. Although the `SortedReader` object does enable you to chain decorators, you must apply the `SortedReader` as a decorator last in the chain, which means that the decorators are not commutative. Decorators are commutative if the following code yields effectively the same behavior, where A and B are both decorators and `decorated` is the decorated object:

```
var a:A = new A(decorated);
var b:B = new B(a);
b.method();

var b:B = new B(decorated);
var a:A = new A(b);
a.method();
```

You can see that `SortedReader` is not commutative because it matters what order it is applied in the chain. For example, if you apply a `WordReader` as a decorator to a `SortedReader` object, you will get different results than if you apply a `SortedReader` to a `WordReader`. This doesn't make the preceding example bad or impractical. It simply illustrates that the Decorator pattern is flexible enough to allow for chainable and non-chainable as well as commutative and non-commutative decorators.

In this next example, you'll have a chance to see how to build visual decorators that are chainable and commutative. This example decorates shapes (circles and rectangles) by making them draggable and by adding bevels to them.

Defining the Common Interface

Define com.peachpit.aas3wdp.shapes.AbstractBasicShape as an abstract class that serves as the common interface. In this example, we're using an abstract class with no implementation rather than an interface because we want all the shapes (decorated and decorator) to be a subtype of Sprite so that all the shapes can rely on the Sprite interface. There is no built-in interface for Sprite or any sort of display object. Normally, it is best to use an actual interface construct. However, in this case, we're going to use an abstract class in place of an interface for two reasons:

1. The required interface is really long. Although this wouldn't excuse not using a proper interface in a typical scenario, we want to simplify things here rather than occupying several printed pages with the interface code.

2. All the concrete classes would have to extend Sprite in order to inherit the critical display object behavior.

For our purposes, we want to create a unique type that implements the entire Sprite interface. Therefore, the simplest thing to do is to create an abstract class that merely inherits from Sprite. It doesn't require any further implementation. Again, we're making a minor exception to our rule that all abstract classes must have some sort of implementation for this example because of the special case it presents.

```
package com.peachpit.aas3wdp.shapes {

  import flash.display.Sprite;

  public class AbstractBasicShape extends Sprite {

    public function AbstractBasicShape() {
    }

  }
}
```

Defining Concrete Decorated Classes

Next, we're going to create a few concrete decorated types. First we'll create a Circle class. Define com.peachpit.aas3wdp.shapes.Circle as a class that draws a circle.

```
package com.peachpit.aas3wdp.shapes {

  import com.peachpit.aas3wdp.shapes.AbstractBasicShape;
  import flash.display.Sprite;

  public class Circle extends AbstractBasicShape {

    public function Circle(radius:Number) {
      var shape:Sprite = new Sprite();
      addChild(shape);
      shape.graphics.lineStyle(0, 0, 0);
      shape.graphics.beginFill(0xFFFFFF);
      shape.graphics.drawCircle(radius, radius, radius);
```

```
            shape.graphics.endFill();
        }

    }
}
```

The second decorated type is the `Rectangle` class. Define `com.peachpit.aas3wdp.decoratorex-ample.shapes.Rectangle` as a class that draws a rectangle.

```
package com.peachpit.aas3wdp.shapes {

    import com.peachpit.aas3wdp.shapes.AbstractBasicShape;
    import flash.display.Sprite;

    public class Rectangle extends AbstractBasicShape {

        public function Rectangle(shapeWidth:Number, shapeHeight:Number,
            center:Boolean = false) {
        var shape:Sprite = new Sprite();
        addChild(shape);
        shape.graphics.lineStyle(0, 0, 0);
        shape.graphics.beginFill(0xFFFFFF);
        shape.graphics.drawRect(center ? -shapeWidth / 2 : 0, center ? -shapeHeight
            / 2 : 0, shapeWidth, shapeHeight);
        shape.graphics.endFill();
        }

    }
}
```

Both of these decorated types are fairly straightforward. They are basic shape types we can decorate with the decorators we're about to create. Apart from the fact that each of these types implement the same interface (which they inherit from `AbstractBasicShape`), there is nothing about these classes that is unique to the Decorator pattern.

Defining Decorator Classes

Now we can create the decorator classes. Define `com.peachpit.aas3wdp.decoratorexample.shapes.DraggableShape` as a decorator class that wraps a `AbstractBasicShape` object and makes it draggable.

```
package com.peachpit.aas3wdp.shapes {

    import com.peachpit.aas3wdp.shapes.AbstractBasicShape;
    import flash.events.MouseEvent;
    import flash.display.Sprite;

    public class DraggableShape extends AbstractBasicShape {

        private var _decorated:AbstractBasicShape;

        public function DraggableShape(AbstractBasicShape:AbstractBasicShape) {
            _decorated = AbstractBasicShape;
            addChild(_decorated);
            addEventListener(MouseEvent.MOUSE_DOWN, onMouseDown);
```

```
            addEventListener(MouseEvent.MOUSE_UP, onMouseUp);
        }

        private function onMouseDown(event:MouseEvent):void {
            startDrag();
        }

        private function onMouseUp(event:MouseEvent):void {
            stopDrag();
        }

    }
}
```

The constructor for this class accepts an instance of a concrete basic shape and then acts as a container for that object. By acting as a container, the drag behaviors added to the `Draggable-Shape` object make the child (the decorated object) draggable by proxy.

NOTE

The *DraggableShape* implementation is purposefully simple. It does not take into account the possibility that the user could move the mouse outside of the object while dragging it. In such a case, the user could inadvertently cause the object to continue to follow the mouse even after releasing the mouse button. We've opted not to show the code to solve that issue because we want to keep this example as focused as possible in demonstrating the Decorator pattern.

Next we'll create a second decorator. Our next decorator class is `BevelShape`, which adds a bevel to the object. Define `com.peachpit.aas3wdp.decoratorexample.shapes.BevelShape` as a class that wraps a `AbstractBasicShape` object and applies a bevel filter.

```
package com.peachpit.aas3wdp.shapes {
    import flash.filters.BevelFilter;

    public class BevelShape extends AbstractBasicShape {

        public function BevelShape(shape:AbstractBasicShape) {
            var filters:Array = shape.filters;
            filters.push(new BevelFilter());
            shape.filters = filters;
            addChild(shape);
        }

    }
}
```

Now we can test that the decorators are commutable and chainable. Define a main class that adds and decorates shapes.

```
package {

    import flash.display.Sprite;
    import flash.display.Stage;
    import flash.display.StageScaleMode;
```

```
import flash.display.StageAlign;
import com.peachpit.aas3wdp.shapes.AbstractBasicShape;
import com.peachpit.aas3wdp.shapes.Circle;
import com.peachpit.aas3wdp.shapes.Rectangle;
import com.peachpit.aas3wdp.shapes.DraggableShape;
import com.peachpit.aas3wdp.shapes.BevelShape;

public class ShapeDecoratorExample extends Sprite {

    public function DecoratorExample() {

        stage.scaleMode = StageScaleMode.NO_SCALE;
        stage.align = StageAlign.TOP_LEFT;

        var shape:AbstractBasicShape;

        // Create a rectangle. Make it draggable first, then
        // add a bevel.
        shape = new Rectangle(200, 200);
        shape = new DraggableShape(shape);
        shape = new BevelShape(shape);
        shape.x = 200;
        shape.y = 200;
        addChild(shape);

        // Create a circle. Apply the bevel, then make it
        // draggable.
        shape = new Circle(100);
        shape = new BevelShape(shape);
        shape = new DraggableShape(shape);
        addChild(shape);

    }
    }
    }
```

Notice that, in the preceding example, it makes no difference if you apply the bevel first or make the object draggable first. Both ways work equally well.

Adding Non-Commutative Decorators

Next, we'll add two non-commutative decorators to see the contrast with the first two decorators. The first non-commutative decorator is ColorableShape. Define com.peachpit.aas3wdp.

shapes.ColorableShape as follows.

```
package com.peachpit.aas3wdp.shapes {
    import flash.geom.ColorTransform;

    public class ColorableShape extends AbstractBasicShape {

        public function ColorableShape(shape:AbstractBasicShape, red:Number,
            green:Number, blue:Number) {
```

```
        shape.transform.colorTransform = new ColorTransform(red, green, blue);
        addChild(shape);
      }

    }
  }
```

The second non-commutative decorator is `ResizableShape`, which adds a resize handler to the shape. The resize handler allows the user to click and drag to change the width and height of the shape. Define `com.peachpit.aas3wdp.shapes.ResizableShape` as follows.

```
package com.peachpit.aas3wdp.shapes {

  import com.peachpit.aas3wdp.shapes.AbstractBasicShape;
  import com.peachpit.aas3wdp.shapes.ColorableShape;
  import flash.display.Sprite;
  import flash.events.MouseEvent;
  import flash.events.Event;

  public class ResizableShape extends AbstractBasicShape {

    private var _isResizing:Boolean;
    private var _resizer:AbstractBasicShape;
    private var _decorated:AbstractBasicShape;

    // Override the width and height setters so when you
    // attempt to set the width and height you set the width
    // and height of the decorated object and move the resizer
    // handle appropriately.
    override public function set width(value:Number):void {
      _decorated.width = value;
      _resizer.x = value;
    }

    override public function set height(value:Number):void {
      _decorated.height = value;
      _resizer.y = value;
    }

    public function ResizableShape(AbstractBasicShape:AbstractBasicShape) {
      _decorated = AbstractBasicShape;
      addChild(_decorated);

      // Create a new rectangle that is centered to serve
      // as the resize handle. Use ColorableShape to make
      // the rectangle gray. Then move the rectangle to
      // the lower-right corner of the decorated shape.
      _resizer = new Rectangle(10, 10, true);
      _resizer = new ColorableShape(_resizer, .8, .8, .8);
      _resizer.x = _decorated.width;
      _resizer.y = _decorated.height;
      addChild(_resizer);
      _resizer.addEventListener(MouseEvent.MOUSE_DOWN, onMouseDown);
      _resizer.addEventListener(MouseEvent.MOUSE_UP, onMouseUp);
    }
```

(CODE CONTINUED)

```
            // When the user clicks on the resize handle, make it
            // draggable, start listening for enterFrame events.
            private function onMouseDown(event:MouseEvent):void {
              addEventListener(Event.ENTER_FRAME, onEnterFrame);
              _resizer.startDrag(true);
              event.stopImmediatePropagation();
            }

            // When the user releases the mouse click, stop making
            // the resize handle draggable, and stop listening for
            // enterFrame events.
            private function onMouseUp(event:MouseEvent):void {
              _resizer.stopDrag();
              removeEventListener(Event.ENTER_FRAME, onEnterFrame);
            }

            private function onEnterFrame(event:Event):void {
              // Don't allow the user to move the resize
              // handle in negative directions.
              if(_resizer.x < 0) {
                _resizer.x = 0;
              }
              if(_resizer.y < 0) {
                _resizer.y = 0;
              }

              // Change the width and height of the decorated
              // object to correspond to the resize handle x
              // and y coordinate values.
              _decorated.width = _resizer.x;
              _decorated.height = _resizer.y;
            }

    }
  }
```

The ResizableShape object wraps decorated objects much like the other decorators we've seen so far in this example. However, it also draws a resize handle within itself. As the user moves the resize handle, the ResizableShape instance adjusts the width and height of the decorated object.

Now that we've created two additional decorators, let's modify the main class so that it uses the two new decorators:

```
package {

  import flash.display.Sprite;
  import flash.display.Stage;
  import flash.display.StageScaleMode;
  import flash.display.StageAlign;
  import com.peachpit.aas3wdp.shapes.AbstractBasicShape;
  import com.peachpit.aas3wdp.shapes.Circle;
  import com.peachpit.aas3wdp.shapes.Rectangle;
  import com.peachpit.aas3wdp.shapes.DraggableShape;
  import com.peachpit.aas3wdp.shapes.BevelShape;
  import com.peachpit.aas3wdp.shapes.ColorableShape;
```

(CODE CONTINUED)

```
import com.peachpit.aas3wdp.shapes.ResizableShape;

public class ShapeDecoratorExample extends Sprite {

    public function DecoratorExample() {

        stage.scaleMode = StageScaleMode.NO_SCALE;
        stage.align = StageAlign.TOP_LEFT;

        var shape:AbstractBasicShape;
        shape = new Rectangle(200, 200);
        shape = new DraggableShape(shape);
        shape = new BevelShape(shape);
        shape = new ColorableShape(shape, 0, 0, 0);
        shape.x = 200;
        shape.y = 200;
        addChild(shape);

        shape = new Circle(100);
        shape = new BevelShape(shape);
        shape = new DraggableShape(shape);
        shape = new ResizableShape(shape);

        addChild(shape);

    }
  }
}
```

When you test this version of the application, you'll notice that although the rectangle is black—as you'd expect because of the ColorableShape decorator—it no longer displays the bevel because the color transform was applied *after* the bevel. Secondly, you'll notice that as you drag the circle, the resize handle does not move with it. That is because the ResizableShape decorator was applied after the DraggableShape decorator.

Next, we can change the order in which the new decorators are applied to illustrate that the order affects the behavior:

```
package {

    import flash.display.Sprite;
    import flash.display.Stage;
    import flash.display.StageScaleMode;
    import flash.display.StageAlign;
    import com.peachpit.aas3wdp.shapes.AbstractBasicShape;
    import com.peachpit.aas3wdp.shapes.Circle;
    import com.peachpit.aas3wdp.shapes.Rectangle;
    import com.peachpit.aas3wdp.shapes.DraggableShape;
    import com.peachpit.aas3wdp.shapes.BevelShape;
    import com.peachpit.aas3wdp.shapes.ColorableShape;
    import com.peachpit.aas3wdp.shapes.ResizableShape;

    public class DecoratorExample extends Sprite {
```

```
        public function DecoratorExample() {

            stage.scaleMode = StageScaleMode.NO_SCALE;
            stage.align = StageAlign.TOP_LEFT;

            var shape:AbstractBasicShape;
            shape = new Rectangle(200, 200);
            shape = new DraggableShape(shape);
            shape = new ColorableShape(shape, 0, 0, 0);
            shape = new BevelShape(shape);
            shape.x = 200;
            shape.y = 200;
            addChild(shape);

            shape = new Circle(100);
            shape = new BevelShape(shape);
            shape = new ResizableShape(shape);
            shape = new DraggableShape(shape);

            addChild(shape);

        }
    }
```

This time, when you test the application, you'll see that the bevel is preserved and that the resize handle moves with the shape. This is because the decorators have been applied in the correct order. The `ColorableShape` and `ResizableShape` decorators are perfectly valid, but they are non-commutative.

Summary

The Decorator pattern allows you to add and modify behavior using composition rather than inheritance. The key advantages of Decorator patterns are that you can add and change behavior at runtime, and you can potentially chain together behaviors without having to write new subclasses for each permutation.

10

Command Pattern

The Command pattern encapsulates functionality into a class. Although the pattern might appear simplistic, don't let its simplicity deceive you. The Command pattern is a powerful way for enabling a range of features that would be difficult to implement using a different approach. Here are some of the most common uses of the Command pattern:

- Building highly reusable components. The Command pattern decouples the functionality from the initiator. Components that use Command pattern objects are highly extensible because they can employ any object that implements the correct interface.

- Queuing requests. When operations must occur in sequence, they must be queued. Because the Command pattern encapsulates the request into an object, it's possible to queue the requests by placing them in an array or similar collection.

- Supporting undo and redo. Because Command pattern objects can be stored in memory, it's possible to keep a history of which operations have occurred. By implementing an undo() and/or redo() method, it's possible to add undo and redo features to an application without difficulty.

- Making transactional or "wizard" operations. An operation often consists of many steps. If any step fails or if the user cancels at any point, it is necessary to roll back any changes that have occurred. The Command pattern enables you to defer execution or to roll back operations by calling the undo() method of a succession of objects.

Understanding the Command Pattern

In its purest form, the Command pattern consists of six elements.

- Command interface
- Concrete command

- Receiver

- Client

- Invoker

The following sections look at these elements in detail.

The Interface

In the simplest form, the command interface defines just one method, often called `execute()` by convention. The `execute()` method is responsible for running the requested operation. That means that in the simplest form, the interface looks like this:

```
package com.peachpit.aas3wdp.commands {
   public interface ICommand {
      function execute():void;
   }
}
```

The command interface is essential to the Command pattern because it allows all implementing command types to use the same interface even though they have different implementations. That way, commands can be called without the calling code having to know much (if anything) about the specific command. Just like you can flip a switch to turn on and off an electrical device without having to know the details of how the particular electrical device operates, the command interface provides a consistent way to operate programmatic objects that might have disparate modes of operation behind the scenes.

This `ICommand` interface is all that is necessary for a basic command. However, sometimes we want command classes to support the possibility of undoable and redoable commands. For that reason, we can define two subtypes called `IUndoableCommand` and `IRedoableCommand`. Here's `IUndoableCommand`.

```
package com.peachpit.aas3wdp.commands {
   public interface IUndoableCommand extends ICommand {
      function undo():void;
   }
}
```

And now here's the `IRedoableCommand` interface:

```
package com.peachpit.aas3wdp.commands {
   public interface IRedoableCommand extends ICommand {
      function redo():void;
   }
}
```

You'll notice that both of these interfaces extend `ICommand`, meaning that all `IUndoableCommand` and `IRedoableCommand` implementing classes also pass the test as implementing `ICommand`.

We'll start by looking at examples that implement just the `ICommand` interface. Later in the chapter, we'll look at a sample application that uses `IUndoableCommand` and `IRedoableCommand`.

The Concrete Command and Receiver

The concrete command is the class that implements the interface in a useful way by defining the execute() method so that it actually runs an operation.

The concrete command usually requires a receiver, which is the object that is the target of the operation. Although it's never strictly necessary, in many cases, the receiver reference is passed to the concrete command constructor. The following is an example of a concrete command that rotates a display object clockwise. In this case, the display object is the receiver.

```
package com.peachpit.aas3wdp.commandexample {

    import com.peachpit.aas3wdp.commands.ICommand;

    public class RotateClockwiseCommand implements ICommand {

        private var _reveiver:DisplayObject;

        public function RotateClockwiseCommand(receiver:DisplayObject) {
            _receiver = receiver;
        }

        public function execute():void {
            _receiver.rotation += 20;
        }

    }
}
```

The Client and Invoker

The *client* is the object that instantiates the command object, and the *invoker* is the object that calls the execute() method of the command object. The client might be the main class of an application, and the invoker might be a button. There are many possible scenarios, and as you'll see throughout the examples in this chapter, there are no definitive rules for what types of objects can be clients and invokers. In fact, in some cases the client and invoker might be the same object.

Building a Simple Command Application

Now that you've had a chance to read the theory behind the Command pattern, let's take a look at a sample application that uses the pattern.

In the sample application in this chapter, you'll use four commands to scale and rotate a display object. Each of the commands is then associated with a draggable display object. By dragging the display objects and dropping them on a button, you'll effectively re-wire the button to apply the new commands associated with the draggable display objects, illustrating the extensibility and interoperability of commands.

This application uses an interface and classes from the AAS3WDP library. Specifically, the application uses the ICommand, IUndoableCommand, and IRedoableCommand interfaces as well as the `BasicButton` class, which are defined in the AAS3WDP library. You'll want to add the AAS3WDP library to the classpath for the project you configure for this example application.

Creating the Commands

First we'll create the command classes this application uses. The first of these commands is the `RotateClockwiseCommand` class. Define the `com.peachpit.aas3wdp.commandexample.commands.RotateClockwiseCommand` class as follows:

```
package com.peachpit.aas3wdp.commandexample.commands {

    import com.peachpit.aas3wdp.commands.ICommand;
    import flash.display.DisplayObject;

    public class RotateClockwiseCommand implements ICommand{

        private var _receiver:DisplayObject;

        public function RotateClockwiseCommand(receiver:DisplayObject) {
            _receiver = receiver;
        }

        public function execute():void {
            _receiver.rotation += 20;
        }

    }
}
```

In this command, the `execute()` method increments the `rotation` property of the receiver object by 20, effectively rotating the object clockwise.

Next, we'll create a command to rotate the object counterclockwise. Define the `com.peachpit.aas3wdp.commandexample.commands.RotateCounterclockwiseCommand` class as follows:

```
package com.peachpit.aas3wdp.commandexample.commands {

    import com.peachpit.aas3wdp.commands.ICommand;
    import flash.display.DisplayObject;

    public class RotateCounterclockwiseCommand implements ICommand {

        private var _receiver:DisplayObject;

        public function RotateCounterclockwiseCommand(receiver:DisplayObject) {
            _receiver = receiver;
        }

        public function execute():void {
            _receiver.rotation -= 20;
        }

    }
}
```

You'll notice that the `RotateCounterclockwiseCommand` class looks almost identical to the `RotateClockwiseCommand` class except that it decrements the receiver object's `rotation` property by 20 rather than incrementing it.

Now we'll create a command class for scaling the receiver object up. Define the `com.peachpit.aas3wdp.commandexample.commands.ScaleUpCommand` class as follows:

```
package com.peachpit.aas3wdp.commandexample.commands {

    import com.peachpit.aas3wdp.commands.ICommand;
    import flash.display.DisplayObject;

    public class ScaleUpCommand implements ICommand {

        private var _receiver:DisplayObject;

        public function ScaleUpCommand(receiver:DisplayObject) {
            _receiver = receiver;
        }

        public function execute():void {
            _receiver.scaleX += .1;
            _receiver.scaleY += .1;
        }

    }
}
```

In this class, the `execute()` method increments the `scaleX` and `scaleY` properties of the receiver object by .1, causing the object to scale up.

And now we'll define a command class that scales the object down. Define the `com.peachpit.aas3wdp.commandexample.commands.ScaleDownCommand` class as follows:

```
package com.peachpit.aas3wdp.commandexample.commands {

    import com.peachpit.aas3wdp.commands.ICommand;
    import flash.display.DisplayObject;

    public class ScaleDownCommand implements ICommand {

        private var _receiver:DisplayObject;

        public function ScaleDownCommand(receiver:DisplayObject) {
            _receiver = receiver;
        }

        public function execute():void {
            _receiver.scaleX -= .1;
            _receiver.scaleY -= .1;
        }

    }
}
```

This command works just like the `ScaleUpCommand` except that it decrements the `scaleX` and `scaleY` properties.

Creating a Receiver Type

The commands we defined in the preceding section require a receiver object. We'll now create a class whose instances we can use as receiver objects for the commands. The receiver objects must be of type DisplayObject, so our receiver type subclasses flash.display.Shape. We'll define com.peachpit.aas3wdp.commandexample.shapes.Rectangle, so that it draws a rectangle you can use as the receiver for the commands.

```
package com.peachpit.aas3wdp.commandexample.shapes {

    import flash.display.Shape;

    public class Rectangle extends Shape {

        public function Rectangle(color:uint, side:Number) {
            graphics.lineStyle();
            graphics.beginFill(color, 1);
            graphics.drawRect(-side / 2, -side / 2, side, side);
            graphics.endFill();
        }

    }

}
```

Creating a Button

Our application requires a button that we can wire up with a command. In order to accomplish this we'll use a subclass of BasicButton from the AAS3WDP library.

Here we define a new subclass of BasicButton called com.peachpit.aas3wdp.commandexample. controls.CommandButton. This class accepts a command and calls the execute() method when clicked.

```
package com.peachpit.aas3wdp.commandexample.controls {

    import com.peachpit.aas3wdp.controls.BasicButton;
    import com.peachpit.aas3wdp.commands.ICommand;
    import flash.events.MouseEvent;

    public class CommandButton extends BasicButton {

        private var _command:ICommand;

        public function set command(value:ICommand):void {
            _command = value;
        }

        public function CommandButton(label:String) {
            super(label);
            addEventListener(MouseEvent.CLICK, onClick);
        }

        private function onClick(event:MouseEvent):void {
            if(_command != null) {
```

(CODE CONTINUED)

```
            _command.execute();
        }
    }

  }
}
```

The `CommandButton` constructor accepts a label parameter just like `BasicButton`, and it passes that along to the super constructor. It also automatically listens for mouse clicks. When the user clicks the button, it attempts to call the `execute()` method of a command object that was passed to it with a setter method. This means that we can assign different command objects to the button, and because the button is programmed to an interface (`ICommand`) rather than a specific implementation, the interface can run the commands successfully even if they have very different implementations.

Creating the Command Containers

For this application, we're going to associate instances of each command type with a draggable display object, which we'll call a command container. For this purpose, we'll define a class called `com.peachpit.aas3wdp.commandcontainers.CommandContainer`. This class is a drag-and-drop `Sprite` subclass that has a command object and applies it to a `CommandButton` instance if it is dropped over the button.

```
package com.peachpit.aas3wdp.commandexample.commandcontainers {

    import flash.display.Sprite;
    import flash.events.MouseEvent;
    import flash.text.TextField;
    import flash.display.DisplayObject;
    import com.peachpit.aas3wdp.commands.ICommand;
    import com.peachpit.aas3wdp.commandexample.controls.CommandButton;

    public class CommandContainer extends flash.display.Sprite {

        private var _command:ICommand;
        private var _x:Number;
        private var _y:Number;

        public function CommandContainer(command:ICommand, labelText:String,
            xValue:Number, yValue:Number) {

            // Store a reference to the command object.
            _command = command;

            // Draw a rectangle.
            graphics.lineStyle();
            graphics.beginFill(0xFFFFFF, 1);
            graphics.drawRect(0, 0, 50, 50);
            graphics.endFill();

            // Create a text field to use as the label.
            var label:TextField = new TextField();
```

```
            label.width = 50;
            label.height = 50;
            label.multiline = true;
            label.wordWrap = true;
            label.text = labelText;
            label.selectable = false;
            addChild(label);

            // Listen for mouse events to enable the
            // drag-and-drop behavior.
            addEventListener(MouseEvent.MOUSE_DOWN, onMouseDown);
            addEventListener(MouseEvent.MOUSE_UP, onMouseUp);

            _x = xValue;
            _y = yValue;
            x = _x;
            y = _y;
        }

        private function onMouseDown(event:MouseEvent):void {
            startDrag();
        }

        private function onMouseUp(event:MouseEvent):void {
            stopDrag();
            x = _x;
            y = _y;

            // Get the current drop target using the inherited
            // dropTarget property. (See ActionScript 3.0
            // documentation for details on the property.)
            var target:DisplayObject = dropTarget;

            // The drop target can sometimes be an object within
            // the object for which you want to test. For
            // the target in this case could be a label inside
            // a command button rather than the command button
            // itself. Use a while statement to get the parent
            // and assign it to the target variable in those
            // cases.
            while(target != null && !(target is CommandButton) && target != root) {
                target = target.parent;
            }

            // If the target is a command button then set the
            // command of the button to the command object
            // associated with this container.
            if(target is CommandButton) {
                CommandButton(target).command = _command;
            }
        }

    }
}
```

The container constructor requires that you associate the container with a command object. The container is draggable. When the user drops the container on a command button, it then sets the command property of the button to the associated command object.

Testing the Application

Finally, we'll define the main class such that it adds an instance of `Rectangle` and `CommandButton` as well as four instances of `CommandContainer`, each with one of the command objects.

```
package {

    import flash.display.Sprite;
    import com.peachpit.aas3wdp.commandexample.commandcontainers.CommandContainer;
    import com.peachpit.aas3wdp.commandexample.shapes.Rectangle;
    import com.peachpit.aas3wdp.commandexample.commands.RotateClockwiseCommand;
    import com.peachpit.aas3wdp.commandexample.commands.RotateCounterclockwiseCommand;
    import com.peachpit.aas3wdp.commandexample.commands.ScaleUpCommand;
    import com.peachpit.aas3wdp.commandexample.commands.ScaleDownCommand;
    import com.peachpit.aas3wdp.commandexample.controls.CommandButton;

    public class CommandExample extends Sprite {

        public function CommandExample() {

            var rectangle:Rectangle = new Rectangle(0xFFFFFF, 50);
            rectangle.x = 200;
            rectangle.y = 200;
            addChild(rectangle);

            var button:CommandButton = new CommandButton("apply command");
            addChild(button);
            button.y = 250;

            var container:CommandContainer = new CommandContainer(new
                RotateClockwiseCommand(rectangle), "rotate clockwise", 0, 0);
            addChild(container);
            container = new CommandContainer(new RotateCounterclockwiseCommand
                (rectangle), "rotate counter-clockwise", 0, 55);
            addChild(container);
            container = new CommandContainer(new ScaleUpCommand(rectangle), "scale up",
                0, 110);
            addChild(container);
            container = new CommandContainer(new ScaleDownCommand(rectangle),
                "scale down", 0, 165);
            addChild(container);

        }
    }
}
```

When you test the sample application, you can drag and drop one of the command containers on the command button instance. That action wires the command button with the corresponding command object. Clicking the button then runs the command. For example, if you drag and drop the rotate clockwise container over the command button and then click the button, the rectangle will rotate clockwise.

Making Commands Undoable and Keeping Command Histories

One of the optional yet powerful features of a command object is that it can enable undoable actions. You'll remember that we've defined the `IUndoableCommand` interface with an `undo()` method earlier in this chapter If we have our command classes implement `IUndoableCommand`, we can define an `undo()` method.

The `undo()` method can be simple or complex, depending on the complexity of the operation in the `execute()` method and the amount of state (how many properties) that must be remembered. Consider the simplest case in which the operation can be undone by simply negating the statement in the `execute()` method. For example, the `execute()` method of the `RotateClockwiseCommand` class from the previous section increments the rotation property of the receiver object by 20. Therefore, the `undo()` method ought to decrement the rotation property by 20. The following code defines the `undo()` method for an undoable version of the `RotateClockwiseCommand` class:

```
public function undo():void {
    _receiver.rotation -= 20;
}
```

The `RotateClockwiseCommand` example is fairly straightforward. If the object was rotated 20 degrees clockwise, the operation is clearly undone by rotating the object counterclockwise by 20 degrees. There is no additional state that the command class has to track. However, consider an example with more complex state options. For example, a `RandomMoveCommand` class can move an object to random coordinates. (For simplicity, we'll define the class so it always selects coordinates within the range defined by a 400-by-400 rectangle with the upper-left corner at 0,0.)

```
public class RandomMoveCommand implements ICommand {

    private var _receiver:DisplayObject;

    public function RandomMoveCommand(receiver:DisplayObject) {
        _receiver = receiver;
    }

    public function execute():void {
        var x:Number = Math.random() * 400;
        var y:Number = Math.random() * 400;
        _receiver.x = x;
        _receiver.y = y;
    }

}
```

In the `RandomMoveCommand` example, the command object needs to track the previous x and y coordinates of the object in order to implement an `undo()` method. The following code shows how to implement an undoable version of the `RandomMoveCommand` class:

```
public class RandomMoveCommand implements IUndoableCommand {

    private var _receiver:DisplayObject;
    private var _x:Number;
    private var _y:Number;

    public function RandomMoveCommand(receiver:DisplayObject) {
        _receiver = receiver;
    }

    public function execute():void {
        _x = _object.x;
        _y = _object.y;
        var x:Number = Math.random() * 400;
        var y:Number = Math.random() * 400;
        _receiver.x = x;
        _receiver.y = y;
    }

    public function undo():void {
        _receiver.x = _x;
        _receiver.y = _y;
    }

}
```

Of course, by itself, an undoable command isn't of much use. You can always store a reference to the most recent command, and that way you can add one level of undo to an application. However, most frequently you'll want to have more than one level of undo in an application. To accomplish that, you'll need to keep track of the command history.

Keeping track of command history isn't difficult. It requires an array and a cursor you can move to point to a specific command in the history. For that purpose, it's useful to define a `CommandStack` class. For the `CommandStack` class, we'll assume that you always want to keep track of command history globally within an application, and we'll therefore write the class as a Singleton class (described in Chapter 4, "Singleton Pattern"). If you wanted to keep track of command histories within unique areas of an application, you could change the implementation of the `CommandStack` class slightly. The following is the `CommandStack` class defined in the `com.peachpit.aas3wdp.commands` package:

```
package com.peachpit.aas3wdp.commands {

    import com.peachpit.aas3wdp.commands.ICommand;

    public class CommandStack {

        private static var _instance:CommandStack;
        private var _commands:Array;
```

(CODE CONTINUED)

```
        private var _index:uint;

        public function CommandStack(parameter:SingletonEnforcer) {
            _commands = new Array();
            _index = 0;
        }

        public static function getInstance():CommandStack {
            if(_instance == null) {
                _instance = new CommandStack(new SingletonEnforcer());
            }
            return _instance;
        }

        public function putCommand(command:ICommand):void {
            _commands[_index++] = command;
            _commands.splice(_index, _commands.length - _index);
        }

        public function previous():ICommand {
            return _commands[--_index];
        }

        public function next():ICommand {
            return _commands[_index++];
        }

        public function hasPreviousCommands():Boolean {
            return _index > 0;
        }

        public function hasNextCommands():Boolean {
            return _index < _commands.length;
        }

    }
}

class SingletonEnforcer {}
```

Building an Undoable Application

In this exercise, we'll update the previous sample application so that all the commands are undoable. This requires the following changes:

- Edit each of the command classes so that they implement IUndoableCommand.

- Edit the command button so that it adds executed commands to a command stack.

- Add an undo button to the main class.

Making Undoable Commands

First, all the command classes must now implement IUndoableCommand. We'll start with
RotateClockwiseCommand:

```
package com.peachpit.aas3wdp.commandexample.commands {

    import com.peachpit.aas3wdp.commands.IUndoableCommand;
    import flash.display.DisplayObject;

    public class RotateClockwiseCommand implements IUndoableCommand {

        private var _receiver:DisplayObject;

        public function RotateClockwiseCommand(receiver:DisplayObject) {
            _receiver = receiver;
        }

        public function execute():void {
            _receiver.rotation += 20;
        }

        public function undo():void {
            _receiver.rotation -= 20;
        }

    }
}
```

Next we'll make a similar edit to RotateCounterclockwiseCommand:

```
package com.peachpit.aas3wdp.commandexample.commands {

    import com.peachpit.aas3wdp.commands.IUndoableCommand;
    import flash.display.DisplayObject;

    public class RotateCounterclockwiseCommand implements IUndoableCommand {

        private var _receiver:DisplayObject;

        public function RotateCounterclockwiseCommand(receiver:DisplayObject) {
            _receiver = receiver;
        }

        public function execute():void {
            _receiver.rotation -= 20;
        }

        public function undo():void {
            _receiver.rotation += 20;
        }

    }
}
```

Likewise we'll edit `ScaleUpCommand`:

```
package com.peachpit.aas3wdp.commandexample.commands {

    import com.peachpit.aas3wdp.commands.IUndoableCommand;
    import flash.display.DisplayObject;

    public class ScaleUpCommand implements IUndoableCommand {

        private var _receiver:DisplayObject;

        public function ScaleUpCommand(receiver:DisplayObject) {
            _receiver = receiver;
        }

        public function execute():void {
            _receiver.scaleX += .1;
            _receiver.scaleY += .1;
        }

        public function undo():void {
            _receiver.scaleX -= .1;
            _receiver.scaleY -= .1;
        }

    }
}
```

And then we'll edit `ScaleDownCommand`:

```
package com.peachpit.aas3wdp.commandexample.commands {

    import com.peachpit.aas3wdp.commands.IUndoableCommand;
    import flash.display.DisplayObject;

    public class ScaleDownCommand implements IUndoableCommand {

        private var _receiver:DisplayObject;

        public function ScaleDownCommand(receiver:DisplayObject) {
            _receiver = receiver;
        }

        public function execute():void {
            _receiver.scaleX -= .1;
            _receiver.scaleY -= .1;
        }

        public function undo():void {
            _receiver.scaleX += .1;
            _receiver.scaleY += .1;
        }

    }
}
```

Each of the changes in the command classes amounts to the same thing: implement `IUndoableCommand` rather than `ICommand`, and add the `undo()` method so that it reverses the effect of the `execute()` method.

Recording Command History

We can next modify the command button so that it records the command history. We'll accomplish this by using `CommandStack`. Each time the command button calls the `execute()` method of a command object, it will also add the command object to the stack.

```
package com.peachpit.aas3wdp.commandexample.controls {

    import com.peachpit.aas3wdp.controls.BasicButton;
    import com.peachpit.aas3wdp.commands.ICommand;
    import flash.events.MouseEvent;
    import com.peachpit.aas3wdp.commands.CommandStack;

    public class CommandButton extends BasicButton {

        private var _command:ICommand;

        public function set command(value:ICommand):void {
            _command = value;
        }

        public function CommandButton(label:String) {
            super(label);
            addEventListener(MouseEvent.CLICK, onClick);
        }

        private function onClick(event:MouseEvent):void {
            if(_command != null) {
                _command.execute();
                CommandStack.getInstance().putCommand(_command);
            }
        }

    }
}
```

With this change, we now have a history of the commands that have been executed.

Adding an Undo Button

Next we add an undo button to the main class. The undo button-click event handler retrieves the last-run command. It then tests to see whether it is an undoable command. If so, it calls `undo()`.

```
package {

    import flash.display.Sprite;
    import com.peachpit.aas3wdp.commandexample.commandcontainers.CommandContainer;
    import com.peachpit.aas3wdp.commandexample.shapes.Rectangle;
    import com.peachpit.aas3wdp.commandexample.commands.RotateClockwiseCommand;
    import com.peachpit.aas3wdp.commandexample.commands.RotateCounterclockwiseCommand;
```

(CODE CONTINUED)

```
import com.peachpit.aas3wdp.commandexample.commands.ScaleUpCommand;
import com.peachpit.aas3wdp.commandexample.controls.CommandButton;
import com.peachpit.aas3wdp.controls.BasicButton;
import com.peachpit.aas3wdp.commandexample.commands.ScaleDownCommand;
import flash.events.MouseEvent;
import com.peachpit.aas3wdp.commands.CommandStack;
import com.peachpit.aas3wdp.commands.ICommand;
import com.peachpit.aas3wdp.commands.IUndoableCommand;

public class CommandExample extends Sprite {

    public function CommandExample() {

        var rectangle:Rectangle = new Rectangle(0xFFFFFF, 50);
        rectangle.x = 200;
        rectangle.y = 200;
        addChild(rectangle);

        var button:CommandButton = new CommandButton("apply command");
        addChild(button);
        button.y = 250;

        var container:CommandContainer = new CommandContainer(new
            RotateClockwiseCommand(rectangle), "rotate clockwise", 0, 0);
        addChild(container);
        container = new CommandContainer(new RotateCounterclockwiseCommand
            (rectangle), "rotate counter-clockwise", 0, 55);
        addChild(container);
        container = new CommandContainer(new ScaleUpCommand(rectangle), "scale up",
            0, 110);
        addChild(container);
        container = new CommandContainer(new ScaleDownCommand(rectangle),
            "scale down", 0, 165);
        addChild(container);


        var undoButton:BasicButton = new BasicButton("undo");
        addChild(undoButton);
        undoButton.y = 280;
        undoButton.addEventListener(MouseEvent.CLICK, onUndo);

    }

    private function onUndo(event:MouseEvent):void {
        var stack:CommandStack = CommandStack.getInstance();
        if(stack.hasPreviousCommands()) {
            var command:ICommand = stack.previous();
            if(command is IUndoableCommand) {
                IUndoableCommand(command).undo();
            }
        }
    }

}
```

With this revision, you can now test the application. As you run commands, you can also undo them by clicking the undo button.

Building a Redoable Application

As is true with making commands undoable, making commands redoable is a matter of implementing the `IRedoableCommand` interface. Next we'll make the commands in our example application redoable. Remember that the `redo()` method effectively redoes whatever was undone by the `undo()` method. In the simplest cases, the `redo()` method can simply call the `execute()` method. For more complex operations, calling the `execute()` method won't work correctly. In those cases, it is necessary to work out what steps are necessary to redo the state changes and then implement the `redo()` method accordingly.

To modify our application to support redoable commands, we'll do the following:

- Modify the command classes so they implement the `IRedoableCommand`.

- Add a redo button to the main class.

Implementing IRedoableCommand

First we'll implement `IRedoableCommand` in all the command classes. So that all our commands are both redoable and undoable, the commands must implement both `IUndoableCommand` and `IRedoableCommand`. Here's `RotateClockwiseCommand`:

```
package com.peachpit.aas3wdp.commandexample.commands {

    import com.peachpit.aas3wdp.commands.IUndoableCommand;
    import com.peachpit.aas3wdp.commands.IRedoableCommand;
    import flash.display.DisplayObject;

    public class RotateClockwiseCommand implements IUndoableCommand, IRedoableCommand {

        private var _receiver:DisplayObject;

        public function RotateClockwiseCommand(receiver:DisplayObject) {
            _receiver = receiver;
        }

        public function execute():void {
            _receiver.rotation += 20;
        }

        public function undo():void {
            _receiver.rotation -= 20;
        }

        public function redo():void {
            execute();
        }

    }
}
```

The remaining command classes follow suit. In each case, we import `IRedoableCommand`, add it to the implements list, and define a `redo()` method that simply calls `execute()`.

Adding the Redo Button

Next we'll add a redo button to the main class. We do this by first adding the following code to the constructor:

```
var redoButton:BasicButton = new BasicButton("redo");
addChild(redoButton);
redoButton.y = 310;
redoButton.addEventListener(MouseEvent.CLICK, onRedo);
```

This code adds the redo button. We still have to define the `onRedo()` method to handle the click event. This is our `onRedo()` method:

```
private function onRedo(event:MouseEvent):void {
   var stack:CommandStack = CommandStack.getInstance();
   if(stack.hasNextCommands()) {
      var command:ICommand = stack.next();
      if(command is IRedoableCommand) {
         IRedoableCommand(command).redo();
      }
   }
}
```

This code is almost identical to the `onUndo()` method except that it tests that the class passes the `IRedoableCommand` test. Then it calls the `redo()` method.

With those few edits, the application now implements redoable commands. Clicking the redo button will re-apply the next command in the command stack.

Using Commands to Build a Proximity Game

The following sample application uses the Command pattern to build a game called Proximity. The game consists of a grid of hexagonal pieces arranged so that each piece is adjacent to 6 pieces (unless the piece is on the edge). The game generally requires two or more players. The game play is as follows.

1. A new game piece is displayed for a game player. The game piece has a numeric value ranging from 2 to 20.

2. The game player clicks on an unoccupied grid space to apply the game piece settings. That grid space then belongs to the game player, and the numeric value is applied to that space.

3. If any of the adjacent grid spaces already belongs to a different player, then a comparison is run between the newly occupied grid space and the adjacent spaces belonging to different players. If the newly occupied space has a higher numeric value than an adjacent space, the owner of the newly occupied space takes ownership of the adjacent space.

4. If any of the adjacent spaces belongs to the same game player as the newly occupied space, those spaces are fortified by adding 1 to their numeric values.

5. Steps 1 through 4 repeat until all grid spaces are occupied.

The application requires a fair number of classes, which we'll build in the following sections.

Defining the Player Data Class

Every game has two or more players. Therefore, we'll first define the class that will serve as the data model for each game player. The GamePlayer class basically just stores the color for the player (each game player must be represented with a unique color on the board).

```
package com.peachpit.aas3wdp.proximity.data {

  public class GamePlayer {

    private var _color:uint;

    public function set color(value:uint):void {
      _color = value;
    }

    public function get color():uint {
      return _color;
    }

    public function GamePlayer() {
      _color = 0xEEEEEE;
    }

  }
}
```

In addition to the standard game player type, we'll also define a null player using NullPlayer. The NullPlayer class extends GamePlayer so that it looks just like a standard player. However, it is a special case we can use in place of an actual player.

```
package com.peachpit.aas3wdp.proximity.data {

  public class NullOwner extends GamePlayer {

  }
}
```

We'll use NullPlayer objects as the default owners for all pieces on the board until another game player takes ownership.

Defining a Collection Class for the Game Players

Every game has a collection of players. To keep track of the game players we'll build a new collection class called GamePlayers. The following code defines a Singleton class called com.peachpit.aas3wdp.proximity.data.GamePlayers to serve as this collection:

```
package com.peachpit.aas3wdp.proximity.data {

    import com.peachpit.aas3wdp.proximity.data.GamePlayers;
    import com.peachpit.aas3wdp.proximity.data.GamePlayer;
    import com.peachpit.aas3wdp.iterators.IIterator;
    import com.peachpit.aas3wdp.iterators.ArrayIterator;

    public class GamePlayers {

        private var _data:Array;
        private static var _instance:GamePlayers;
        private static const COLORS:Array = [0xFFCCCC, 0xCCFFCC, 0xCCCCFF, 0xFFFFCC,
           0xCCFFFF, 0xFFCCFF];

        public function GamePlayers(parameter:SingletonEnforcer) {
            _data = new Array();
        }

        public static function getInstance():GamePlayers {
            if(_instance == null) {
                _instance = new GamePlayers(new SingletonEnforcer());
            }
            return _instance;
        }

        public function addGamePlayer(gamePlayer:GamePlayer):void {
            gamePlayer.color = COLORS[_data.length];
            _data.push(gamePlayer);
        }

        public function iterator():IIterator {
            return new ArrayIterator(_data);
        }

    }
}

class SingletonEnforcer {}
```

Note that this class has just two instance methods: addGamePlayer() to add game player instances and iterator() to retrieve an iterator to access the collection.

Defining Game Pieces

Now that we've defined the game player classes and created a collection for them, we next need to define another basic building block of the game: the game pieces. The com.peachpit.aas3wdp. proximity.data.PieceData class serves as the data model for game pieces and grid spaces.

```
package com.peachpit.aas3wdp.proximity.data {

    import flash.events.EventDispatcher;
    import flash.events.Event;
    import com.peachpit.aas3wdp.proximity.data.GamePlayer;
    import com.peachpit.aas3wdp.proximity.data.NullOwner;

    public class PieceData extends EventDispatcher {
```

```
protected var _row:int;
protected var _column:int;
protected var _count:uint;
protected var _owner:GamePlayer;
protected var _radius:Number;

// Keep track of the radius to use for the game piece
// when it is displayed.
public function set radius(value:Number):void {
   _radius = value;
   dispatchEvent(new Event(Event.CHANGE));
}

public function get radius():Number {
   return _radius;
}

// Keep track of the count (the value) for the game piece.
public function set count(value:uint):void {
   _count = value;
   dispatchEvent(new Event(Event.CHANGE));
}

public function get count():uint {
   return _count;
}

// Every game piece belongs to a game player.
public function set owner(value:GamePlayer):void {
   _owner = value;
   dispatchEvent(new Event(Event.CHANGE));
}

public function get owner():GamePlayer {
   return _owner;
}

// Which row is the game piece in?
public function set row(value:int):void {
   _row = value;
}

public function get row():int {
   return _row;
}

// Which column is the game piece in?
public function set column(value:int):void {
   _column = value;
}

public function get column():int {
   return _column;
}

// Use the constructor to set default property values.
```

(CODE CONTINUED)

```
        public function PieceData() {
          _row = -1;
          _column = -1;
          _count = 0;

          // Use a NullOwner by default.
          _owner = new NullOwner();
        }

      }
    }
```

This class is yet another basic data model class. This time, however, it's important to note that `PieceData` inherits from `EventDispatcher`; when the values change, it dispatches events notifying listeners that the data model has changed.

Defining the Game Board Data Class

The game needs a game board. Our game board data model keeps track of all the pieces, placing them in rows and columns. Because there can be only one game board per game, the game board data model class is defined as a Singleton class.

```
package com.peachpit.aas3wdp.proximity.data {

  import com.peachpit.aas3wdp.proximity.data.PieceData;
  import com.peachpit.aas3wdp.proximity.data.GameboardData;
  import com.peachpit.aas3wdp.iterators.IIterator;
  import flash.events.EventDispatcher;
  import flash.events.Event;
  import com.peachpit.aas3wdp.iterators.ArrayIterator;

  public class GameboardData extends EventDispatcher {

    private var _pieces:Array;
    private var _rows:uint;
    private var _columns:uint;
    private var _newGamePiece:PieceData;
    private var _iterator:IIterator;

    private static var _instance:GameboardData;

    // Set the number of rows in the game board.
    public function set rows(value:uint):void {
      _rows = value;
      update();
    }

    // Set the number of columns in the garme board.
    public function set columns(value:uint):void {
      _columns = value;
      update();
    }

    // Request a new game piece. The game board is responsible
```

```
          // for returning the next game piece to play.
          public function get newGamePiece():PieceData {
            return _newGamePiece;
          }

          // Set defaults for all the properties.
          public function GameboardData(parameter:SingletonEnforcer) {
            _rows = 10;
            _columns = 10;
            _newGamePiece = new PieceData();
            _newGamePiece.radius = 40;
            _iterator = GamePlayers.getInstance().iterator();
            update();
          }

          public static function getInstance():GameboardData {
            if(_instance == null) {
              _instance = new GameboardData(new SingletonEnforcer());
            }
            return _instance;
          }

          // Re-add the game pieces. This method is called every time
          // one of the properties changes (columns, rows, etc.) This
          // code then creates all the game pieces, sets the rows and
          // columns, and adds the pieces to the pieces array.
          public function update():void {
            var i:uint;
            var j:uint;
            var piece:PieceData;
            _pieces = new Array();
            for(i = 0; i < _rows; i++) {
              for(j = 0; j < _columns; j++) {
                piece = new PieceData();
                piece.row = i;
                piece.column = j;
                piece.radius = 20;
                addPiece(piece);
              }
            }
            dispatchEvent(new Event(Event.CHANGE));
          }

          private function addPiece(piece:PieceData):void {
            if(_pieces[piece.row] == null) {
              _pieces[piece.row] = new Array();
            }
            _pieces[piece.row][piece.column] = piece;
          }

          // Return an iterator that allows access to each game
          // piece.
          public function iterator():IIterator {
            var pieces:Array = new Array();
            var i:uint;
            var j:uint;
```

```
            for(i = 0; i < _rows; i++) {
              for(j = 0; j < _columns; j++) {
                pieces.push(_pieces[i][j]);
              }
            }
            return new ArrayIterator(pieces);
        }

        // Calculate all the pieces that are adjacent to a given
        // piece, and return an iterator that allows access to
        // those pieces.
        public function getProximityPieces(piece:PieceData):IIterator {
          var pieces:Array = new Array();
          var row:uint = piece.row;
          var column:uint = piece.column;
          if(piece.row > 0) {
            pieces.push(_pieces[row - 1][column]);
            if(row % 2 == 0 && column > 0) {
              pieces.push(_pieces[row - 1][column - 1]);
            }
            else if(row % 2 != 0 && column < _pieces[row - 1].length - 1) {
              pieces.push(_pieces[row - 1][column + 1]);
            }
          }
          if(piece.column > 0) {
            pieces.push(_pieces[row][column - 1]);
          }
          if(column < _pieces[row].length - 1) {
            pieces.push(_pieces[row][column + 1]);
          }
          if(row < _pieces.length - 1) {
            pieces.push(_pieces[row + 1][column]);
            if(row % 2 == 0 && column > 0) {
              pieces.push(_pieces[row + 1][column - 1]);
            }
            else if(row % 2 != 0 && column < _pieces[row + 1].length - 1) {
              pieces.push(_pieces[row + 1][column + 1]);
            }
          }
          return new ArrayIterator(pieces);
        }
        // Advance to the next game piece to play.
        public function nextGamePiece():void {
          if(!_iterator.hasNext()) {
            _iterator.reset();
          }
          _newGamePiece.count = Math.round(Math.random() * 18) + 2;
          _newGamePiece.owner = GamePlayer(_iterator.next());
          if(!_iterator.hasNext()) {
            _iterator.reset();
          }
        }
    }
  }

  class SingletonEnforcer {}
```

The `GameboardData` class is responsible for several things. First, it is responsible for keeping track of all the game pieces. Additionally, it is responsible for determining what game pieces are adjacent to other game pieces. And it is also responsible for keeping track of the game piece that can next be played. The `nextGamePiece()` method accomplishes this task by retrieving the next item from the game player iterator and generating a random number from 2 to 20, assigning those values to the `_newGamePiece` instance.

Defining the Game Play Command Class

Now that we've defined all the data model classes, we'll next create the command class used for game play. The `com.peachpit.aas3wdp.proximity.commands.GamePlayCommand` class encapsulates the command for game play.

```
package com.peachpit.aas3wdp.proximity.commands {

    import com.peachpit.aas3wdp.proximity.data.PieceData;
    import com.peachpit.aas3wdp.proximity.data.GamePlayer;
    import com.peachpit.aas3wdp.proximity.data.GamePlayers;
    import com.peachpit.aas3wdp.proximity.data.GameboardData;
    import com.peachpit.aas3wdp.proximity.data.NullOwner;
    import com.peachpit.aas3wdp.commands.ICommand;
    import com.peachpit.aas3wdp.iterators.IIterator;

    public class GamePlayCommand implements ICommand {

        protected var _piece:PieceData;

        public function GamePlayCommand(piece:PieceData) {
            _piece = piece;
        }

        public function execute():void {
            var gameboard:GameboardData = GameboardData.getInstance();
            var newGamePiece:PieceData = gameboard.newGamePiece;
            var currentGamePlayer:GamePlayer = newGamePiece.owner;
            // If the game piece's owner is a NullOwner (and
            // only if) then it's a valid click, so apply the
            //command.
            if(_piece.owner is NullOwner) {

                _piece.owner = currentGamePlayer;
                _piece.count = newGamePiece.count;

                // Retrieve all adjacent pieces.
                var iterator:IIterator = gameboard.getProximityPieces(_piece);
                var piece:PieceData;
                while(iterator.hasNext()) {
                    piece = iterator.next() as PieceData;

                    // If the game piece has the same
                    // owner as the clicked game piece,
                    // increment the count. If they have
                    // different owners (and the owner
                    // isn't NullOwner) then test if the
```

(CODE CONTINUED)

```
                      // clicked game piece has a higher
                      // count. If so, make it the new
                      // owner.
                      if(piece.owner == _piece.owner) {
                        piece.count++;
                      }
                      else if(!(piece.owner is NullOwner)) {
                        if(piece.count < _piece.count) {
                            piece.owner = currentGamePlayer;
                        }
                      }
                    }
                  }

                  // Get the next game piece.
                  GameboardData.getInstance().nextGamePiece();
                }
              }

          }
        }
```

In this command type, the game piece is the receiver. When the user triggers the execute() method, the method requests the new game piece from the game board and applies it to the receiver. The method also requests all the adjacent pieces and uses game play rules to determine how and if to change those values.

Defining the Game Factory Class

In the next chapter, we'll update the application by adding undo and redo functionality in the context of a our discussion of the Memento pattern. To minimize the impact of those future changes to the code we're creating now, we'll use a factory (see Chapter 5, "Factory Method Pattern") to make the command objects. Define com.peachpit.aas3wdp.proximity.commands. CommandFactory as follows:

```
package com.peachpit.aas3wdp.proximity.commands {

    import com.peachpit.aas3wdp.commands.ICommand;
    import com.peachpit.aas3wdp.proximity.commands.GamePlayCommand;
    import com.peachpit.aas3wdp.proximity.data.PieceData;

    public class CommandFactory {

        private static var _type:String = NORMAL;

        public static const NORMAL:String = "normal";
        public static const UNDOABLE:String = "undoable";
        public static const REDOABLE:String = "redoable";

        public static function set type(value:String):void {
            _type = value;
        }

        public static function getGamePlayCommand(data:PieceData):ICommand {
```

```
            if(_type == NORMAL) {
                return new GamePlayCommand(data);
            }
            return null;
        }


    }
}
```

This class allows us to globally set the type of commands it should create. Then we can use `getGamePlayCommand()` to request the command for a specific receiver. Currently, we're only ever returning one type, but subsequently, we'll enable undoable and redoable versions.

Defining the Game Piece View and Controller Class

The `com.peachpit.aas3wdp.proximity.views.Piece` class is the view (and controller) for the game pieces/grid spaces. The `Piece` class uses a `PieceData` object as its data model, and it draws itself based on the data model values. It also stores a command object that it executes when the user clicks the object.

```
package com.peachpit.aas3wdp.proximity.views {

    import flash.display.Sprite;
    import flash.text.TextField;
    import flash.events.Event;
    import flash.events.MouseEvent;
    import flash.text.TextFormat;
    import flash.text.TextFieldAutoSize;
    import com.peachpit.aas3wdp.proximity.data.PieceData;
    import com.peachpit.aas3wdp.proximity.commands.CommandFactory;
    import com.peachpit.aas3wdp.commands.ICommand;

    public class Piece extends Sprite {

        private var _background:Sprite;
        private var _label:TextField;
        private var _data:PieceData;
        private var _command:ICommand;

        public function set data(value:PieceData):void {
            _data = value;
            _data.addEventListener(Event.CHANGE, draw);

            // Retrieve the command from the factory.
            _command = CommandFactory.getGamePlayCommand(_data);
            draw();
        }

        public function get data():PieceData {
            return _data;
        }

        public function Piece() {
```

```
        // Listen for mouse events.
        addEventListener(MouseEvent.MOUSE_OVER, onMouseOver);
        addEventListener(MouseEvent.MOUSE_OUT, onMouseOut);
        addEventListener(MouseEvent.CLICK, onClick);

        // Create the background into which to draw the
        // hexagon.
        _background = new Sprite();
        addChild(_background);

        // Create the text field into which to display the
        // count.
        _label = new TextField();
        addChild(_label);
        _label.selectable = false;
        _label.autoSize = TextFieldAutoSize.LEFT;
    }

    // Draw the game piece based on the data model.
    public function draw(event:Event = null):void {
        var color:uint = _data.owner.color;
        var newX:Number;
        var newY:Number;
        var angle:Number = -Math.PI / 6;
        var angleDelta:Number = Math.PI / 3;
        _background.graphics.clear();
        _background.graphics.lineStyle(0, 0, 0);
        _background.graphics.beginFill(color, 1);
        newX = Math.cos(angle) * _data.radius;
        newY = Math.sin(angle) * _data.radius;
        _background.graphics.moveTo(newX, newY);
        for(var i:uint = 0; i < 6; i++) {
            angle += angleDelta;
            newX = Math.cos(angle) * _data.radius;
            newY = Math.sin(angle) * _data.radius;
            _background.graphics.lineTo(newX, newY);
        }
        _background.graphics.endFill();
        if(_data.row != -1) {
            x = (_data.row % 2 == 0 ? 0 : _data.radius) + _data.column * _data.radius * 2;
            y = _data.row * _data.radius * 2;
        }
        _label.text = String(_data.count);
        _label.x = -_label.width / 2;
        _label.y = -_label.height / 2;
    }

    private function onMouseOver(event:MouseEvent):void {
        _background.alpha = .1;
    }

    private function onMouseOut(event:MouseEvent):void {
        _background.alpha = 1;
    }

    // When the user clicks on the game piece, call the
```

(CODE CONTINUED)

```
      // command's execute() method
      private function onClick(event:MouseEvent):void {
        _command.execute();
      }
    }
  }
}
```

The key thing about this class is that it uses a command object to neatly encapsulate its behavior. When the user clicks the piece, it executes the command. However, the exact command implementation might change because we can simply change what is getting returned by the factory (as we'll see in subsequent versions of this application).

Defining the Game Board View and Controller

The game board also requires a view and controller, for which we'll define com.peachpit. aas3wdp.proximity.Gameboard. The Gameboard class uses a GameboardData object as its data model.

```
package com.peachpit.aas3wdp.proximity.views {

  import flash.display.Sprite;
  import com.peachpit.aas3wdp.proximity.data.GameboardData;
  import com.peachpit.aas3wdp.iterators.IIterator;
  import com.peachpit.aas3wdp.proximity.data.PieceData;
  import flash.events.Event;

  public class Gameboard extends flash.display.Sprite {

    private var _data:GameboardData;
    private var _newGamePiece:Piece;

    public function set data(value:GameboardData):void {
      _data = value;
      onUpdate();
      // Redraw the gameboard every time the data model
      // changes.
      _data.addEventListener(Event.CHANGE, onUpdate);
    }

    public function Gameboard() {
    }

    private function onUpdate(event:Event = null):void {
      _pieces = new Sprite();
      addChild(_pieces);
      var iterator:IIterator = _data.iterator();
      var piece:Piece;
      while(iterator.hasNext()) {
        piece = new Piece();
        piece.data = PieceData(iterator.next());
        _pieces.addChild(piece);
      }

      if(_newGamePiece == null) {
```

```
                    // The new game piece shows what piece can
                    // next be played.
                    _newGamePiece = new Piece();
                    _newGamePiece.data = _data.newGamePiece;
                    _newGamePiece.data.radius = 40;
                    addChild(_newGamePiece);
                }
                _newGamePiece.x = _pieces.width / 2;
                _newGamePiece.y = _pieces.height + _pieces.y + 40;
            }
        }
    }
```

Because most of the work is already handled in the data model classes and in the game piece view/controller, the implementation for Gameboard is relatively simple. All it has to do is add the game pieces based on the data model, and it has to display the new game piece as well.

Defining the Main Class

Next we have to create a main class to put the application together and test it. The main class for the application is called Proximity and is defined as follows:

```
package {

    import flash.display.Sprite;
    import flash.display.StageScaleMode;
    import flash.display.StageAlign;
    import flash.events.MouseEvent;
    import com.peachpit.aas3wdp.commands.ICommandStack;
    import com.peachpit.aas3wdp.proximity.views.Piece;
    import com.peachpit.aas3wdp.proximity.data.GameboardData;
    import com.peachpit.aas3wdp.proximity.data.PieceData;
    import com.peachpit.aas3wdp.proximity.data.GamePlayer;
    import com.peachpit.aas3wdp.proximity.data.GamePlayers;
    import com.peachpit.aas3wdp.proximity.data.NullOwner;
    import com.peachpit.aas3wdp.proximity.commands.CommandFactory;
    import com.peachpit.aas3wdp.iterators.IIterator;
    import com.peachpit.aas3wdp.iterators.NullIterator;
    import com.peachpit.aas3wdp.commands.ICommand;
    import com.peachpit.aas3wdp.proximity.views.Gameboard;

    public class Proximity extends Sprite {

        private var _newGamePiece:Piece;

        public function Proximity() {
            // Set the command type. The valid types are NORMAL,
            // UNDOABLE, and REDOABLE. This determines
            // what sort of commands the factory returns.
            CommandFactory.type = CommandFactory.NORMAL;

            // Set the stage scaleMode and align properties.
            stage.scaleMode = StageScaleMode.NO_SCALE;
```

(CODE CONTINUED)

```
            stage.align = StageAlign.TOP_LEFT;

            // Add a new gameboard and its datamodel.
            var gameboard:Gameboard = new Gameboard();
            var gameboardData:GameboardData = GameboardData.getInstance();

            // Set the number of columns for the gameboard to 20
            // (the default is 10).
            gameboardData.columns = 20;
            gameboard.data = gameboardData;
            addChild(gameboard);
            gameboard.x = 20;
            gameboard.y = 20;

            // Add game players.
            var gamePlayers:GamePlayers = GamePlayers.getInstance();
            gamePlayers.addGamePlayer(new GamePlayer());
            gamePlayers.addGamePlayer(new GamePlayer());

            GameboardData.getInstance().nextGamePiece();

        }

    }
}
```

When you test the application, you will see an image like the one shown in **Figure 10.1**.

Clicking a grid space applies the game piece settings (the player who owns the piece and the value of the piece) by calling the command object's execute() method. The execute() method also advances the game play to the next player.

Figure 10.1

The Proximity gameboard with 10 rows and 20 columns.

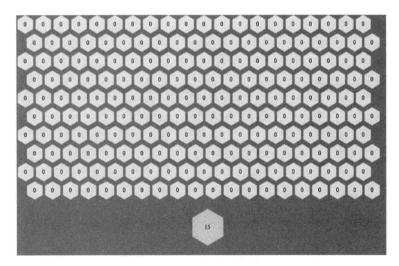

Summary

This chapter discusses the Command pattern, which is a way of encapsulating an action and its parameters. The Command pattern is useful as a solution to a variety of scenarios such as the need for transactional behavior or undoable actions. Regardless of the way in which a command is used, it always implements a known interface that has, at a minimum, a method (`execute()`) that runs the action. In most cases, the command also has a receiver of the action, a client that instantiates the command, and an invoker that calls the method that runs the action. As shown by the examples in this chapter, the receiver, client, and invoker for a command change based on the way in which the command is used. In some cases, the client and invoker are the same object.

In the next chapter, we'll look at the Memento pattern, which is often used in conjunction with the Command pattern. In fact, in the next chapter we'll continue building the Proximity game application to use the Memento pattern.

11

Memento Pattern

The Memento pattern is a way of recording an object's current state without breaking the rules of encapsulation. The rules of encapsulation say that an object should manage its own state, and that it should allow external objects to influence its state only through a well-defined API. For example, it is perfectly acceptable for a class to define a setter method that changes the value of a private property. However, it would be bad design to use public properties that can be set without going through a method of the class. Public properties allow external objects to change the object's state without the object knowing what has occurred.

There are many reasons you might want to record an object's state at a point in time. Frequently you want to record an object's state so that you can return to that point if necessary. For example, an application with panel sets might enable the user to configure the panels by moving them and resizing them. You might then want to record the configuration so that the user can make changes but be able to return to the saved configuration. The difficulty is in how to record the state without breaking encapsulation. One option that might jump out immediately is to add methods that return each of the required values. For example, if you want to record a panel's state, you might want to record the x and y coordinates as well as the width and height. That might seem simple enough. However, consider that an object's internal state might be complex, and it might well be inappropriate to expose certain elements of the internal state in that way.

The Memento pattern elegantly solves this dilemma. The Memento pattern consists of three basic elements called the memento, the originator, and the caretaker. The originator is the class that needs to record a snapshot of its state. It accomplishes that by way of an instance of a memento class. The caretaker is the object that stores the memento until which time it needs to restore it to the originator. The originator class has an API that allows a caretaker class to request a memento object. The caretaker class stores the memento, and it then passes it back to the originator if requested.

The Memento pattern does not impose a very precise API that must be followed. However, the Memento pattern generally uses at least three classes for a basic implementation: the originator, the memento, and the caretaker.

The originator can be any sort of class for which you need to record the state at a point in time. The originator class must define methods to get and set the memento, which is used to save and restore state. The memento is usually tightly coupled with the originator. Because a memento records state for an originator, the memento must know about the type of state that the originator maintains. At this point, a very simple example will be helpful.

Consider the case of a `Circle` class like the following:

```
package {
    import flash.display.Sprite;
    public class Circle extends Sprite {
        private var _radius:Number;
        private var _color:Number;

        public function set radius(value:Number):void {
            _radius = value;
            draw();
        }

        public function set color(value:Number):void {
            _color = value;
            draw();
        }

        public function Circle(radiusValue:Number, colorValue:Number) {
            _radius = radiusValue;
            _color = colorValue;
            draw();
        }

        private function draw():void {
            graphics.clear();
            graphics.lineStyle(1, _color, 1);
            graphics.beginFill(_color, 1)
            graphics.drawCircle(0, 0, _radius);
            graphics.endFill();
        }
    }
}
```

This example is purposefully simple. This `Circle` class simply draws a circle. The only state it needs to maintain is the radius and the color with which to draw the circle. Here's an example of code that creates a new `Circle` and adds it to the display list:

```
var circle:Circle = new Circle(10, 0xFFFFFF);
addChild(circle);
```

That code creates a white circle with a radius of 10. If you want, you can change the color to red and the radius to 20, like this:

```
circle.color = 0xFF0000;
circle.radius = 20;
```

But what happens if you then want to return to the previous state with the white color and the radius of 10? Clearly you must record the state before changing it so that you can restore it at a later time. The Memento pattern says that in order to record the state for the Circle class, we must create a memento type that we will call CircleMemento. The CircleMemento is capable of storing the radius and color values.

```
package {
   public class CircleMemento {
      private var _radius:Number;
      private var _color:Number;
      public function get radius():Number {
         return _radius;
      }
      public function get color():Number {
         return _color;
      }
      public function CircleMemento(radiusValue:Number, colorValue:Number) {
         _radius = radiusValue;
         _color = colorValue;
      }
   }
}
```

The memento class is a data-only class that simply stores all the values for the state that you want to record for a particular type. In the case of CircleMemento we want to record the radius and color values for a Circle instance.

Next, we need a way for the originator (Circle) to be responsible for saving and restoring its state. For that purpose, we add getMemento() and setMemento() methods to Circle.

```
package {
   import flash.display.Sprite;
   public class Circle extends Sprite {
      private var _radius:Number;
      private var _color:Number;

      public function set radius(value:Number):void {
         _radius = value;
         draw();
      }

      public function set color(value:Number):void {
         _color = value;
         draw();
      }

      public function Circle(radiusValue:Number, colorValue:Number) {
         _radius = radiusValue;
         _color = colorValue;
```

(CODE CONTINUED)

```
            draw();
        }

        private function draw():void {
          graphics.clear();
          graphics.lineStyle(1, _color, 1);
          graphics.beginFill(_color, 1)
          graphics.drawCircle(0, 0, _radius);
          graphics.endFill();
        }

        public function getMemento():CircleMemento {
          return new CircleMemento(_radius, _color);
        }

        public function setMemento(memento:CircleMemento):void {
          _radius = memento.radius;
          _color = memento.color;
          draw();
        }

      }
  }
```

You can see that the getMemento() method constructs and returns a new CircleMemento object that stores the current state. The setMemento() method accepts a CircleMemento parameter and then restores the Circle object's state to the state values from the memento.

The only object we haven't yet looked at is the caretaker. The caretaker is the object that calls getMemento() to retrieve and store the current memento, and it then can pass that memento back to the object using setMemento(). In this case, the caretaker is whatever object is constructing the Circle instance. Here's an example that creates a Circle instance: Every time the user clicks the circle, it changes the state randomly. The caretaker also records the current state by retrieving a memento from the Circle instance. Then the user can use the right and left keys on the keyboard to move backward and forward through the sequence of state changes.

```
package {
    import flash.display.Sprite;
    import flash.events.KeyboardEvent;
    import flash.events.MouseEvent;
    import flash.ui.Keyboard;

    public class MementoExample extends Sprite {

        private var _circle:Circle;
        private var _previousMementos:Array;
        private var _nextMementos:Array;

        public function MementoExample() {
        // Create arrays to store the next and previous states.
        _previousMementos = new Array();
        _nextMementos = new Array();

        // Create a circle.
```

(CODE CONTINUED)

```
            _circle = new Circle(10, 0xFFFFFF);
            addChild(_circle);

            // Listen for click events on the circle. Listen for
            // keyboard events globally.
            _circle.addEventListener(MouseEvent.CLICK, onClick);
            stage.addEventListener(KeyboardEvent.KEY_UP, onKey);
        }

        // When thye user clicks on the circle retrieve the current
        // memento from the circle, and store it in the _previousMementos
        // array. Then set the state of the circle to random values.
        private function onClick(event:MouseEvent):void {
          _nextMementos = new Array();
          _previousMementos.push(_circle.getMemento());
          _circle.radius = Math.random() * 40 + 10;
          _circle.color = Math.random() * (255 * 255 * 255);
        }

        // When the user presses the right and left keys restore the
        // state of the circle by retrieving a memento from the appropriate
        // array and passing it to the setMemento() method of the circle.
        private function onKey(event:KeyboardEvent):void {
          var memento:CircleMemento;
          if(event.keyCode == Keyboard.LEFT) {
            if(_previousMementos.length > 0) {
              memento = _previousMementos.pop();
            _nextMementos.push(memento);
              _circle.setMemento(memento);
            }
          }
          else if(event.keyCode == Keyboard.RIGHT) {
            if(_nextMementos.length > 0) {
              memento = _nextMementos.pop();
            _previousMementos.push(memento);
              _circle.setMemento(memento);
            }
          }
        }
      }
    }
  }
```

This should give you a basic idea of the structure of a relatively simple Memento pattern implementation. Throughout the chapter, we'll look at additional examples.

Using Mementos to Make Actions Undoable in the Proximity Game

Often, mementos are used in conjunction with commands in order to implement complex undoable and redoable commands. The following application applies mementos to the Proximity game application you created in the previous chapter, "Command Pattern"; the mementos will make the commands undoable in the Proximity game.

Defining the Memento Type

The first thing we'll do is define a memento class. The class com.peachpit.aas3wdp.proximity.
mementos.GamePieceMemento serves as the memento type used to store game piece state.

```
package com.peachpit.aas3wdp.proximity.mementos {

    import com.peachpit.aas3wdp.proximity.data.GamePlayer;

    public class GamePieceMemento {

        private var _count:uint;
        private var _owner:GamePlayer;

        public function get count():uint {
            return _count;
        }

        public function get owner():GamePlayer {
            return _owner;
        }

        public function GamePieceMemento(count:uint, owner:GamePlayer) {
            _count = count;
            _owner = owner;
        }

    }
}
```

You can see that the memento in this case stores values for count and owner. These values represent state for a PieceData object.

Creating the Originator

In the Proximity game, the mementos we want to store are for PieceData objects. Therefore, we'll need to make the PieceData class an originator by adding getMemento() and setMemento() methods. Here's PieceData with the new methods (we've omitted some of the code here just for the purposes of saving printed space):

```
package com.peachpit.aas3wdp.proximity.data {

    import flash.events.EventDispatcher;
    import flash.events.Event;
    import com.peachpit.aas3wdp.proximity.data.GamePlayer;
    import com.peachpit.aas3wdp.proximity.data.NullOwner;
    import com.peachpit.aas3wdp.proximity.mementos.GamePieceMemento;

    public class PieceData extends EventDispatcher {

        // Existing code goes here.

        public function getMemento():GamePieceMemento {
            return new GamePieceMemento(_count, _owner);
```

```
      }

      public function setMemento(memento:GamePieceMemento):void {
        _count = memento.count;
        _owner = memento.owner;
        dispatchEvent(new Event(Event.CHANGE));
      }

   }
 }
```

You can see that the getMemento() method simply constructs and returns a new GamePieceMemento object. The setMemento() method takes a GamePieceMemento instance, restores the PieceData state, and dispatches an event to notify listeners that the data model has changed.

Defining the Undoable Command Type

Next we'll define an undoable command type. The undoable command should inherit from the standard command type (GamePlayCommand). In addition, the command needs to implement the IUndoableCommand interface. The class, com.peachpit.aas3wdp.proximity.commands. UndoableGamePlayCommand is as follows:

```
package com.peachpit.aas3wdp.proximity.commands {

    import com.peachpit.aas3wdp.proximity.data.PieceData;
    import com.peachpit.aas3wdp.proximity.data.GamePlayer;
    import com.peachpit.aas3wdp.proximity.data.GamePlayers;
    import com.peachpit.aas3wdp.proximity.data.GameboardData;
    import com.peachpit.aas3wdp.proximity.commands.GamePlayCommand;
    import com.peachpit.aas3wdp.iterators.IIterator;
    import com.peachpit.aas3wdp.proximity.mementos.GamePieceMemento;
    import com.peachpit.aas3wdp.proximity.data.GameboardData;
    import com.peachpit.aas3wdp.proximity.data.NullOwner;
    import com.peachpit.aas3wdp.proximity.data.PieceData;
    import com.peachpit.aas3wdp.commands.CommandStack;
    import com.peachpit.aas3wdp.commands.IUndoableCommand;

    public class UndoableGamePlayCommand extends GamePlayCommand implements
       IUndoableCommand {

       protected var _gamePieceMementos:Array;
       protected var _gameboardMemento:GamePieceMemento;


       public function UndoableGamePlayCommand(piece:PieceData) {
         super(piece);
         _gamePieceMementos = new Array();
       }

       override public function execute():void {
         var gameboard:GameboardData = GameboardData.getInstance();
         if(_piece.owner is NullOwner) {

            // Get the memento for the clicked game piece.
```

(CODE CONTINUED)

```
            _gamePieceMementos.push({object: _piece, memento: _piece.getMemento()});

            var iterator:IIterator = gameboard.getProximityPieces(_piece);
            var piece:PieceData;
            while(iterator.hasNext()) {
              piece = PieceData(iterator.next());

              // Add a memento for the adjacent
              // game piece.
              _gamePieceMementos.push({object: piece, memento: piece.getMemento()});
            }

            // Add a memento for the new game piece and for the gameboard.
            _gameboardMemento = gameboard.getMemento();
          }
          super.execute();
          CommandStack.getInstance().putCommand(this);
        }

        public function undo():void {
          for(var i:uint = 0; i < _gamePieceMementos.length; i++) {
            _gamePieceMementos[i].object.setMemento(_gamePieceMementos[i].memento);
          }
          GameboardData.getInstance().setMemento(_gameboardMemento);
        }

      }
    }
```

This class overrides the execute() method so that it can retrieve all the mementos for the affected game pieces before changing their state. Then the undo() method loops through all the mementos and restores the originator state for each affected game piece.

Updating the Command Factory

Next we want to edit CommandFactory so that it returns a UndoableGamePlayCommand instance when the option is set correctly. Here's the updated getGamePlayCommand() method:

```
        public static function getGamePlayCommand(data:PieceData):ICommand {
          if(_type == NORMAL) {
            return new GamePlayCommand(data);
          }
          else if(_type == UNDOABLE) {
            return new UndoableGamePlayCommand(data);
          }
          return null;
        }
```

Updating the Main Class

Next we can edit the main class to enable undoable commands in the game. The behavior we are striving for is to undo commands when the user presses the left-arrow key.

The first thing we need to do in the main class is edit the constructor and assign UNDOABLE rather than NORMAL to the CommandFactory.type property:

```
CommandFactory.type = CommandFactory.UNDOABLE;
```

Next we'll add keyboard control. To do this the class must import the Keyboard and KeyboardEvent classes:

```
import flash.events.KeyboardEvent;
import flash.ui.Keyboard;
```

Then we'll add the following line of code to the main class constructor to listen for keyboard events:

```
stage.addEventListener(KeyboardEvent.KEY_DOWN, onKeyboard);
```

Add an onKeyboard() method to the main class. Define the method as follows:

```
private function onKeyboard(event:KeyboardEvent):void {
   var stack:CommandStack = CommandStack.getInstance();
   var command:ICommand;

   // If the user pressed the left arrow and there are
   // previous commands in the stack,
   // and if the command is undoable, call undo().
   if(event.keyCode == Keyboard.LEFT && stack.hasPreviousCommands()) {
      command = stack.previous();
      if(command is IUndoableCommand) {
         IUndoableCommand(command).undo();
      }
      else {
         stack.next();
      }
   }
}
```

Those few changes make the game's play actions undoable. When you test the Proximity application now, you can use the left-arrow key to undo the actions you have applied.

Using Mementos to Make Actions Redoable in the Proximity Game

Now that we have added an undo feature to the Proximity game, we'll complete our modifications to the game by adding code that redoes actions we have just undone.

Defining the Redoable Command

The first step in making the commands redoable is to create a redoable command class. Define a class, com.peachpit.aas3wdp.proximity.commands.RedoableGamePlayCommand, that extends UndoableGamePlayCommand and adds redo functionality by implementing IRedoableCommand.

```
package com.peachpit.aas3wdp.proximity.commands {

    import com.peachpit.aas3wdp.proximity.data.PieceData;
    import com.peachpit.aas3wdp.proximity.data.GamePlayer;
    import com.peachpit.aas3wdp.proximity.data.GamePlayers;
    import com.peachpit.aas3wdp.proximity.data.GameboardData;
    import com.peachpit.aas3wdp.proximity.commands.UndoableGamePlayCommand;
    import com.peachpit.aas3wdp.iterators.IIterator;
    import com.peachpit.aas3wdp.proximity.mementos.GamePieceMemento;
    import com.peachpit.aas3wdp.commands.IRedoableCommand;
    import com.peachpit.aas3wdp.proximity.data.NullOwner;

    public class RedoableGamePlayCommand extends UndoableGamePlayCommand implements
        IRedoableCommand {

        private var _nextGamePieceMemento:GamePieceMemento;

        public function RedoableGamePlayCommand(piece:PieceData) {
            super(piece);
        }

        override public function undo():void {
            _nextGamePieceMemento = GameboardData.getInstance().newGamePiece.getMemento();
            super.undo();
        }

        public function redo():void {
            var gameboard:GameboardData = GameboardData.getInstance();
            var newGamePiece:PieceData = gameboard.newGamePiece;
            var currentGamePlayer:GamePlayer = newGamePiece.owner;
            _piece.owner = currentGamePlayer;
            _piece.count = newGamePiece.count;

            // Retrieve all adjacent pieces.
            var iterator:IIterator = gameboard.getProximityPieces(_piece);
            var piece:PieceData;
            while(iterator.hasNext()) {
                piece = PieceData(iterator.next());

                // If the game piece has the same owner as
                // the clicked game piece, increment the
                // count. If they have different owners (and
                // the owner isn't NullOwner) then test if
                // the clicked game piece has a higher
                // count. If so, make it the new owner.
                if(piece.owner == _piece.owner) {
                    piece.count++;
                }
                else if(!(piece.owner is NullOwner)) {
                    if(piece.count < _piece.count) {
                        piece.owner = currentGamePlayer;
                    }
                }
            }
            GameboardData.getInstance().setMemento(_nextGamePieceMemento);
        }

    }

}
```

The redoable command redoes a command by essentially replaying based on the new game piece. It then uses a memento to restore the next new game piece state.

Editing the Factory Class

Next we'll edit the `CommandFactory` class so that it returns a `RedoableGamePlayCommand` object when the `type` property is set to `REDOABLE`. Here's the updated `getGamePlayCommand()` method:

```
public static function getGamePlayCommand(data:PieceData):ICommand {
   if(_type == NORMAL) {
      return new GamePlayCommand(data);
   }
   else if(_type == UNDOABLE) {
      return new UndoableGamePlayCommand(data);
   }
   else if(_type == REDOABLE) {
      return new RedoableGamePlayCommand(data);
   }
   return null;
}
```

Editing the Main Class

Now we can edit the main class by assigning a value of `REDOABLE` rather than `UNDOABLE` to the `CommandFactory.type` property.

```
CommandFactory.type = CommandFactory.REDOABLE;
```

Add an `if` clause to the `onKeyboard()` method so that it calls the `redo()` method of the next command object in the stack when the user presses the right-arrow key:

```
private function onKeyboard(event:KeyboardEvent):void {
   var stack:CommandStack = CommandStack.getInstance();
   var command:ICommand;

   if(event.keyCode == Keyboard.LEFT && stack.hasPreviousCommands()) {
      command = stack.previous();
      if(command is IUndoableCommand) {
         IUndoableCommand(command).undo();
      }
      else {
         stack.next();
      }
   }

   // If the user pressed the right arrow key and there are next
   // commands in the stack, and if the command is redoable, call
   // redo().
   if(event.keyCode == Keyboard.RIGHT && stack.hasNextCommands()) {
      command = stack.next();
      if(command is IRedoableCommand) {
         IRedoableCommand(command).redo();
      }
      else {
         stack.previous();
      }
   }
}
```

When you test the application now, you can press the right-arrow key to redo any action that you've previously undone.

Summary

This chapter discusses the Memento pattern, which provides an elegant way to store an object's state while at the same time breaking no rules of encapsulation. An object for which you need to record state is called the originator. The originator is responsible for returning a memento object that stores the object's current state, and the originator is also responsible to managing its own state by applying a stored state from a memento. The memento objects can be stored by a caretaker object until they are reapplied to the originator.

CHAPTER 12

State Pattern

The State pattern is a valuable pattern in ActionScript development. It allows an object to change its behavior when its internal state changes. Take a toggle button as an example. The toggle button must maintain two separate states: one for selected and one for unselected. The two states share the same structure, but they have very different functionality. In addition to the visual display being different, they most likely handle a click event differently, too. This is where the State pattern becomes valuable. The State pattern defines a standard methodology for handling encapsulated states.

There are many ways to implement the State pattern, but they all come to the same result: The object's class appears to change. Obviously, we aren't talking about changing the object's *type* at run-time, but we are talking about changing nearly every operation in a class based on its internal state.

The best way to demonstrate the State pattern is with an example. Therefore, we're going to build a basketball shooter. Our example will build a shooter object with three different states: lay up, free throw, and three-pointer. Each of these states has characteristics such as accuracy and point value. We'll use this shooter object in the context of a basketball game. When we tell the shooter to shoot the ball, we can calculate whether the shot was made and for how many points based on the internal state of the shooter object.

Simple State Example

Our first attempt at representing the basketball shooter and its various states is very simple. In fact, you've probably built classes just like this before. This shooter class meets all the criteria of the State pattern but is a naive and inelegant solution that presents further problems. We'll look at this example first to understand how we can later improve on this.

Create the Simple Shooter Class

The SimpleShooter class holds all the shooter functionality for each state. The state is set in the setState() method. This method takes a stateName as the parameter. The value of this parameter is saved in a class property called stateName.

There are three constants defined in this class that represent the three state names: LAY_UP_STATE, FREE_THROW_STATE, and THREE_POINTER_STATE. They should be used when calling the setState() method to ensure accuracy.

The SimpleShooter class also has a getAccuracy() method to determine the percentage of shots made from that state. And there is a getPointValue() method that returns the point value of a made shot from that state. Each of these methods has a switch statement that determines the state in which the object is.

```
package com.peachpit.aas3wdp.stateexample {

  public class SimpleShooter {

    private var stateName:String;
    public static const LAY_UP_STATE:String = "lay_up_state";
    public static const FREE_THROW_STATE:String = "free_throw_state";
    public static const THREE_POINTER_STATE:String = "three_pointer_state";

    public function SimpleShooter() {}

    // Returns the shot accuracy percent of the current state
    public function getAccuracy():Number {
      switch(stateName) {
        case LAY_UP_STATE:
          return 0.9;
        case FREE_THROW_STATE:
          return 0.7;
        case THREE_POINTER_STATE:
          return 0.4;
        default:
          return 0;
      }
    }

    // Returns the made shot point value of the current state
    public function getPointValue():Number {
      switch(stateName) {
        case LAY_UP_STATE:
          return 2;
        case FREE_THROW_STATE:
          return 1;
        case THREE_POINTER_STATE:
          return 3;
        default:
          return 0;
      }
    }

    // Sets the current state of the object
```

(CODE CONTINUED)

```
        public function setState(stateName:String):void {
            this.stateName = stateName;
        }

    }

}
```

Create the Main Example Class

We'll build a class called `SimpleShooterExample`, which serves as the starting point for this example. This class creates the shooter object, sets the state, initiates ten shots at a constant time interval, calculates the outcome (whether or not the ball went through the hoop) based on the accuracy property, and keeps track of the points. After each shot, we output the outcome of the shot. The outcome of the shot and the point value are determined by the internal state of the shooter object. The following is the code for our implementation class:

```
package {

    import flash.display.Sprite;
    import flash.utils.Timer;
    import flash.events.TimerEvent;
    import com.peachpit.aas3wdp.stateexample.SimpleShooter;

    public class SimpleShooterExample extends Sprite {

        private var _points:Number;
        private var _shooter:SimpleShooter;

        public function SimpleShooterExample() {
            // Initially set the points to zero
            _points = 0;
            // Create the SimpleShooter instance and set its state
            _shooter = new SimpleShooter();
            _shooter.setState(SimpleShooter.THREE_POINTER_STATE);

            var shotInterval:Timer = new Timer(1000, 10);
            shotInterval.addEventListener(TimerEvent.TIMER, onShot);
            shotInterval.start();
        }

        private function calculateShot(accuracy:Number):Boolean {
            return Math.random() < accuracy;
        }

        private function onShot(event:TimerEvent):void {
            if(calculateShot(_shooter.getAccuracy())) {
                _points += _shooter.getPointValue();
                trace("Made the Shot!   " + _points + " point(s)");
            }else {
                trace("Missed the Shot!")
            }
        }
    }
}
```

The `SimpleShooterExample` class has two properties: `points` and `shooter`. The `points` property holds the running total of our points across all ten shots; the `shooter` property holds the instance of the `SimpleShooter` object. Inside the constructor, we create that `SimpleShooter` object and set the state of it.

The shot is calculated by grabbing the accuracy of the current shot. This is a percentage at which shots from that state are typically made. We run that though a simple probability function called `calculateShot()`. If the accuracy is 80%, the `calculateShot()` method returns true 80% of the times it is called and false for the remaining 20%.

Problems with This Example

Although the example we just described works and is simple to understand, there are a couple major problems with it.

The first problem is scalability. This solution simply will not scale well. Consider an option with 100 states and 20 methods per state. The resulting class would be huge. And each time you add or remove a state, you'd have to modify every method.

This transitions us nicely to our second problem: maintainability. If we have to modify massive amounts of code for each change request, we're opening ourselves up to having a lot of bugs. To prevent this from happening, we should encapsulate each of the states in its own class and close those states for modification. This makes the application easier to perform Quality Assurance (QA) testing and debugging.

Encapsulating the States

Let's try this again. This time we're going to encapsulate each state into its own class so that the code is easier to maintain and scales well. Figure 12.1 shows what our solution looks like.

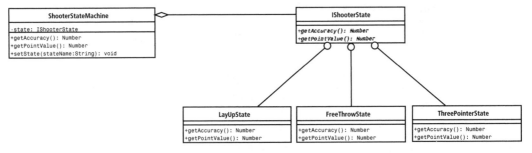

Figure 12.1

Encapsulating the states.

The Shooter State Interface

First, we create an interface that all of our state classes implement. All our state objects implement the IShooterState interface, therefore, we can treat them interchangeably. This is known as *polymorphism*. The IShooterState interface has two methods: getAccuracy() and getPointValue(). Notice that we typed the state property in the ShooterStateMachine class to IShooterState so that we can store an instance of any object that implements that interface.

```
package com.peachpit.aas3wdp.stateexample {

    public interface IShooterState {

        function getAccuracy():Number;

        function getPointValue():Number;

    }
}
```

State Objects

All our state objects are basically the same. They encapsulate the state-specific information for our application. For example, the LayUpState defines an accuracy of 90% and a point value of 2. By encapsulating all the state specific logic into objects, we make them easier to manage and more flexible. They're easier to manage because modifications to one state don't affect the other states. It's also easier to add new states.

```
package com.peachpit.aas3wdp.stateexample {

    import com.peachpit.aas3wdp.statepattern.IShooterState;

    internal class LayUpState implements IShooterState {

        public function getAccuracy():Number {
            return 0.9;
        }

        public function getPointValue():Number {
            return 2;
        }

    }

}

package com.peachpit.aas3wdp.stateexample {

    import com.peachpit.aas3wdp.statepattern.IShooterState;

    internal class FreeThrowState implements IShooterState {

        public function getAccuracy():Number {
            return 0.7;
```

(CODE CONTINUED)

```
        }

        public function getPointValue():Number {
           return 1;
        }

     }

  }

  package com.peachpit.aas3wdp.stateexample {

     import com.peachpit.aas3wdp.stateexample.IShooterState;

     internal class ThreePointerState implements IShooterState{

        public function getAccuracy():Number {
           return 0.4;
        }

        public function getPointValue():Number {
           return 3;
        }

     }

  }
```

The `Shooter State Machine` Class

The `ShooterStateMachine` class serves as a proxy to our state objects. It implements the same methods as our states and delegates the calls to the current state object. It is also responsible for switching states.

TIP

State machines are also sometimes referred to as the *context* in the State pattern.

Much like the `SimpleShooter` class, `ShooterStateMachine` has three constants that represent the three states. One of these three values should be used when calling the `setState()` method.

The `setState()` method has a little more functionally in this implementation of the basketball application. Instead of putting `switch` statements in each method, we put it in only the `setState()` method. The `switch` statement is responsible for creating the correct state object based on the state name.

```
  package com.peachpit.aas3wdp.stateexample {

     import com.peachpit.aas3wdp.stateexample.IShooterState;
     import com.peachpit.aas3wdp.stateexample.LayUpState;
     import com.peachpit.aas3wdp.stateexample.FreeThrowState;
     import com.peachpit.aas3wdp.stateexample.ThreePointerState;
```

```
public class ShooterStateMachine {

    private var _state:IShooterState;
    public static const LAY_UP_STATE:String = "lay_up_state";
    public static const FREE_THROW_STATE:String = "free_throw_state";
    public static const THREE_POINTER_STATE:String = "three_pointer_state";

    public function ShooterStateMachine() {}

    public function getAccuracy():Number {
      return _state.getAccuracy();
    }

    public function getPointValue():Number {
      return _state.getPointValue();
    }

    public function setState(stateName:String):void {
      switch(stateName) {
        case LAY_UP_STATE:
          _state = new LayUpState();
          break;
        case FREE_THROW_STATE:
          __state = new FreeThrowState();
          break;
        case THREE_POINTER_STATE:
          _state = new ThreePointerState();
          break;
        default:
          _state = null;
      }
    }

  }
```

The creation of state objects is done inside the setState() method. There are two options for creating and destroying state objects: The first is what we did in the preceding code. This is preferable because we create the states only when they are needed and we avoid creating states that are never used.

The second option is to create all the state objects in the constructor and simply change the reference to the current state. This second approach is valuable when you have to maintain some data across state switches. In the preceding example, the LayUpState object is re-created each time the state changes to LAY_UP_STATE. This is good for memory management, but what if we wanted to count how many lay-ups were made? If we used the same object each time that state was set, then a counter at the LayUpState level could persist across state changes. The second approach can also be good if your application has a lot of rapid state changing and you want to incur the performance hit of creating the objects only once.

Creating the Main Example Class

The main class for this implementation is nearly identical to the one for our first implementation. We'll name this class ShooterImp; it will create an instance of ShooterStateMachine instead of SimpleShooter.

```
package {

    import flash.display.Sprite;
    import flash.utils.Timer;
    import flash.events.TimerEvent;
    import com.peachpit.aas3wdp.stateexample.ShooterStateMachine;

    public class ShooterExample extends Sprite {

        private var _points:Number;
        private var _shooter:ShooterStateMachine;

        public function ShooterExampe() {
            _points = 0;
            _shooter = new ShooterStateMachine();
            _shooter.setState(ShooterStateMachine.LAY_UP_STATE);
            var shotInterval:Timer = new Timer(1000, 10);
            shotInterval.addEventListener(TimerEvent.TIMER, onShot);
            shotInterval.start();
        }

        private function calculateShot(accuracy:Number):Boolean {
            return Math.random() < accuracy;
        }

        private function onShot(event:TimerEvent):void {
            if(calculateShot(_shooter.getAccuracy())) {
                _points += _shooter.getPointValue()
                trace("Made the Shot!  " + _points + " point(s)");
            }else {
                trace("Missed the Shot!")
            }
        }

    }

}
```

When you debug this implementation (ShooterExample), you'll see that the result is exactly the same as SimpleShooterExample. However, we now have a design that is both scalable and easy to maintain.

Using Abstract Classes

As mentioned earlier in this chapter, there are many ways to implement a State pattern. In the previous example, we used an interface to define the methods that each state must implement. But what if we wanted to share a common implementation? One option would be to copy the implementation to each state class. This would work fine, but it would be difficult to manage as the number of states grew and change requests came in. A better option would be to use an abstract base class in addition to an interface. An abstract base class allows us to reuse a common implementation and still define methods that need to be overridden by each state class. In the next example, we're going to encapsulate the shooting functionality inside each state as a shoot() method. The method is the same across all states; therefore, each state object does not override it. Figure 12.2 shows how the design changes to work with an abstract class in place of an interface.

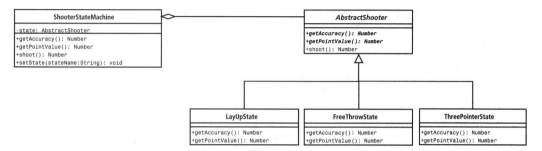

Figure 12.2
Using abstract classes.

The Abstract Shooter State

The biggest change between this example and the previous example is that we're now using an abstract base class for all our state objects. We're going to name this class AbstractShooterState.

TIP

It's common convention to start abstract class names with the word *Abstract*. The naming convention is especially important for ActionScript classes because there is no programmatic way to enforce an abstract class.

The abstract class implements the private calculateShot() method from our original implementation class. This method is called from the shoot() method. The shoot() method uses the getAccuracy() and getPointValue() methods to calculate whether the shot was made and how many points the shot was worth. However, the getAccuracy() and getPointValue() methods are overridden by the state objects.

NOTE

This is actually an example of the Template Method pattern described in Chapter 5.

Notice that both the getAccuracy() and getPointValue() methods throw errors in this class (if they are not overridden, and someone tries to call one of the methods). And because the shoot() method depends on the results of getAccuray() and getPointValue(), the shoot() method would also throw the error. When these abstract methods are overridden, the errors are not thrown. This is a nice way to get around the fact that ActionScript 3.0 doesn't officially support abstract classes.

NOTE

The state classes are made internal because they should be available only inside the com.peachpit.aas3wdp.stateexample package.

```
package com.peachpit.aas3wdp.stateexample {

    internal class AbstractShooterState {

        private function calculateShot(accuracy:Number):Boolean {
            return Math.random() < accuracy;
        }

        public function getAccuracy():Number {
            throw new Error("AbstractShooterState.getAccuracy() is an Abstract method
                            and must be overridden.");
        }

        public function getPointValue():Number {
            throw new Error("AbstractShooterState.getPointValue() is an Abstract method
                            and must be overridden.");
        }

        public function shoot():Number {
            if(calculateShot(getAccuracy())) {
                trace("Made the Shot!");
                return getPointValue();
            }
            trace("Missed the Shot.");
            return 0;
        }

    }

}
```

State Objects

The state objects in this example vary only slightly from the original implementation. Instead of implementing the IShooterState interface, now the state classes extend the AbstractShooterState abstract class. Notice the use of the override keyword. It is necessary to use this keyword to override the methods of the base class. The method signatures must also match the base class's methods exactly.

```
package com.peachpit.aas3wdp.stateexample {

    import com.peachpit.aas3wdp.statepattern.AbstractShooterState;

    internal class LayUpState extends AbstractShooterState {

        public override function getAccuracy():Number {
            return 0.9;
        }

        public override function getPointValue():Number {
            return 2;
```

```
        }

    }

}

package com.peachpit.aas3wdp.stateexample {

    import com.peachpit.aas3wdp.statepattern.AbstractShooterState;

    internal class FreeThrowState extends AbstractShooterState {

        public override function getAccuracy():Number {
            return 0.7;
        }

        public override function getPointValue():Number {
            return 1;
        }

    }

}

package com.peachpit.aas3wdp.stateexample {

    import com.peachpit.aas3wdp.statepattern.AbstractShooterState;

    internal class ThreePointerState extends AbstractShooterState {

        public override function getAccuracy():Number {
            return 0.4;
        }

        public override function getPointValue():Number {
            return 3;
        }

    }

}
```

Although using an interface and an abstract class are both valid ways to implement the State pattern, each has its own use case. As a rule, you should use interfaces; however, if you have states that share an implementation, abstract classes are the better option.

The Shooter State Machine

The state machine changes only slightly for this example. We need to type the state property to the AbstractStateShooter abstract class instead of to the IShooterState interface. And we also need to implement a shoot() method that is delegated to the current state.

```
package com.peachpit.aas3wdp.stateexample {

    import com.peachpit.aas3wdp.stateexample.AbstractShooterState;
```

(CODE CONTINUED)

```
import com.peachpit.aas3wdp.stateexample.LayUpState;
import com.peachpit.aas3wdp.stateexample.FreeThrowState;
import com.peachpit.aas3wdp.stateexample.ThreePointerState;

public class ShooterStateMachine {

    private var state:AbstractShooterState;
    public static const LAY_UP_STATE:String = "lay_up_state";
    public static const FREE_THROW_STATE:String = "free_throw_state";
    public static const THREE_POINTER_STATE:String = "three_pointer_state";

    public function ShooterStateMachine() {}

    public function getAccuracy():Number {
        return state.getAccuracy();
    }

    public function getPointValue():Number {
        return state.getPointValue();
    }

    public function shoot():Number {
        return state.shoot();
    }

    public function setState(stateDesc:String):void {
        switch(stateDesc) {
            case LAY_UP_STATE:
                state = new LayUpState();
                break;
            case FREE_THROW_STATE:
                state = new FreeThrowState();
                break;
            case THREE_POINTER_STATE:
                state = new ThreePointerState();
                break;
            default:
                state = null;
        }
    }

}
```

Creating the Main Example Class

The main class changes for this implementation because we encapsulated the shoot logic into the state objects. Therefore, we don't need to calculate whether a shot was made—we only need to call the state object's shoot() method, and that method tells us the points for that shot (0 for a missed shot and 1, 2, or 3 for a made shot).

```
package {

    import flash.display.Sprite;
```

(CODE CONTINUED)

```
import flash.utils.Timer;
import flash.events.TimerEvent;
import com.peachpit.aas3wdp.stateexample.ShooterStateMachine;

public class AbstractShooterExample extends Sprite {

    private var _points:Number;
    private var _shooter:ShooterStateMachine;

    public function AbstractShooterImp() {
        _points = 0;
        _shooter = new ShooterStateMachine();
        _shooter.setState(ShooterStateMachine.FREE_THROW_STATE);
        var shotInterval:Timer = new Timer(1000, 10);
        shotInterval.addEventListener(TimerEvent.TIMER, onShot);
        shotInterval.start();
    }

    private function onShot(event:TimerEvent):void {
        _points += _shooter.shoot();
        trace(_points);
    }

}
```

Transitions

When Flash developers hear the word *transistion*, they first think of animations between screens or view states. However, in the context of the State pattern, a transition is simply what triggers our application to move from one state to another. This is not necessarily a visual thing, it's simply how a state gets changed. You probably noticed in the previous examples that we had no way to move from one state to the other. The state was defined in the main class. In this section, we'll look at two ways to handle transitions within the abstract state example we just completed.

Transitions Defined in the State Machine

The first implementation is the easiest. We set the current state in the state machine; therefore, why not also manage when that state changes? In this example, we switch the state after each shot. We do this by iterating through an array of the three state objects.

Our state machine is getting two new properties: _stateList and _index. The stateList property is an array that holds all the state names available to our state machine, and it holds them in the order in which they should be run. The index holds the current position of the state machine in the stateList array.

Inside the constructor, set the index to 0 and populate the stateList with the state names. Because we want the state machine to manage when the state is set, we're removing the setState() call from our main class. Instead, we put the initial setState() call at the end of the state machine's constructor.

The only other change is in the shoot() method. Now, instead of just returning the value of the current state's shot, it also sets the next state.

```
package com.peachpit.aas3wdp.stateexample {

    import com.peachpit.aas3wdp.stateexample.AbstractShooterState;
    import com.peachpit.aas3wdp.stateexample.LayUpState;
    import com.peachpit.aas3wdp.stateexample.FreeThrowState;
    import com.peachpit.aas3wdp.stateexample.ThreePointerState;

    public class ShooterStateMachine {

        private var _state:AbstractShooterState;
        private var _stateList:Array;
        private var _index:Number;
        public static const LAY_UP_STATE:String = "lay_up_state";
        public static const FREE_THROW_STATE:String = "free_throw_state";
        public static const THREE_POINTER_STATE:String = "three_pointer_state";

        public function ShooterStateMachine() {
            _index = 0;
            _stateList = new Array();
            _stateList.push(ShooterStateMachine.LAY_UP_STATE);
            _stateList.push(ShooterStateMachine.FREE_THROW_STATE);
            _stateList.push(ShooterStateMachine.THREE_POINTER_STATE);
            setState(_stateList[_index]);
        }

        public function getAccuracy():Number {
            return _state.getAccuracy();
        }

        public function getPointValue():Number {
            return _state.getPointValue();
        }

        public function shoot():Number {
            var shotResult:Number = state.shoot();
            if(++_index >= _stateList.length) _index = 0;
            setState(_stateList[_index]);
            return shotResult;
        }

        public function setState(stateDesc:String):void {
            switch(stateDesc) {
                case LAY_UP_STATE:
                    _state = new LayUpState();
                    break;
                case FREE_THROW_STATE:
                    _state = new FreeThrowState();
                    break;
                case THREE_POINTER_STATE:
                    _state = new ThreePointerState();
                    break;
                default:
                    _state = null;
            }
        }
    }
}
```

Transitions Defined in the State Objects

The other option for where to put the transition logic is a little more involved because it requires putting the transition logic inside the state objects. For this implementation, we'll revert back to the state machine used in the original abstract state example, with two minor changes. We're going to pass a reference to the state machine into each of the state objects' constructors, and we're going to set the first state in the state machine's constructor.

```
package com.peachpit.aas3wdp.stateexample {

    import com.peachpit.aas3wdp.stateexample.AbstractShooterState;
    import com.peachpit.aas3wdp.stateexample.LayUpState;
    import com.peachpit.aas3wdp.stateexample.FreeThrowState;
    import com.peachpit.aas3wdp.stateexample.ThreePointerState;

    public class ShooterStateMachine {

        private var _state:AbstractShooterState;
        public static const LAY_UP_STATE:String = "lay_up_state";
        public static const FREE_THROW_STATE:String = "free_throw_state";
        public static const THREE_POINTER_STATE:String = "three_pointer_state";

        public function ShooterStateMachine() {
            setState(ShooterStateMachine.LAY_UP_STATE);
        }

        public function getAccuracy():Number {
            return _state.getAccuracy();
        }

        public function getPointValue():Number {
            return _state.getPointValue();
        }

        public function shoot():Number {
            return _state.shoot();
        }

        public function setState(stateDesc:String):void {
            switch(stateDesc) {
                case LAY_UP_STATE:
                    _state = new LayUpState(this);
                    break;
                case FREE_THROW_STATE:
                    _state = new FreeThrowState(this);
                    break;
                case THREE_POINTER_STATE:
                    _state = new ThreePointerState(this);
                    break;
                default:
                    _state = null;
            }
        }
    }
}
```

The state objects do most of the work for us. Each stores a reference to the state machine and calls its setState() method when the state object wants to move to the next state. We're still triggering that move on the shoot() method call, so we need to override that method. We still call the abstract state's shoot() method using the super keyword, but we need to override it so that we can add the setState() call to it. The following are the new state objects with these changes:

```
package com.peachpit.aas3wdp. stateexample {

    import com.peachpit.aas3wdp. stateexample.AbstractShooterState;

    internal class LayUpState extends AbstractShooterState {

        private var _stateMachine:ShooterStateMachine;

        public function LayUpState(_stateMachine:ShooterStateMachine) {
            this._stateMachine = _stateMachine;
        }

        public override function getAccuracy():Number {
            return 0.9;
        }

        public override function getPointValue():Number {
            return 2;
        }

        public override function shoot():Number {
            var pointValue:Number = super.shoot();
            _stateMachine.setState(ShooterStateMachine.FREE_THROW_STATE);
            return pointValue;
        }

    }

}

package com.peachpit.aas3wdp.stateexample {

    import com.peachpit.aas3wdp.stateexample.AbstractShooterState;
    import com.peachpit.aas3wdp.stateexample.ShooterStateMachine;

    internal class FreeThrowState extends AbstractShooterState {

        private var _stateMachine:ShooterStateMachine;

        public function FreeThrowState(_stateMachine:ShooterStateMachine) {
            this._stateMachine = _stateMachine;
        }

        public override function getAccuracy():Number {
            return 0.7;
        }

        public override function getPointValue():Number {
            return 1;
```

(CODE CONTINUED)

```
        }

        public override function shoot():Number {
           var pointValue:Number = super.shoot();
           _stateMachine.setState(ShooterStateMachine.THREE_POINTER_STATE);
           return pointValue;
        }

    }

}

package com.peachpit.aas3wdp.stateexample {

    import com.peachpit.aas3wdp.stateexample.AbstractShooterState;

    internal class ThreePointerState extends AbstractShooterState {

        private var _stateMachine:ShooterStateMachine;

        public function ThreePointerState(_stateMachine:ShooterStateMachine) {
           this._stateMachine = _stateMachine;
        }

        public override function getAccuracy():Number {
           return 0.4;
        }

        public override function getPointValue():Number {
           return 3;
        }

        public override function shoot():Number {
           var pointValue:Number = super.shoot();
           _stateMachine.setState(ShooterStateMachine.LAY_UP_STATE);
           return pointValue;
        }

    }

}
```

This logic could have gone into the abstract class, but it's left on the state subclasses because it demonstrates the flexibility of defining the transitions this way. If you're going to treat all the transitions the same, and you have a set methodology for how you trigger the transitions, then the state machine should manage that. However, if each state has different criteria for triggering a transition, defining the transition on the state object provides the most flexibility.

For example, maybe we want to change the way the LayUpState transitions. We'll require a shooter to make a lay-up before we move on to the free throw. All we need to do is add a condition to the shoot() method. The following code shows the simple change:

```
package com.peachpit.aas3wdp.stateexample {

    import com.peachpit.aas3wdp.stateexample.AbstractShooterState;

    internal class LayUpState extends AbstractShooterState {

        private var _stateMachine:ShooterStateMachine;

        public function LayUpState(stateMachine:ShooterStateMachine) {
            this._stateMachine = _stateMachine;
        }

        public override function getAccuracy():Number {
            return 0.9;
        }

        public override function getPointValue():Number {
            return 2;
        }

        public override function shoot():Number {
            var pointValue:Number = super.shoot();
            if(pointValue > 0) {
                _stateMachine.setState(ShooterStateMachine.FREE_THROW_STATE);
            }
            return pointValue;
        }

    }

}
```

Summary

The State pattern is a great way to manage states within your application. By encapsulating the states into their own objects, we make the code more scalable and maintainable. There are many ways to implement the State pattern. In this chapter, we looked at how to build states using both an interface and an abstract class; and we discussed when to use each of these approaches.

Transitions are the action of switching states. They can be defined in the context or inside the state objects. Although defining transitions inside the state objects gives you more flexibility, doing so can produce code that is difficult to maintain.

Advanced ActionScript Topics

13

Working with Events

Events drive applications. Nearly everything that happens in an ActionScript 3.0 application is triggered by events. There are two basic types of events: user and system. When a user clicks a button or types on the keyboard events are fired. These are examples of user events. System events are those which occur because of something based on time or asynchronous operations. For example, loading an external resource might trigger a load complete or a load error event.

In this chapter, we'll look at what events are, what design problems they solve, how they related to known design patterns, and how they are used in ActionScript 3.0.

Understanding Events

Traditional, non-event-driven applications are susceptible to problems that give rise to the motivation for events and a unified event model. There are two primary problems with the traditional approach:

- **Tight coupling:** In a traditional approach, the object that initiates something and the object that responds are tightly coupled, typically in a one-to-one relationship. For example, in the traditional approach, when a user clicks a button, the button might trigger the invocation of a callback method. Although this technique might work, it has significant shortcomings. What happens when you want several objects to respond to a button click rather than just one? What happens if you accidentally override the callback method? These problems highlight some of the reasons we strive for loosely coupled objects when designing applications.

- **Inconsistent manner of responding to operations:** In a traditional approach to application design, synchronous and asynchronous operations require different ways of handling results. It's far more advantageous to use a single consistent way to handle results. Events provide that.

Earlier versions of ActionScript use many different ways of responding to occurrences within the application. However, ActionScript 3.0 has one unified event model used across the board. At the core of this event model is the flash.events package of classes—namely the Event class and the EventDispatcher class.

The EventDispatcher class provides all the functionality to allow objects to register for event notifications. When an object registers with an event dispatcher for notifications for a particular event, the event dispatcher adds that object to a queue. When the event occurs, the event dispatcher notifies all the objects in the queue. The objects in the queue are called *listeners*, and in ActionScript 3.0 all listeners are functions/methods. When a listener is notified, it gets called and passed a parameter of type Event (or a subtype specific to the type of event). The event parameter provides the context for the event, including the type of event and the object that dispatched the event. This arrangement allows for the event dispatcher and the listener to know virtually nothing about one another at compile time, but at runtime, the listener can obtain a reference back to the dispatcher using the event parameter. This powerful design means that the dispatchers and listeners are loosely coupled. It also means that many listeners can register for notifications when an event occurs for just one dispatcher. Figure 13.1 illustrates this concept.

Figure 13.1

An event is handled.

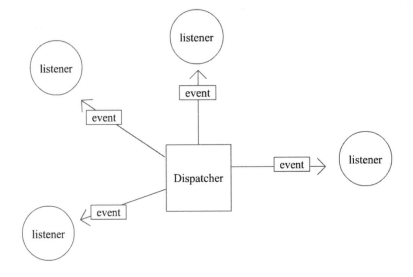

In ActionScript 3.0, the event model is closely related to a well-known design pattern called the Observer pattern. Although the Observer pattern is an important pattern, we don't discuss it in any detail in this book because the built-in event model in ActionScript 3.0 already solves all the design patterns the Observer pattern is intended to solve.

Using Events

If you're reading this book, we assume that you already know the basics of working with events because they are so fundamental to ActionScript. However, developers often know how to work with events without really understanding how they work at a basic level. In this section, we'll look at the mechanics of events in ActionScript 3.0.

Understanding Event Elements

There are at least three elements required when working with events: event objects, event dispatchers, and event listeners. We've already talked about each of these briefly, but here we'll discuss the mechanics of each.

All *event objects* are of type `flash.events.Event` or a subtype. Event subtypes are simply types that are specific to a particular sort of behavior. For example, events raised by mouse behavior are of type `MouseEvent` while events that occur because of a timer are of type `TimerEvent`. Usually subtypes define additional properties that provide information about the type of event. For example, `MouseEvent` defines a property called `buttonDown`, which indicates whether or not the mouse button is down at the time the event occurs. This is information that is important for events related to mouse behavior, but it wouldn't be important for an event that occurs when data loads. Yet all event objects always have type and target properties that tell the listener what type of event it is and what object dispatched the event.

The second element that is always required is an event dispatcher. An *event dispatcher* is sometimes called a *subject* and sometimes called a *target*. The event dispatcher is the object that broadcasts an event. In ActionScript 3.0, all event dispatchers are instances of `EventDispatcher`, the built-in Flash Player class. Event dispatchers must allow listeners to register for notifications for events. The `EventDispatcher` API allows listeners to register. We'll discuss this in more detail in the next section.

Event listeners in ActionScript 3.0 are always functions. You must register a listener with an event dispatcher for a specific event. When that event occurs, the dispatcher notifies the listener, and the listener gets called with an event parameter.

Registering Listeners

Listener objects register with the dispatcher object by calling the dispatcher's `addEventListener()` method. At a minimum, the `addEventListener()` method requires two parameters: the name of the event and the listener.

```
dispatcher.addEventListener(eventName, listener);
```

ActionScript 3.0 implements proper method closure, which means that functions and methods always maintain their original scope. This is a significant change from previous versions of ActionScript which required workarounds to ensure that a listener would be called within the proper scope.

The following example creates a rectangular sprite, and it uses an event listener to move the rectangle to a random location each time the user clicks on it.

```
package {
    import flash.display.Sprite;
    import flash.events.MouseEvent;
    import flash.display.StageScaleMode;
    import flash.display.StageAlign;

    public class Test extends Sprite {

        private var _rectangle:Sprite;

        public function Test() {

            stage.scaleMode = StageScaleMode.NO_SCALE;
            stage.align = StageAlign.TOP_LEFT;

            _rectangle = new Sprite();
            _rectangle.graphics.lineStyle(0, 0, 0);
            _rectangle.graphics.beginFill(0xFFFFFF, 1);
            _rectangle.graphics.drawRect(0, 0, 100, 50);
            _rectangle.graphics.endFill();
            addChild(_rectangle);

            _rectangle.addEventListener(MouseEvent.CLICK, onClick);
        }

        public function onClick(event:MouseEvent):void {
            event.target.x = Math.random() * 400;
            event.target.y = Math.random() * 400;
        }
    }
}
```

Because the event listener moves the event target to a random location, you can also use that same listener for a different target. In this next example, two event dispatchers use the same event listener. In this case, both the rectangle and the circle move to random locations when clicked.

```
package {
    import flash.display.Sprite;
    import flash.events.MouseEvent;
    import flash.display.StageScaleMode;
    import flash.display.StageAlign;

    public class Test extends Sprite {

        private var _rectangle:Sprite;
        private var _circle:Sprite;

        public function Test() {

            stage.scaleMode = StageScaleMode.NO_SCALE;
            stage.align = StageAlign.TOP_LEFT;

            _rectangle = new Sprite();
            _rectangle.graphics.lineStyle(0, 0, 0);
```

```
            _rectangle.graphics.beginFill(0xFFFFFF, 1);
            _rectangle.graphics.drawRect(0, 0, 100, 50);
            _rectangle.graphics.endFill();
            addChild(_rectangle);

            _circle = new Sprite();
            _circle.graphics.lineStyle(0, 0, 0);
            _circle.graphics.beginFill(0xFFFFFF, 1);
            _circle.graphics.drawCircle(0, 0, 50);
            _circle.graphics.endFill();
            _circle.x = 100;
            _circle.y = 100;
            addChild(_circle);

            _rectangle.addEventListener(MouseEvent.CLICK, onClick);
            _circle.addEventListener(MouseEvent.CLICK, onClick);
        }

        public function onClick(event:MouseEvent):void {
            event.target.x = Math.random() * 400;
            event.target.y = Math.random() * 400;
        }
    }
}
```

Removing Event Listeners

On the flip side of adding event listeners is removing event listeners. Generally it's advisable to remove event listeners whenever you no longer need to listen for a particular event. You can achieve this by using the removeEventListener() method. The removeEventListener() method accepts two parameters: the event name and the listener, and it removes the listener for the particular event for the dispatcher from which you call the method. The following code removes onClick() as an event listener for the click event.

```
    _circle.removeEventListener(MouseEvent.CLICK, onClick);
```

Understanding Event Phases

There are two types of event dispatches: display objects on the display list and all other types. When an object that is not on the display list dispatches an event, it notifies only those listeners that are registered directly with the dispatcher. For example, when a URLLoader object dispatches a complete event, the only listeners that receive the notification are those registered directly with the URLLoader. However, when a display object on the display list dispatches events, the event flow is triggered. The event flow consists of three phases: capture, target, and bubble. We'll talk about each of these phases next.

The Capture Phase

The first phase of the event flow is called the *capture phase*. In this phase, Flash Player is looking for the object that triggered the event. In doing so, it starts at the root display object and uses a drill-down approach through the hierarchy of the display list until it finds the event's target, meaning the object that actually dispatched the event.

By default, event listeners do not receive notifications during the capture phase. Instead, if you want to register a listener for the capture phase, you must pass a value of true for the third parameter of the addEventListener() method. Otherwise, if the parameter is omitted or false, the listener only receives notifications during the target and bubble phases. Here is an example that registers a listener for the capture phase:

```
object.addEventListener(MouseEvent.CLICK, onClick, true);
```

The capture phase may seem strange at first. And, in fact, it is not often used. However, it's an important part of the event flow because it allows the application to trap events before they reach child targets. When you want to trap events and stop them from propagating to child elements, you must call the stopImmediatePropagation() method of the event object in the event handler. Here's an example that adds to the previous examples by trapping click events so that they are never handled by the listeners for child elements:

```
package {
    import flash.display.Sprite;
    import flash.events.MouseEvent;
    import flash.display.StageScaleMode;
    import flash.display.StageAlign;

    public class Test extends Sprite {

        private var _rectangle:Sprite;
        private var _circle:Sprite;
        private var _loader:Loader;

        public function Test() {

            stage.scaleMode = StageScaleMode.NO_SCALE;
            stage.align = StageAlign.TOP_LEFT;

            _rectangle = new Sprite();
            _rectangle.graphics.lineStyle(0, 0, 0);
            _rectangle.graphics.beginFill(0xFFFFFF, 1);
            _rectangle.graphics.drawRect(0, 0, 100, 50);
            _rectangle.graphics.endFill();
            addChild(_rectangle);

            _circle = new Sprite();
            _circle.graphics.lineStyle(0, 0, 0);
            _circle.graphics.beginFill(0xFFFFFF, 1);
            _circle.graphics.drawCircle(0, 0, 50);
            _circle.graphics.endFill();
            _circle.x = 100;
            _circle.y = 100;
```

(CODE CONTINUED)

```
            addChild(_circle);

            addEventListener(MouseEvent.CLICK, onStageClick, true);

            _rectangle.addEventListener(MouseEvent.CLICK, onClick);
            _circle.addEventListener(MouseEvent.CLICK, onClick);

        }

        public function onClick(event:MouseEvent):void {
            event.target.x = Math.random() * 400;
            event.target.y = Math.random() * 400;
        }

        public function onStageClick(event:MouseEvent):void {
            event.stopImmediatePropagation();
        }
    }
}
```

The Target Phase

After the capture phase is the *target phase*. The target phase occurs when the event target (the event dispatcher responsible for the event) is reached in the event flow. This is probably the most commonly used phase of the event flow because it is the phase during which listeners that are registered directly with an event dispatcher are notified. This is the phase illustrated by most of the examples throughout this chapter and this book.

The Bubble Phase

The last phase of the event flow is the *bubble phase*. It allows for events to bubble up the display list. The bubble phase occurs in the reverse order of the capture phase: starting from the target and moving upward to parent containers until the root is reached.

You don't need to do anything different for event bubbling to work. You can simply register a listener to a container for any event that any child can dispatch, and the event listener will receive the notification during the bubble phase. For example, the following code achieves the same effect as an earlier example, but it registers the listener with the container rather than with the children:

```
package {
    import flash.display.Sprite;
    import flash.events.MouseEvent;
    import flash.display.StageScaleMode;
    import flash.display.StageAlign;

    public class Test extends Sprite {

        private var _rectangle:Sprite;
        private var _circle:Sprite;
```

(CODE CONTINUED)

```
        public function Test() {

            stage.scaleMode = StageScaleMode.NO_SCALE;
            stage.align = StageAlign.TOP_LEFT;

            _rectangle = new Sprite();
            _rectangle.graphics.lineStyle(0, 0, 0);
            _rectangle.graphics.beginFill(0xFFFFFF, 1);
            _rectangle.graphics.drawRect(0, 0, 100, 50);
            _rectangle.graphics.endFill();
            addChild(_rectangle);

            _circle = new Sprite();
            _circle.graphics.lineStyle(0, 0, 0);
            _circle.graphics.beginFill(0xFFFFFF, 1);
            _circle.graphics.drawCircle(0, 0, 50);
            _circle.graphics.endFill();
            _circle.x = 100;
            _circle.y = 100;
            addChild(_circle);

            addEventListener(MouseEvent.CLICK, onClick);

        }

        public function onClick(event:MouseEvent):void {
            event.target.x = Math.random() * 400;
            event.target.y = Math.random() * 400;
        }
    }
}
```

Notice in this example that the event object parameter's target property still references the actual target of the event (the circle or rectangle in this example) rather than the object for which the listener is registered (the container). If you want to retrieve a reference to the object to which the listener is registered, you can use the currentTarget property.

It's also important to note that not all event types can bubble. Only those events for which the bubbles property is set to true can bubble.

NOTE

When you create a custom event, you can specify whether the event will bubble. The default is true.

Event Priority

Event priority is a little-used concept, but it is important to understand what it can do. When you add an event, you have the ability to set your listener's priority. The higher the priority setting, the sooner your listener will get called. You can set the priority for a listener using the fourth parameter of the addEventListener() method.

Two listeners with the same priority level are called in the order they were added. It's important to note that priorities are relevant only within a phase (capture, target, or bubble). The order of the phases of the event flow supersedes the priority level.

Weak References

The concept of *weak references* is particularly useful when adding listeners to objects. To understand why weak references are so good, you first need to understand a little about garbage collection. Garbage collection is how Flash Player cleans up memory that isn't needed anymore; it's important because otherwise applications would use more and more RAM until they required the system to restart. Flash Player 9 uses two systems called *reference counting* and *mark and sweep*.

Reference counting is not new to Flash Player. It is the traditional way in which Flash Player has run garbage collection. When you create an object in ActionScript, that object exists in memory. However, the object is useful only as long as there are references (such as variables) to that object. When no more references exist, it is safe to assume that the object is no longer used and can be garbage collected. Although this system is efficient, it is not accurate because it is possible, through circular references, to have references still in existence even though none of the references is actually accessible. For example, two objects can have references to one another. If the references to those objects are deleted, we would expect that the objects themselves would be garbage collected. However, because they have references to one another, they remain in memory.

The mark-and-sweep garbage collection system solves the circular reference problem by traversing all active (accessible) nodes within an application. Any objects that exist outside of the active nodes can be assumed to be no longer in use, and they can be garbage collected.

Although the two garbage collection systems work in conjunction to efficiently and effectively manage memory usage, they do not compensate for incorrect programming. It's important that you always remove event listeners when you no longer need to use them. If you register an event listener using normal references, it will not get garbage collected even if you delete the listener or the object containing the listener because the event dispatcher will still have a reference to it. Removing the event listener using `removeEventListener()` ensures that the event target no longer has a reference to the listener, and that action will allow it to be properly garbage collected after you've deleted the listener.

However, sometimes we can't remove the listeners because our object is deleted elsewhere. This is where weak references come in handy. They allow for normal event listening functionality, but when the listener object is removed, the listener is removed from memory properly because the reference is weak and not counted by the reference counting function of the garbage collector.

You can specify that a listener should use a weak reference by registering it using a value of true for the fifth parameter to the `addEventListener()` method.

```
target.addEventListener(MouseEvent.CLICK, onClick, false, 0, true);
```

Creating Event Dispatchers

Dispatchers (also known as *subjects* or *targets*) are the source of events. These are the objects that fire events. Earlier in this chapter, you saw how to listen for events. Many classes are already capable of dispatching events. However, now we'll look at how to create custom classes that dispatch events.

Understanding Event Objects

All events use event objects. In the following sections, we'll look at how to dispatch events, but first we need to look at how to create an event object.

All event objects must be instances of the `flash.events.Event` class (or one of its subclasses). `Event` objects have properties that store information about the event and methods for manipulating the event.

The simplest way to create an event object is to use the constructor of the `Event` class or one of its subclasses in a new statement. The constructor requires that you pass it a string indicating the event type. The following example creates a new event object for a change event:

```
var event:Event = new Event(Event.CHANGE);
```

Often it is easiest and most effective to use an existing event type (`Event`, `MouseEvent`, and so on) when possible. However, when that's not possible, you can create a custom event type by subclassing `Event`. The following is an example of a custom event that extends the `Event` class:

```
package {

    import flash.events.Event;

    public class CustomEvent extends Event {

        private var _customData:Object;

        public function customData(value:Object):void {
            _customData = value;
        }

        public function get customData():Object {
            return _customData;
        }

        public function CustomEvent(type:String, bubbles:Boolean = false,
    cancelable:Boolean = false) {
            super(type, bubbles, cancelable);
        }

    }

}
```

Understanding Event Target Properties

Events have both a `target` and a `currentTarget` property. This is relevant when an event is being dispatched into the event flow. It tells us the difference between the object we registered with and the object that dispatched the event. The `target` is the object that originates the event, while the `currentTarget` is the object with which you registered the listener. During the target phase, those two properties reference the same object. However, if you get an event during the capture or bubble phase, the two properties are different.

Default Behavior of Events

When most events are fired, the responses to those events are defined in the listeners. But in some cases, the responses are so common and predictable that there are default behaviors that occur inside Flash Player. A good example of this is the use case of a user typing in a text field. The default behavior is that the keystrokes fire events that populate the text field with the corresponding characters. However, there may be times when you don't want this default behavior to happen. To stop the default behavior, you simply call the `preventDefault()` method of the event object. You can check the status of this behavior by calling the `isDefaultPrevented()` method. Only events with the `cancelable` property set to true can be canceled.

Stopping Propagation

In some cases, you might want to stop the event flow dead in its tracks. To accomplish this, you use the `stopPropagation()` or `stopImmediatePropogation()` method of the event object. The methods are nearly identical and differ only in regards to when the stop is executed. If you call `stopPropagation()`, the event is not allowed to continue up the display list, but the `currentTarget` is allowed to finish dispatching the event to its listeners. The `stopImmediatePropogation()` method stops the event flow completely, and the `currentTarget` is not allowed to finish.

Dispatching Events Through Inheritance

The `flash.events.EventDispatcher` class is at the heart of the event model in ActionScript 3.0. All native Flash Player classes that dispatch events inherit from `EventDispatcher`. This is the simplest and most common way to add event dispatching functionality to a class. You can do this directly by creating a class that extends `EventDispatcher`. Optionally, because `MovieClip`, `Sprite`, and many other core classes already extend `EventDispatcher`, you can inherit the event functionality indirectly by extending those classes as well.

The `EventDispatcher` class defines the behavior that adds, queues, and removes event listeners. It also enables the dispatcher to actually dispatch the event to the listeners. We've already seen the behavior for adding and removing events using `addEventListener()` and `removeEventListener()`. Now we'll look at how to actually dispatch events.

The `dispatchEvent()` method is a method of `EventDispatcher`, and it is what triggers an event to be broadcast. When you extend `EventDispatcher`, you can call `dispatchEvent()` within the class.

CAUTION

Although the *dispatchEvent()* method is public, it's a good idea to leave event dispatching up to the subject objects. Objects triggering events to be dispatched from other subject objects can lead to un-maintainable code that is difficult for other developers to read. Subjects should always be responsible for dispatching their own events.

The only parameter you need to pass into the `dispatchEvent()` method is an Event object. We'll talk more about Event objects and their behavior later in this chapter. However, here is a basic example:

```
dispatchEvent(new Event(Event.CHANGE));
```

This example dispatches a change event to all listeners that are currently registered to receive notifications for change events for instances of the class within which the `dispatchEvent()` method appears.

The IEventDispatcher Interface

ActionScript 3.0 supports only single inheritance. This means that if you're already extending a class that doesn't itself extend the EventDispatcher class, you must find another way to access the event dispatching functionality. For this reason, Flash Player includes an IEventDispatcher interface. By programming to this interface, you can get the EventDispatcher functionality into your class through composition instead of through inheritance. The following is an example of how you'd implement the IEventDispatcher interface:

```
package {

   import flash.events.Event;
   import flash.events.IEventDispatcher;
   import flash.events.EventDispatcher;

   public class Dispatcher implements IEventDispatcher {

      private var eventDispatcher:EventDispatcher;

      public function Dispatcher() {
         eventDispatcher = new EventDispatcher(this);
      }

      public function addEventListener(type:String, listener:Function,
   useCapture:Boolean=false, priority:int=0.0, useWeakReference:Boolean=false):void {
         eventDispatcher.addEventListener(type, listener, useCapture, priority,
   useWeakReference);
      }

      public function dispatchEvent(event:Event):Boolean {
         return eventDispatcher.dispatchEvent(event);
      }

      public function hasEventListener(type:String):Boolean {
         return eventDispatcher.hasEventListener(type);
      }
```

(CODE CONTINUED)

```
        public function removeEventListener(type:String, listener:Function, useCapture:
    Boolean=false):void {
            eventDispatcher.removeEventListener(type, listener, useCapture);
        }

        public function willTrigger(type:String):Boolean {
            return eventDispatcher.willTrigger(type);
        }

    }

}
```

Passing a target reference into the EventDispather constructor is necessary when using composition. The reference tells the EventDispatcher which object to use as the target for events dispatched by your class. This is not necessary for classes that extend EventDispatcher.

An Example Working with Events

In this example, we're going to create and implement a custom icon button in order to better understand events. The button has three elements: an icon, a text field, and a background. Each of these elements triggers different events. We can examine these events to see exactly how the event flow works.

Creating the IconButton Class

The first thing we need to do is create our IconButton class. We will generate all the elements for this class inside its constructor. The background will be a Shape object. We'll simply draw a gray rectangle on that shape. The next element is our icon. For our example, this icon is a simple square, so we'll use a Sprite. Even though we're still just drawing a shape, we want to use the Sprite class because it allows the icon to dispatch mouseOver and mouseOut events. The last element is the label, which is a text field that will hold the button label text.

We'll also add a couple listeners to the icon Sprite so we can have a rollover on that item. When the user rolls over the icon, we'll use a ColorTransform object to make the icon white. When the user rolls off the icon, it will go back to grey.

```
package {

    import flash.display.Shape;
    import flash.display.Sprite;
    import flash.events.MouseEvent;
    import flash.geom.ColorTransform;
    import flash.text.TextField;
    import flash.text.TextFieldAutoSize;

    public class IconButton extends Sprite {
```

```
        public function IconButton(text:String) {

            // Create the button background, drawing a
            // rectangle.
            var background:Shape = new Shape();
            background.graphics.beginFill(0xEEEEEE, 1);
            background.graphics.drawRect(0, 0, 100, 20);
            background.graphics.endFill();
            addChild(background);

            // Create the icon, and also draw a rectangle
            // within the icon.
            var icon:Sprite = new Sprite();
            icon.graphics.beginFill(0xAAAAAA, 1);
            icon.graphics.drawRect(4, 4, 12, 12);
            icon.graphics.endFill();

            // Listen for mouse events on the icon.
            icon.addEventListener(MouseEvent.MOUSE_OVER, onIconMouseOver, false, 0, true);
            icon.addEventListener(MouseEvent.MOUSE_OUT, onIconMouseOut, false, 0, true);
            addChild(icon);

            // Create a text field to use as a label.
            var label:TextField = new TextField();
            label.height = 20;
            label.x = 22;
            label.text = text;
            label.selectable = false;
            label.autoSize = TextFieldAutoSize.LEFT;
            addChild(label);
        }

        private function onIconMouseOver(event:MouseEvent):void {
            var colorTransform:ColorTransform = new ColorTransform();
            colorTransform.color = 0xFFFFFF;
            (event.target as Sprite).transform.colorTransform = colorTransform;
        }

        private function onIconMouseOut(event:MouseEvent):void {
            var colorTransform:ColorTransform = new ColorTransform();
            colorTransform.color = 0xAAAAAA;
            (event.target as Sprite).transform.colorTransform = colorTransform;
        }

    }

}
```

The preceding code is fairly basic. When the user moves the mouse over the icon, the icon changes color using events. Next we'll look at how to use this button.

Creating the Main Class

Now that we have our IconButton class, we need to create a simple main class that uses the button We'll do this with a ButtonExample class that will serve as the main class for this project. In the constructor, we create an instance of the IconButton class, add a couple event listeners, and add the IconButton instance to our display list. Notice that we add two listeners that are nearly the same. We're doing this to illustrate the useCapture functionality. The second listener has the useCapture parameter set to true. Each of these listeners is treated separately, so our class should get the MOUSE_UP event twice: once during the capture phase and the second during either the target or bubble phase.

That last statement may seem a bit confusing. What determines whether the MOUSE_UP event will be dispatched to our ButtonImp class during the target phase versus the bubble phase? Well, it all comes down to which element inside our button is clicked on. If the user clicks on the icon Sprite, then the icon is going to be the target of the event. Because our ButtonImp class registered itself directly to the IconButton class, we wouldn't get that event during the target phase. However, the MOUSE_OVER and MOUSE_OUT events inside the IconButton class would occur in the target phase because the IconButton registered itself directly to the icon Sprite. The same would be true if the user clicked on the TextField. Therefore, the ButtonImp gets those events through bubbling.

Recall that we also have a third element in our button: the background Shape. If the user clicks on it, the Shape does nothing because Shape doesn't dispatch a MOUSE_UP event. Therefore, the IconButton would dispatch the event and our ButtonImp would get its event during the target phase.

The following code is our ButtonImp class. Notice the trace statements in the listener function. These trace statements allow you to see the event's phase and the difference between the target and currentTarget properties for each event.

```
package {

    import flash.display.Sprite;
    import flash.events.MouseEvent;

    public class ButtonExample extends Sprite {

        public function ButtonExample() {
            var button:IconButton = new IconButton("Test");
            button.addEventListener(MouseEvent.MOUSE_UP, onMouseUp, false, 0, true);
            button.addEventListener(MouseEvent.MOUSE_UP, onMouseUp, true, 0, true);
            addChild(button);
        }

        private function onMouseUp(event:MouseEvent):void {
            trace("phase: " + event.eventPhase);
            trace("target: " + event.target);
            trace("currentTarget: " + event.currentTarget);
        }

    }

}
```

Summary

The event framework in ActionScript 3.0 offers a solid and consistent way to handle events. It improves on earlier versions of Flash by unifying all events under one standardized system. The new event bubbling and weak reference features are also very valuable. Overall, the new event framework is a great addition to ActionScript 3.0 and will surely play a major part in all your ActionScript projects.

CHAPTER 14

Sending and Loading Data

Flash platform applications almost always use data in one form or another. Generally, applications need to have some form of client-server data communication. In the simplest example, an application might have to load plain text. For example, an application might have one responsibility: displaying the day's news post. And some applications might have significantly more complex data communication requirements. For example, a more sophisticated version of the news application might need to retrieve an index of all the top news stories, the contents of news stories, user comments for each news story, and it might even incorporate live data that broadcasts the transcript of a live commentator.

There are many different types of data you can use with Flash Platform applications, including these:

- Text (including Unicode support)
- XML
- AMF (Action Message Format, a binary messaging format)
- Binary data

In addition to the many types of data, there are many ways you can transmit that data, including the following:

- HTTP
- RTMP
- XML socket connection
- Binary socket connection

In this chapter, we'll look at each of these topics with the exception of the socket connection topics, which are outside the scope of this book. Then we'll look at relevant design patterns and how they apply to sending and loading data.

Loading Text

One of the simplest ways to work with data is to load blocks of text either from a text file or from an Internet resource. Although you can certainly embed text in an SWF file, loading text at runtime has the following advantages:

- You can manage when the text is loaded. When you embed text in an .SWF, the text loads as part of the SWF file. However, when you load text at runtime, you can load the text only when the application requires it. For large amounts of text, this can be a significant advantage.

- Editing text files is generally easier than assembling strings with ActionScript. This is especially true when the text contains HTML elements or lots of non-standard Unicode characters.

- Loading text at runtime allows you to update the context without having to recompile and redeploy a new .swf. This is especially true when the text is loaded from a dynamic resource such as a ColdFusion page where the content is retrieved from a Web service, a database, or some other source that is updated frequently.

Although you can load text with any of the techniques described in this chapter, this section focuses on the simplest mechanism for loading blocks of text. Using the flash.net.URLLoader class, you can load data from a URL. When you use URLLoader, you also must use the flash.net.URLRequest class to specify the URL from which you want to load the content. The following statement constructs a new URLRequest object that points to a text file called data.txt that is stored in the same directory as the SWF file:

```
var request:URLRequest = new URLRequest("data.txt");
```

You must then create a URLLoader object before you can load data using the URLRequest object. The URLLoader constructor does not require any parameters, as you can see here:

```
var loader:URLLoader = new URLLoader();
```

NOTE

Although it is not required, you can optionally pass a *URLRequest* object to a *URLLoader* constructor to begin a data request immediately.

URLLoader objects dispatch complete events when the data loads. For that reason, you'll almost always want to register a listener for the complete event:

```
loader.addEventListener(Event.COMPLETE, onData);
```

You can then use the load() method to load the data. The load() method requires that you pass it a URLRequest object specifying the URL of the data to load, like this:

```
loader.load(request);
```

The load() method initiates the request for the data and works asynchronously. Flash Player does not wait for the response before continuing to execute the code. It simply makes the request; when the data loads, the URLLoader object dispatches events, including the complete event when the data has completely loaded.

When the complete event occurs, the URLLoader object notifies all listeners. The listeners receive an event parameter with a target property that references the URLLoader object dispatching the event. The URLLoader class defines a data property that contains the data that was loaded. The following event listener uses trace() to output the data that was loaded:

```
private function onData(event:Event):void {
    trace(event.target.data);
}
```

Next, we'll look at a simple example that uses the Model View Controller (MVC) pattern (described in Chapter 3) to load and display four different limericks from text files. This example uses four text files called limerick0.txt, limerick1.txt, limerick2.txt, and limerick3.txt. The files contain the following text (each block of text is a different file):

```
There was an Old Man on a hill,
Who seldom, if ever, stood still;
He ran up and down,
In his Grandmother's gown,
Which adorned that Old Man on a hill.
- Edward Lear

There was a Young Lady whose chin,
Resembled the point of a pin;
So she had it made sharp,
And purchased a harp,
And played several tunes with her chin.
- Edward Lear

There was a Young Lady whose eyes,
Were unique as to colour and size;
When she opened them wide,
People all turned aside,
And started away in surprise.
- Edward Lear

There was a Young Lady of Bute,
Who played on a silver-gilt flute;
She played several jigs,
To her uncle's white pigs,
That amusing Young Lady of Bute.
- Edward Lear
```

Creating the LimerickData Class

Next, we'll create a model class called LimerickData that essentially acts as a wrapper for a URL-Loader object:

```
package com.peachpit.aas3wdp.limerickreader.data {
    import flash.events.EventDispatcher;
    import flash.net.URLLoader;
    import flash.net.URLRequest;
```

(CODE CONTINUED)

```
      import flash.events.Event;
      import flash.net.URLVariables;
      import flash.net.URLRequestMethod;
      import flash.net.URLLoaderDataFormat;

      public class LimerickData extends EventDispatcher {

        private var _loader:URLLoader;
        private var _limerick:String;
        private var _ids:Array;

        // Retrieve the current limerick string.
        public function get limerick():String {
          return _limerick;
        }

        public function LimerickData() {
          _loader = new URLLoader();
          _loader.addEventListener(Event.COMPLETE, onData);
          _limerick = "";
          // Store indices to use to reference each of the
          // text files.
          _ids = [0, 1, 2, 3];
        }

        // Advance to the next limerick.
        public function next():void {
          // Retrieve a random element from _ids.
          var index:uint = uint(_ids[Math.floor(Math.random() * _ids.length)]);

          // Load the text from one of the files.
          var request:URLRequest = new URLRequest("limerick" + index + ".txt");
          _loader.load(request);
        }

        // The data has loaded. Set the limerick text, and dispatch
        // an event to notify listeners.
        private function onData(event:Event):void {
          _limerick = _loader.data;
          dispatchEvent(new Event(Event.CHANGE));
        }

      }
    }
```

We'll use the LimerickData class as a data model for the application. As the limerick changes, it will notify listeners.

Creating the LimerickView Class

The LimerickView class listens for change events dispatched by a model object, and it then draws itself using the data passed into the constructor:

```
    package com.peachpit.aas3wdp.limerickreader.views {
      import flash.display.Sprite;
```

```
import com.peachpit.aas3wdp.limerickreader.data.LimerickData;
import flash.text.TextField;
import flash.text.TextFieldAutoSize;
import flash.events.Event;

public class LimerickView extends Sprite {

   private var _data:LimerickData;
   private var _textField:TextField;

   // Pass in the data model to use.
   public function LimerickView(data:LimerickData) {
     _data = data;

     // Listen for change events.
     _data.addEventListener(Event.CHANGE, draw);

     // Create the text field to use to display the
     // limerick.
     _textField = new TextField();
     _textField.border = true;
     _textField.autoSize = TextFieldAutoSize.LEFT;
     addChild(_textField);
     draw();
   }

   // The data has changed, so display the new text.
   public function draw(event:Event = null):void {
     _textField.text = _data.limerick;
   }

  }
}
```

This class simply creates a text field that displays the current limerick text value from the data model.

Creating the Main Class

The main class simply creates an instance of the model and an instance of the view and uses a timer to load a random limerick every five seconds:

```
package {

   import flash.display.Sprite;
   import com.peachpit.aas3wdp.limerickreader.views.LimerickView;
   import com.peachpit.aas3wdp.limerickreader.data.LimerickData;
   import flash.utils.Timer;
   import flash.events.TimerEvent;
   import flash.events.Event;

   public class LimerickExample extends Sprite  {

      private var _data:LimerickData;

      public function LimerickExmmple() {
```

(CODE CONTINUED)

```
        _data = new LimerickData();
        var view:LimerickView = new LimerickView(_data);
        addChild(view);
        startTimer(null);
    }

    private function startTimer(event:Event):void {
        var timer:Timer = new Timer(5000);
        timer.addEventListener(TimerEvent.TIMER, onTimer);
        timer.start();
        onTimer();
    }

    private function onTimer(event:TimerEvent = null):void {
        _data.next();
    }

  }
}
```

This class creates an instance of both the model and the view. It uses a timer to advance the model to the next limerick every 5 seconds. When you run this code, you should see the limericks displayed on the screen, changing every 5 seconds.

Sending and Loading Variables

The preceding technique is appropriate when you want to simply load blocks of text from static URLs. However, often an application requires a greater degree of variability. In such cases, you need to send and/or load variables either by themselves or in conjunction with loading text.

Although there are lots of ways to send and load variables, the following sections look specifically at sending and loading URL-encoded variables using HTTP requests and responses through a URLLoader object, building on what we discussed in the preceding section regarding loading text.

NOTE

The URL-encoded format serializes values into a string that uses Web-safe characters. Variables are grouped into name/value pairs, which consist of the name of the variable and the value delimited by an equal sign. For example, a=1 is a name/value pair for a variable called a with a value of 1. If there are multiple name/value pairs, they are delimited by ampersands. For example, a=1&b=2 represents two variables: a and b.

Sending Variables

Sending variables requires that the resource receiving the request is capable of receiving the variables. For example, you can send variables to a PHP or ColdFusion page, but you cannot meaningfully send variables to a text file.

When you want to send variables, you have two basic options: appending the query string to the URL in the URLRequest object or using a URLVariables object.

When you construct a URLRequest object, you can simply append a query string to the URL. The following example constructs a URLRequest object that points to a URL with a query string:

```
var request:URLRequest = new URLRequest("data.php?index=0");
```

Sending data using this first technique has the advantage of being relatively simple to implement when the query string is simple. However, there are two primary disadvantages:

- Adding lots of variables with dynamic values to the query string makes the code more difficult to read.

- You can send the data only using HTTP GET.

The second technique uses a flash.net.URLVariables object. The URLVariables constructor does not require any parameters. After you've constructed a URLVariables object, you can assign arbitrary properties and values to the instance. Each property corresponds to a variable you want to send.

```
var variables:URLVariables = new URLVariables();
variables.a = 1;
variables.b = 2;
```

You can then assign the URLVariables object to the data property of the URLRequest object, like this:

```
var request:URLRequest = new URLRequest("data.php");
request.data = variables;
```

Regardless of which technique you use to assign the variables, you employ the load() method of a URLLoader object to send the request just as you would when loading text. The only difference occurs when you want to send the variables using POST rather than GET. URLRequest objects send all requests using GET by default. If you want to specify the method explicitly, you can use the method property and assign to it either the GET or the POST constant of the flash.net.URLRequestMethod class, like this:

```
request.method = URLRequestMethod.POST;
loader.load(request);
```

The following revision to the LimerickData class presented earlier in this chapter uses a PHP script as the request URL, and it sends two variables:

```
package com.peachpit.aas3wdp.limerickreader.data {
    import flash.events.EventDispatcher;
    import flash.net.URLLoader;
    import flash.net.URLRequest;
    import flash.events.Event;
    import flash.net.URLVariables;
    import flash.net.URLRequestMethod;
    import flash.net.URLLoaderDataFormat;

    public class LimerickData extends EventDispatcher {

        private var _loader:URLLoader;
        private var _limerick:String;
```

```
        private var _ids:Array;

        public function get limerick():String {
          return _limerick;
        }

        public function LimerickData() {
          _loader = new URLLoader();
          _loader.addEventListener(Event.COMPLETE, onData);
          _limerick = "";
          _ids = [0, 1, 2, 3];
        }

        public function next():void {
          var index:uint = uint(_ids[Math.floor(Math.random() * _ids.length)]);
          var variables:URLVariables = new URLVariables();
          variables.limerickIndex = index;
          variables.html = 0;
          var request:URLRequest = new URLRequest("http://www.rightactionscript.com/
            limerick/limerick.php");
          request.method = URLRequestMethod.POST;
          request.data = variables;
          _loader.load(request);
        }

        private function onData(event:Event):void {
          _limerick = _loader.data;
          dispatchEvent(new Event(Event.CHANGE));
        }

      }
    }
```

Now the `LimerickData` class is configured to send a request with variables to a PHP script. The result is the same as before when it was loading data from four text files, but now it is able to point to a single PHP script.

Loading Variables

Not only can you send variables, you can also load variables. Loading variables differs from loading text only in how you ask Flash Player to interpret the return value. By default, Flash Player treats the `data` property of the `URLLoader` object as plain text. However, if you set the `URLLoader.dataFormat` property, you can specify that you want Flash Player to automatically attempt to decode the return value as variables. When that occurs, the `data` property is a `URLVariables` object, and you can simply retrieve the variable values by using the variable names.

To set the `dataFormat` property, use the `VARIABLES` constant of the `flash.net.URLLoaderDataFormat` class, like this:

```
    loader.dataFormat = URLLoaderDataFormat.VARIABLES;
```

In the preceding examples, we've had to assume that there were four limericks, and we had to hard-code the indices that would return the limericks. In this example, we'll first load variables from a PHP script to retrieve the valid indices. The PHP script returns a string in the following format: limerickIds=0,1,2,3. Next we'll revise the LimerickData class so that it loads the data and parses it into an array before loading any of the limericks. Because the model cannot load the limericks until it has first loaded the variables, that introduces a dilemma: Currently, the main class calls the next() method immediately. There is no guarantee that the limerick IDs will have loaded before the next() method is called, and that will result in an unhandled error with the current implementation (because the _ids will be null.) You have two basic options:

- Require a change to the main class so that it doesn't call next() until the IDs have loaded. This option entails dispatching and listening for an additional event.

- Change the implementation of next() so that it handles requests elegantly if the IDs haven't yet loaded.

We'll opt for the second option. The next() method will test that _ids is not null before trying to make a request to the server. We'll add a property that keeps track of whether or not the next() method has been called. If that property is true, then the code will automatically call next() when the IDs load. Here's the updated class:

```
package com.peachpit.aas3wdp.limerickreader.data {
    import flash.events.EventDispatcher;
    import flash.net.URLLoader;
    import flash.net.URLRequest;
    import flash.events.Event;
    import flash.net.URLVariables;
    import flash.net.URLRequestMethod;
    import flash.net.URLLoaderDataFormat;

    public class LimerickData extends EventDispatcher {

        private var _loader:URLLoader;
        private var _limerick:String;
        private var _idsLoader:URLLoader;
        private var _ids:Array;
        private var _pendingNext:Boolean;

        public function get limerick():String {
            return _limerick;
        }

        public function LimerickData() {
            _loader = new URLLoader();
            _loader.addEventListener(Event.COMPLETE, onData);
            _limerick = "";
            _idsLoader = new URLLoader();
            _idsLoader.addEventListener(Event.COMPLETE, setIds);
            _idsLoader.load(new URLRequest("http://localhost/limerick/limerickIndex.php"));
            _idsLoader.dataFormat = URLLoaderDataFormat.VARIABLES;
        }

        private function setIds(event:Event):void {
```

(CODE CONTINUED)

```
            _ids = _idsLoader.data.limerickIds.split(",");
            if(_pendingNext) {
              next();
            }
        }

        public function next():void {
          if(_ids != null) {
            var variables:URLVariables = new URLVariables();
            variables.limerickIndex = _ids[Math.floor(Math.random() * _ids.length)];
            variables.html = 0;
            var request:URLRequest = new URLRequest("http://localhost/limerick/
              limerick.php");
            request.method = URLRequestMethod.POST;
            request.data = variables;
            _loader.load(request);
          }
          else {
            _pendingNext = true;
          }
        }

        private function onData(event:Event):void {
          _limerick = _loader.data;
          dispatchEvent(new Event(Event.CHANGE));
        }

    }
}
```

Now the code loads limerick IDs from the PHP script first. After it loads the IDs, it can load limericks from the limerick PHP script just as it did previously. This configuration is much more flexible because it allows us to change the IDs of the limericks by changing the output of the limerickIndex.php script rather than having to recompile the SWF with new IDs.

Sending and Loading XML

XML (eXtensible Markup Language) is a standard for storing and transferring data. Flash Player has built-in support for working with XML data. You can read about working with XML in Chapter 15, "E4X (XML)." In this chapter, we'll focus on how to send and load XML data.

When you send and load XML from Flash Player, it is always converted to a string. That enables you to send and load XML data (as a string) using the same techniques you use to send and load text. To send and load XML, you use the same URLLoader and URLRequest classes you used to send and load text.

Sending XML

When you send XML data, you generally send the raw XML data using HTTP POST. The ActionScript code required to accomplish this task is similar to that for sending variables.

However, rather than using a `URLVariables` object, you simply assign the XML string to the `data` property of the `URLRequest` object. You then generally want to set the MIME type of the request using the `URLRequest.contentType` property. The following example sends an XML string to a PHP script:

```
var loader:URLLoader = new URLLoader();
var request:URLRequest = new URLRequest("saveSettings.php");
request.contentType = "text/xml";
request.method = URLRequestMethod.POST;
request.data = "<settings><email>email@domain.com</email><phone>555-1212</phone></
settings>";
loader.load(request);
```

Loading XML

Loading XML is exactly the same as loading text with one additional step after the data has loaded. The XML constructor allows you to pass it a string that the constructor will parse into the XML object. You can simply pass the value from the `data` property of the `URLLoader` object.

```
var xml:XML = new XML(_loader.data);
```

NOTE

You can optionally cast the data as XML rather than passing it to an XML constructor.

Some XML you load might have additional whitespace (carriage returns and tabs) added for human readability. Unless you tell Flash Player to watch for the extra whitespace, it will interpret whitespace as XML elements. That's generally not the desired behavior. The simple solution is to set `XML.ignoreWhitespace` before parsing the string to the XML object, like this:

```
XML.ignoreWhitespace = true;
var xml:XML = new XML(_loader.data);
```

Using Web Services

Web services are a popular standard for client-server data communication. However, Flash Player has no built-in classes specifically designed for working with Web services. If you are using the Flex framework, you can employ the `mx.rpc.soap.WebService` class. In this book, we're concerned primarily with solutions that rely exclusively on the Flash Player API. For a description of the `WebService` class, see the Flex documentation.

If you are interested in a Web services solution that does not rely on the Flex framework, you have two options:

- Write your own Web services framework in ActionScript. Although Web services appear in many forms, one of the most popular uses SOAP, an XML-based protocol that is sent over HTTP. Writing a Web service framework requires sending and loading XML data using `URLLoader` along with a custom SOAP parser.

- Make standard requests to a server-side script that makes the Web service calls. The server-side script can return URL-encoded data or XML data.

NOTE

Another option is to manually create and parse SOAP requests and responses. This is advisable for only very simple cases. You can see an example of this in Chapter 15.

The second option is often the best. One obvious reason that server-side Web service proxies are a good idea is that server-side languages generally have robust Web service capabilities that can work with a variety of protocols—not just SOAP. Server-side scripts can also generally parse Web service responses more quickly. They can relay the responses back to the client in a format that is more compact than SOAP (to limit the bandwidth overhead), and the server can even cache responses when applicable to limit the number of Web service requests.

Using Flash Remoting

Flash Remoting is a technology for making remote procedure calls from Flash Player to server-side services. The concept is similar to that of Web services: The client makes a request to a method that's exposed using a server-side service. The request is serialized in a specific format, sent over HTTP (or HTTPS), and the response is likewise serialized and sent back to the client. This approach enables remote clients and services to interact to create integrated applications. Like Web services, Flash Remoting has the advantage of automatically serializing and deserializing to and from native data types.

However, there are significant differences between Flash Remoting and Web services. Following are a few of those differences:

- Flash Remoting uses AMF (Action Message Format) as the protocol for packaging data. Although this might initially sound like yet another non-standardized, proprietary format, AMF is actually a binary form of SOAP that has a significant advantage over SOAP. SOAP packets have a lot of overhead that increases the bandwidth requirements. Over time, the extra bandwidth costs can add up. AMF can send the same amount of data in a much more compact (i.e., binary) format than its SOAP counterparts.

- AMF is supported natively by Flash Player. In addition to its use with Flash Remoting, AMF is the format Flash Player uses for shared objects and local connections. Because AMF is supported natively in Flash Player, that means that serializations and deserializations to and from native ActionScript types is automatic and fast.

- AMF support is not built into most server technologies. However, adding the necessary AMF gateway on the server is simple. Gateways are available for most major platforms including ColdFusion, Java, Perl, .NET, and PHP. There are even reliable and enterprise-ready open-source options available.

Understanding Flash Remoting Basics

When you want to use Flash Remoting, there are two elements that communicate: a client and a service. The service is generally a class that has been exposed so that it is available to Flash Remoting. Flash Remoting is a request-response model, which means the client must initiate all requests. The client must make all calls through an intermediary called a gateway. The gateway is a web-accessible resource on the server that is capable of accepting AMF requests, deserializing them, and delegating the requests to the appropriate services.

There are many Flash Remoting gateway products, including the following:

- OpenAMF (www.openamf.org): an open-source Java gateway

- WebORB (www.themidnightcoders.com): gateway products for .NET, Java, Ruby on Rails, and PHP

- AMFPHP (www.amfphp.org): an open-source PHP gateway

Each gateway has its specific installation instructions. However, after you've installed the gateway, the general instructions to use it are the same. The following section looks at the Action-Script required to make Flash Remoting calls. In each case, you'll need to know the URL to the gateway resource for your server. The documentation for the specific gateway you are using will tell you what you need to know to locate the correct resource. It is always a web-accessible resource such as a page (a PHP page, a .NET page, and so on) or a servlet.

Making Flash Remoting Calls

Although the Flex framework and the Flash Remoting components for Flash provide a high-level API for working with Flash Remoting, at a lower level, all Flash Remoting calls go through a flash.net.NetConnection object. In this section, we'll look exclusively at working directly with NetConnection objects to make Flash Remoting calls.

The first step in making Flash Remoting calls is to construct a NetConnection object using the constructor. The constructor does not require any parameters, as you can see here:

```
var netConnection:NetConnection = new NetConnection();
```

Next, you must specify the gateway URL using the connect() method. Despite its name, the connect() method does not actually attempt to make a connection to the resource. It simply sets the gateway URL for the object so that subsequent Flash Remoting calls can be routed through the correct gateway resource.

```
netConnection.connect("http://localhost/gateway");
```

After you've set the gateway URL, you can make calls to methods of available services using the call() method. The call() method requires at least two parameters: the name of the service and method as a string, and an object indicating how to handle responses.

The name of the service and method must be the fully qualified service name and method name, all in dot notation. That means that if the service is in a package, you must specify the package as well as the name of the service. The name of the service and the name of the method are also separated by a dot. The following statement makes a call to the test method of the Example service:

```
netConnection.call("Example.test", null);
```

The second parameter can be null (as in the preceding example) if and when you do not need to listen for a response from the service method. However, if you do need to listen for a response, you can use a flash.net.Responder object. The Responder constructor requires that you specify two functions to handle the possible responses: a result and an error. The following statement makes a call to the test method, this time handling the response:

```
netConnection.call("Example.call", new Responder(onResult, onError));
```

When the service method returns a valid value, the result method gets called and is passed the return value as a parameter. When an error occurs, the error method gets called with an Object parameter whose properties detail the error.

You can also pass parameters to the service method by adding additional parameters to the call() method parameter list. For example, the following code passes the parameters 1, true, and "a" to the service method:

```
netConnection.call("Example.call", new Responder(onResult, onError), 1, true, "a");
```

The following rewrite of the LimerickData class uses Flash Remoting instead of loading data using URLLoader. For the sake of simplicity, this example does not handle errors. In an actual application, you might want to handle errors by bubbling up error events (as described in Chapter 13, "Working with Events").

```
package com.peachpit.aas3wdp.limerickreader.data {
    import flash.events.EventDispatcher;
    import flash.events.Event;
    import flash.net.NetConnection;
    import flash.net.Responder;

    public class LimerickData extends EventDispatcher {

        private var _limerick:String;
        private var _ids:Array;
        private var _pendingNext:Boolean;
        private var _netConnection:NetConnection;

        public function get limerick():String {
            return _limerick;
        }

        public function LimerickData() {
            _limerick = "";

            // Use a NetConnection object rather than the
            // URLLoader object used previously.
```

(CODE CONTINUED)

```
      _netConnection = new NetConnection();
      _netConnection.connect("http://www.rightactionscript.com/limerick/gateway.php");
      _netConnection.call("LimerickService.getIds", new Responder(setIds, null));
   }

   private function setIds(ids:Array):void {
      _ids = ids;
      if(_pendingNext) {
         next();
      }
   }

   public function next():void {
      if(_ids != null) {
         var index:uint = _ids[Math.floor(Math.random() * _ids.length)];
         _netConnection.call("LimerickService.getLimerick", new Responder(onData,
            null), index, false);
      }
      else {
         _pendingNext = true;
      }
   }

   private function onData(limerick:String):void {
      _limerick = limerick;
      dispatchEvent(new Event(Event.CHANGE));
   }

   }
}
```

This version accomplishes the same basic tasks as previous versions. However, it now uses Flash Remoting to accomplish these goals.

Optimizing Data Communication

When you work with data, it is frequently important that you optimize the manner in which you work with the data. The following sections look at several specific ways you can optimize your work with data.

Caching Data

When an application makes calls to services, it is typically either submitting or requesting data. When an application requests data, there are two ways it can use that data: temporarily or persistently. If the data is used temporarily, it can and should be discarded when the application no longer needs it. However, when the data is used persistently, it can sometimes be useful to store that data in a persistent data model rather than discarding it and re-requesting it when the application needs the data again.

The technique of caching persistent data allows you to minimize the number of requests made to the server when the same data is used over and over. The sample limerick application is a good case in point. The application uses just a handful of pieces of data. The implementation thus far makes requests for each limerick every time the data is needed by the application. If the application displays one of the limericks fifty times, it also makes a request for the data fifty times from the server. Yet the cost of making those network requests is expensive, both in terms of bandwidth usage and latency in the application. In this particular case, a better solution is to store the limerick data client-side rather than making the request to the server each time.

There are two ways you can handle retrieving persistent data: requesting all the data at once or requesting the data one piece at a time as the user needs it, but caching the data rather than discarding it. The first technique has the advantage of ensuring the immediate availability of data when the user requests it. Yet the first technique also requires a potentially large initial download, even though the user may or may not be using all the data. The second technique allows the application to download data only when it is first requested by the user. Which technique you select depends on the requirements for the application. If the application allows for an initial wait for the user but requires low latency and immediate responsiveness after that initial wait, then you should download the data as part of an initialization. If the data set is very large and the average user of the application is not likely to use all the data every time she uses the application, it is generally better to download data on demand and cache it for later use.

We'll look at how to rewrite the LimerickData class so that it uses the on-demand technique—caching data so the class doesn't have to download the same data twice. For this purpose, we'll introduce a new class called LimerickItem. This class is a simple data model for a single limerick that stores the limerick text and its index.

```
package com.peachpit.aas3wdp.limerickreader.data {
    import flash.events.EventDispatcher;
    import flash.events.Event;

    public class LimerickItem extends EventDispatcher {

        private var _index:uint;
        private var _text:String;

        public function LimerickItem(index:uint) {
            _index = index;
        }

        public function getIndex():uint {
            return _index;
        }

        public function getText():String {
            return _text;
        }

        public function setText(value:String):void {
            _text = value;
            dispatchEvent(new Event(Event.CHANGE));
        }

    }
}
```

Next, modify the existing LimerickData class so that it stores LimerickItem objects in an array. When the application requests a limerick that's already been loaded, the data model returns the cached data rather than request it from the server again.

```
package com.peachpit.aas3wdp.limerickreader.data {
    import flash.events.EventDispatcher;
    import flash.events.Event;
    import flash.net.NetConnection;
    import flash.net.Responder;

    public class LimerickData extends EventDispatcher {

        private var _limerick:String;
        private var _ids:Array;
        private var _pendingNext:Boolean;
        private var _netConnection:NetConnection;
        private var _limericks:Array;

        public function get limerick():String {
            return _limerick;
        }

        public function LimerickData() {
            _limerick = "";
            _netConnection = new NetConnection();
            _netConnection.connect("http://localhost/limerick/gateway.php");
            _netConnection.call("LimerickService.getIds", new Responder(setIds, null));

            // This is the array in which the model stores each
            // of the LimerickItem objects.
            _limericks = new Array();
        }

        private function setIds(ids:Array):void {
            _ids = ids;
            if(_pendingNext) {
                next();
            }
        }

        public function next():void {
            if(_ids != null) {
                var index:uint = _ids[Math.floor(Math.random() * _ids.length)];

                // Test if the data has already been
                // requested. If not, request it. If so,
                // set current limerick to the cached
                // value.
                if(_limericks[index] == undefined) {
                    var item:LimerickItem = new LimerickItem(index);

                    // Listen for the change event that
                    // the item dispatches when the value
                    // is set, and then call onItem().
                    item.addEventListener(Event.CHANGE, onItem);
                    _limericks[index] = item;
```

(CODE CONTINUED)

```
                    // Use item.setText as the result
                    // event handler method.
                    netConnection.call("LimerickService.getLimerick", new Responder
                    (item.setText, null), index, false);
                }
                else {
                    onData(_limericks[index].getText());
                }
            }
            else {
                _pendingNext = true;
            }
        }

        // When the data is returned and assigned to the limerick
        // item, then call onData() wuith the data.
        private function onItem(event:Event):void {
            onData(event.target.getText());
        }

        private function onData(limerick:String):void {
            _limerick = limerick;
            dispatchEvent(new Event(Event.CHANGE));
        }

    }
}
```

Queuing and Pooling Requests

When you have lots of service calls, there are two ways you can call them: back to back, or all together. The back-to-back technique is what we call *queuing*. The technique of calling all the methods at once is what we call *pooling*. Each has advantages and disadvantages.

A novice approach to remote procedure calls is to simply make the calls when it's convenient. This approach means that some calls are queued and some calls are pooled, but never intentionally. This is not generally a good approach because there are cases in which calls must be queued and cases in which it is better if they are pooled. It is better to specifically select the manner in which you make service method calls.

The limerick application has a perfect example of a case in which method calls must be queued. Two service methods are called in the example: getIds() and getLimerick(). It is essential that getIds() is called before getLimerick() because getLimerick() requires a parameter whose value is determined by the result of the getIds() method call. This means you must queue the method calls to ensure that getIds() returns a value before getLimerick() is called. In the existing example, this order is achieved by using an if statement to test that the _ids array (which is populated by the return value from getIds()) is defined before calling getLimerick().

Pooling requests is rarely if ever required. However, pooling does significantly reduce network overhead. If there are several method calls that do not have dependencies (which would require that they be queued), and if those methods are likely to be called in relatively close succession anyway, it is better to make the requests all at the same time. Flash Player automatically bundles together all requests made in the same frame (which basically amounts to all requests made in the same routine) into a single AMF request packet.

Summary

Working with data is integral to the majority of Flash Platform applications. In this chapter, you learned how to load text, send and load variables, work with the transfer of XML, and use Flash Remoting. You also learned techniques for optimizing your work with data.

CHAPTER 15

E4X (XML)

XML got a major overhaul with the release of ActionScript 3.0. The much-anticipated E4X has finally made its way into Flash Player 9. This makes working with XML in Flash much simpler and reduces the need for complex XML logic. Nearly everything you know about working with XML in Flash has changed with this release.

In this chapter, we examine the new features of E4X, look at how loading external XML files has changed, review the classic XML API, and create an example application that uses a few of these advanced features.

E4X stands for ECMAScript for XML. ECMAScript is the language ActionScript is based on. The E4X specification was developed by ECMA International and was released in the summer of 2004. The goal of E4X is to simplify the way developers use XML inside ECMAScript languages. It also introduces features that were not available in ActionScript 2.0.

NEW CLASSES IN ACTIONSCRIPT 3.0

Because E4X is not simply an upgrade of the previous XML functionality, the class structure is not exactly the same. ActionScript 3.0 has the following top-level classes for working with E4X functionality: XML, XMLList, QName, and Namespace.

XML

The new XML class is nothing like the XML class in ActionScript 2.0. ActionScript 2.0 had two classes that represented the XML structure: XML and XMLNode. The XMLNode class was always a little silly because technically each node is a self-contained XML document. Therefore, in ActionScript 3.0, Adobe corrected this confusion by removing the XMLNode class. Now the XML type represents all elements, attributes, processing instructions, and text.

XMLList

ActionScript 3.0 introduces a new class called XMLList. In ActionScript 2.0, you could get an array of XMLNode objects by calling the childNodes property of any XMLNode object. Now, instead of working with a generic Array, you can use the XML.children() method to return an XMLList with the same functionality. A nice feature of the XMLList class is that if you have a case where there is only one XML object in the list, the XMLList delegates calls to that object. It basically functions as though it *is* that XML object. In the following example, lines 2 and 3 are identical because there is only one item:

```
var data:XML = <data><item>Test Value</item.</data>;
var value1:String = data.item[0].toString();
var value2:String = data.item.toString();
```

The first line in the preceding example might seem a bit strange if you are completely new to E4X. It is a new way to define XML objects in ActionScript 3.0 using literals. We'll talk more about literals later in this chapter.

QName

The QName class, also new to ActionScript 3.0, is used to represent the qualified names of elements and attributes in an XML object. There are two parts to qualified names: The first part is a local name that conforms to XML standards, and the second part is a namespace URI (Uniform Resource Identifier). The namespace is optional.

Namespace

The Namespace class is used to define XML namespaces. Namespace support is a new feature included in E4X that is also used to define namespaces in your code not related to XML. It's important to understand that this class has multiple uses, only one of which relates to XML.

Creating XML Objects

ActionScript 3.0 provides two basic ways to create XML objects: using a constructor or using literal notation. The constructor works just as you would expect:

```
var xml:XML = new XML();
```

Optionally you can pass a string to the constructor that you want to parse into XML:

```
var xml:XML = new XML("<data><value>a</value></data>");
```

However, using literal notation is often far easier and more readable. The following example shows a simple XML object that is created with literal syntax:

```
var catalog:XML = <catalog>
    <product id="0">
        <name>Product One</name>
        <price>50</price>
    </product>
    <product id="1">
        <name>Product Two</name>
        <price>35</price>
    </product>
</catalog>;
```

You can see that literal notation is easier and more readable, especially when you compare the literal notation with the equivalent constructor notation, shown here:

```
var catalog:XML = new XML('<catalog><product id="0"><name>Product One</
name><price>50</price></product><product id="1"><name>Product Two</name><price>35</
price></product></catalog>');
```

You can also use literals to declare XMLList objects. When using XMLList literal notation, you should use <></> as the root tag. The following example creates two XML objects named product in an XMLList object:

```
var products:XMLList = <>
    <product id="0">
        <name>Product One</name>
        <price>50</price>
    </product>
    <product id="1">
        <name>Product Two</name>
        <price>35</price>
    </product>
</>;
```

Sometimes you'll have a situation in which you need variable values in your XML object. You can achieve this by using curly braces ({}) to surround the variable within the XML literal. The following example shows how you can create a XML object named product using variable values for both name and price:

```
var productName:String = "Product One";
var productPrice:Number = 50;
var product:XML = <product id="0">
    <name>{productName}</name>
```

(CODE CONTINUED)

```
      <price>{productPrice}</price>
    </product>;
    var catalog:XML = <catalog>
    {product}
    </catalog>;
```

NOTE

The name of the variable *product* is the same as the first element of the *XML* object. Although this is not required, we do this for simplicity. If we were to use a different name for the variable, we would treat that variable name as though it were the name of the first element of our *XML* object. By naming them the same, we minimize confusion.

Property Accessors

E4X syntax reuses and extends the property accessor syntax already familiar to ActionScript developers. For example, ActionScript developers are already familiar with how to use dot-notation to access a property such as the x or y properties of a display object.

```
sprite.x = 100;
sprite.y = 100;
```

Because of this familiarity, the learning curve for XML in ActionScript 3.0 is lowered.

For the following discussion we'll use this XML object.

```
var catalog:XML = <catalog>
  <product id="0">
    <name>Product One</name>
    <price>50</price>
  </product>
  <product id="1">
    <name>Product Two</name>
    <price>35</price>
  </product>
</catalog>;
```

First, we'll access the XMLList that is a child of the root node. Because the child nodes of the root are called product, you can use dot notation to access a property of that same name which will reference the XMLList:

```
var products:XMLList = catalog.product;
```

XMLList objects allow you to use array-access notation to access the elements of the list. For example, the following code retrieves a reference to the first product XML node.

```
var firstProduct:XML = catalog.product[0];
```

Although up to this point the syntax has been familiar, we'll now introduce one new syntax that uses an @ symbol to reference attributes. By using the @ symbol, you can target attributes of an

XML object as shown in the following example. This code retrieves the `id` attribute value of the first product node.

```
var id:Number = Number(catalog.product[0].@id);
```

If you use the `@` symbol for an `XMLList`, it will return an `XMLList` of all the attributes of that name for all the `XMLList` elements. Here's an example that retrieves all the `id` attributes for all the `product` nodes:

```
var allProductIds:XMLList = catalog.product.@id;
```

You can use an asterisk as a wildcard to get all the items at a given level. For example, the following code retrieves all the product nodes without having to know the name of the nodes:

```
var firstLevel:XMLList = catalog.*;
```

You can also use wildcards with attributes. This example retrieves all the attributes of all the product nodes:

```
var firstLevel:XMLList = catalog.product.@*;
```

XML Filtering

Arguably, the most powerful and useful feature of E4X is its ability to filter data. This new feature replaces the need for XPath libraries and the loops previously used to search an XML document in earlier versions of ActionScript. Now you can do all this natively in ActionScript 3.0 using as little as one line of code.

To use filtering, you can enclose expressions in parentheses as part of an E4X expression. The following examples show a few uses of filtering. We'll use the same XML object for all our examples:

```
var catalog:XML = <catalog>
  <product id="0">
    <name>Product One</name>
    <price>50</price>
  </product>
  <product id="1">
    <name>Product Two</name>
    <price>35</price>
  </product>
</catalog>;
```

The following line retrieves the `product` element that has an `id` attribute equal to 1. This example returns just one XML object, but it would return an `XMLList` if more than one element matches the criteria.

```
var product1:XML = catalog.product.(@id == 1);
```

This next line grabs the name of the `product` element that has a `price` less than 50. It's important to understand that this would return an `XMLList` if more than one element met the criteria:

```
var cheapestProductName:String = catalog.product.(price < 50).name;
```

This example retrieves the `product` elements that have a `price` greater than 35 and less than 50:

```
var productRange:XMLList = catalog.product.(price >= 35 && price <= 50);
```

Iterating Through an XMLList

Developers must often *iterate*, or loop, through an `XMLList` object. ActionScript 3.0 provides a few ways to do this. We'll use the same `catalog` example to demonstrate three different ways to iterate through the products and add up the `price` values. Here again is the literal syntax for creating the `catalog` object:

```
var catalog:XML = <catalog>
   <product id="0">
      <name>Product One</name>
      <price>50</price>
   </product>
   <product id="1">
      <name>Product Two</name>
      <price>35</price>
   </product>
</catalog>;
```

The first method of iterating through an `XMLList` is a simple `for` loop. We use the `XMLList.length()` method to get the number of items in the `XMLList`. Then we simply iterate that number of times, incrementing the index (`i`) with each iteration. You use a similar syntax to loop through an indexed array.

```
var total:Number = 0;
for(var i:int = 0; i < catalog.product.length(); i++) {
   total += (catalog.product[i].price as Number);
}
```

The second method is a `for...in` loop that iterates over the `XMLList`. This method is commonly used to loop over an associative array or an object.

```
var total:Number = 0;
for(var i:String in catalog.product) {
total += (catalog.product[i].price as Number);
}
```

The third method is new to ActionScript 3,0. It's a `for each..in` loop and provides a cleaner way to loop over XML.

```
var total:Number = 0;
for each(var product:XML in catalog.product) {
   total += (product.price as Number);
}
```

It's also possible to use the new `for each..in` loop structure to iterate over attributes in an `XML` object.

```
var product:XML = <product id="0" name="Product One" price="50" />;
for each(var attribute:XML in product.@*) {
   trace(attribute.name() + ": " + attribute.toXMLString());
}
```

Namespaces

E4X has the added capability of XML *namespaces*. Namespaces are used to avoid element name conflicts. Namespaces are most commonly found in complex XML documents that contain XML data from multiple sources. SOAP, the XML format behind many Web services, is one of the most common examples of XML documents that use namespaces. Many developers never use namespaces in their XML documents, but if you do, there are some new ways to work with them in ActionScript 3.0.

We'll use a simple SOAP envelope to show how you can work with namespaces. The following code shows how to create an XML namespace using literals:

```
var envelope:XML = <soap:envelope xmlns:soap="http://www.w3.org/2003/05/
soap-envelope" />;
```

Next, we'll add a `body` element to the envelope. The body should have the same namespace as the envelope. We can do this a few different ways. We can use the literal syntax to create the body element, as in this example:

```
envelope.body = <soap:body xmlns:soap="http://www.w3.org/2003/05/soap-envelope" />
```

We can also create the `body` element by declaring the namespace and using the :: operator, like this:

```
var soap:Namespace = new Namespace("http://www.w3.org/2003/05/soap-envelope");
envelope.soap::body = new XML();
```

Both of these examples create an `XML` object that looks like the following:

```
<soap:envelope xmlns:soap="http://www.w3.org/2003/05/soap-envelope">
 <soap:body />
</soap:envelope>
```

We can also create an `XML` object using a default namespace, like this:

```
default xml namespace = new Namespace("http://www.w3.org/2003/05/soap-envelope");
var envelope:XML = <envelope><body /></envelope>;
```

Sending and Loading XML Data

The two main classes that send or load data in ActionScript 3.0 are `URLRequest` and `URLLoader`. The `URLRequest` class is used to create any HTTP request, and the `URLLoader` class is used to transfer the request and listen for the response. Chapter 14, "Sending and Loading Data," explains how to use `URLLoader` to send and load data. Here in the following sections we'll revisit this information in the context of sending and loading XML.

Simple Soap Example

To demonstrate many of the new features of E4X, we'll create a simple example that uses SOAP-formatted XML to send and receive data from a remote Web service. The service accepts an IP address and returns the geographical location it resolves to.

NOTE

For more information on sending and loading XML, see Chapter 14.

The following example sends and loads data using a public Web service whose WSDL document is located at http://ws.cdyne.com/ip2geo/ip2geo.asmx. You can read more about the Web service at http://ws.cdyne.com/ip2geo/ip2geo.asmx?op=ResolveIP.

Before we create the example, we'll first look at the format of the request and response packets. The request packet is a standard SOAP-formatted request. The heart of the request is inside the `<m:ResolveIP>` tags. It has two child elements: the first is the IP address value, and the second is the license key. Here's an example of what the packet might look like:

```
<SOAP-ENV:Envelope xmlns:SOAP-ENV="http://schemas.xmlsoap.org/soap/envelope/"
xmlns:SOAP-ENC="http://schemas.xmlsoap.org/soap/encoding/" xmlns:xsi="http://www.
w3.org/2001/XMLSchema-instance" xmlns:xsd="http://www.w3.org/2001/XMLSchema">
   <SOAP-ENV:Body>
      <m:ResolveIP xmlns:m="http://ws.cdyne.com/">
         <m:IPaddress>24.118.19.171</m:IPaddress>
         <m:LicenseKey>0</m:LicenseKey>
      </m:ResolveIP>
   </SOAP-ENV:Body>
</SOAP-ENV:Envelope>
```

In this example, notice that the license key is 0. This particular Web service allows us to test the service by using a license key of 0.

The response packet is a SOAP-formatted response. Inside the `<ResolveIPResult>` tag are the values for the response:

```
<soap:Envelope xmlns:soap="http://schemas.xmlsoap.org/soap/envelope/" xmlns:
xsi="http://www.w3.org/2001/XMLSchema-instance" xmlns:xsd="http://www.w3.org/2001/
XMLSchema">
   <soap:Body>
      <ResolveIPResponse xmlns="http://ws.cdyne.com/">
         <ResolveIPResult>
            <City>Chicago</City>
            <StateProvince>IL</StateProvince>
            <Country>USA</Country>
            <Latitude>41.5000000</Latitude>
            <Longitude>-87.4100000</Longitude>
            <HasDaylightSavings>false</HasDaylightSavings>
            <Certainty>16</Certainty>
         </ResolveIPResult>
      </ResolveIPResponse>
   </soap:Body>
</soap:Envelope>
```

You can see that the response includes information such as the city, state, and country to which the IP address resolves. This example contains specific data such as Chicago, IL, and USA. The actual Web service responses will contain data specific to the IP address passed in using the request.

Now that we've looked at the structure of the request and response packets, we can build the sample application.

Building the Custom Event

The very first thing we'll need to build in this example is a custom event type. Because our event has data associated with it, we will create a custom event class called `LocationEvent`. This class extends the built-in `Event` class and simply adds five public properties. These properties are later populated from the data returned by the Web service.

```
package com.peachpit.aas3wdp.e4xexample {

  import flash.events.Event;

  public class LocationEvent extends Event {

    private var _city:String;
    private var _stateProvince:String;
    private var _country:String;
    private var _latitude:String;
    private var _longitude:String;

    public function get city():String {
      return _city;
    }

    public function set city(value:String):void {
      _city = value;
    }

    public function get stateProvince():String {
      return _stateProvince;
    }

    public function set stateProvince(value:String):void {
      _stateProvince = value;
    }

    public function get country():String {
      return _country;
    }

    public function set country(value:String):void {
      _country = value;
    }

    public function get latitude():String {
      return _latitude;
    }

    public function set latitude(value:String):void {
      _latitude = value;
    }

    public function get longitude():String {
      return _longitude;
    }

    public function set longitude(value:String):void {
```

```
            _longitude = value;
        }

        public function LocationEvent(type:String, bubbles:Boolean = false,
    cancelable:Boolean = false) {
            super(type, bubbles, cancelable);
        }

    }

}
```

This class requires a fair amount of code, but it is quite simple. It merely extends Event and adds additional properties specific to location. We'll see how to use this event type in the next few sections.

Building the Web Service Class

The ResolveIP class does all the heavy lifting in this example. It is responsible for making the request and listening for the response. All the SOAP communication is encapsulated in this class.

The first thing our class does in the constructor is to create the URLRequest object. This object is where we define the request data (the request SOAP packet), headers, URL, methods, and content type. Notice the use of curly braces to populate the request data with the IP address that is passed into the constructor. The URLLoader object is used to execute this request.

The onComplete() event handler is where we respond to the URLLoader.COMPLETE event. Here we create a custom event object using our LocationEvent class.

```
package com.peachpit.aas3wdp.e4xexample {

    import com.peachpit.aas3wdp.e4xexample.LocationEvent;
    import flash.events.Event;
    import flash.events.EventDispatcher;
    import flash.net.URLLoader;
    import flash.net.URLRequest;
    import flash.net.URLRequestHeader;


    public class ResolveIP extends EventDispatcher {

        private var urlLoader:URLLoader;

        public function ResolveIP(ipAddress:String) {
            var urlRequest:URLRequest = new URLRequest();
            urlRequest.contentType = "text/xml; charset=utf-8";
            urlRequest.method = "POST";
            urlRequest.url = "http://ws.cdyne.com/ip2geo/ip2geo.asmx";
            var soapAction:URLRequestHeader = new URLRequestHeader("SOAPAction",
                "http://ws.cdyne.com/ResolveIP");
            urlRequest.requestHeaders.push(soapAction);
            urlRequest.data = <SOAP-ENV:Envelope xmlns:SOAP-ENV="http://schemas.xmlsoap.
                org/soap/envelope/" xmlns:SOAP-ENC="http://schemas.xmlsoap.org/soap/
                encoding/" xmlns:xsi="http://www.w3.org/2001/XMLSchema-instance" xmlns:
                xsd="http://www.w3.org/2001/XMLSchema">
```

```
            <SOAP-ENV:Body>
                <m:ResolveIP xmlns:m="http://ws.cdyne.com/">
                    <m:IPaddress>{ipAddress}</m:IPaddress>
                    <m:LicenseKey>0</m:LicenseKey>
                </m:ResolveIP>
            </SOAP-ENV:Body>
        </SOAP-ENV:Envelope>;

        urlLoader = new URLLoader();
        urlLoader.addEventListener(Event.COMPLETE, onComplete);
        urlLoader.load(urlRequest);
    }

    private function onComplete(event:Event):void {
        var envelope:XML = XML(urlLoader.data);
        var soap:Namespace = envelope.namespace("soap");
        var response:Namespace = new Namespace("http://ws.cdyne.com/");
        var result:XMLList = envelope.soap::Body.response::ResolveIPResponse.
            response::ResolveIPResult;
        var locationEvent:LocationEvent = new LocationEvent(Event.COMPLETE, true, true);
        locationEvent.city = result.response::City.toString();
        locationEvent.stateProvince = result.response::StateProvince.toString();
        locationEvent.country = result.response::Country.toString();
        locationEvent.latitude = result.response::Latitude.toString();
        locationEvent.longitude = result.response::Longitude.toString();
        dispatchEvent(locationEvent);
    }

    }

}
```

Creating the Main Class

Invoking the ResolveIP class is simple. Just create a new instance of the class and pass an IP address into the constructor during creation. Then register for the complete event and the error event. The complete event returns a LocationEvent object. The error events are not actually thrown by ResolveIP, but instead are thrown by the URLLoader object inside the ResolveIP object. Because the error events aren't caught by the ResolveIP object, they bubble up to our WebServiceExample object.

Here's the main class for our SOAP-parsing Web service example:

```
package {

    import com.peachpit.aas3wdp.e4xexample.LocationEvent;
    import com.peachpit.aas3wdp.e4xexample.ResolveIP;
    import flash.events.Event;
    import flash.events.IOErrorEvent;
    import flash.events.SecurityErrorEvent;
    import flash.events.KeyboardEvent;
    import flash.ui.Keyboard;
    import flash.display.Sprite;
```

```
import flash.text.TextField;
import flash.text.TextFieldType;


public class WebServiceExample extends Sprite {

   private var _resolveIP:ResolveIP;
   private var _text:TextField;

   public function WebServiceExample() {

      // Create a text field to accept user input and
      // display the response.
      _text = new TextField();
      _text.type = TextFieldType.INPUT;
      _text.width = 200;
      _text.height = 22;
      _text.background = true;
      _text.border = true;

      // Initially populate the text field with a valid
      // IP address. This makes it easy to test the
      // application. You can also change this at runtime
      // if you want to test a different IP address.
      _text.text = "24.118.19.171";

      // Listen for keyboard events.
      _text.addEventListener(KeyboardEvent.KEY_UP, onKey);
      addChild(_text);
   }

   private function onKey(event:KeyboardEvent):void {

      // If the user presses the Enter key then createa a
      // new ResolveIP object, passing it the text from
      // the text field. Then listen for events.
      if(event.keyCode == Keyboard.ENTER) {
         _resolveIP = new ResolveIP(_text.text);
         _resolveIP.addEventListener(Event.COMPLETE, onComplete);
         _resolveIP.addEventListener(IOErrorEvent.IO_ERROR, onError);
         _resolveIP.addEventListener(SecurityErrorEvent.SECURITY_ERROR, onError);
      }
   }

   // When the response is returned, display the location
   // to which the IP address resolves.
   private function onComplete(locationEvent:LocationEvent):void {
      _text.text = locationEvent.city + ", " + locationEvent.stateProvince;
   }

   private function onError(event:Event):void {
      _text.text = "error: " + event.type;
   }

   }

}
```

You can test this example by entering a valid IP address in the text field and pressing the Enter key. The Web service will respond shortly, and the result will be displayed in the text field.

CLASSIC XML API

The old way of working with XML still exists in ActionScript 3.0 in the form of the XMLDocument and XMLNode classes. These classes are included in ActionScript 3.0 mainly for backwards compatibility. All new projects should use E4X because it is the new standard for working with XML in ActionScript.

Summary

E4X is one of the biggest improvements to ActionScript in years. This enhancement increases the power of XML and makes it an even more robust option for ActionScript programmers. In this chapter, you learned about the new features of E4X and created a simple Web service application.

Regular expressions enable you to look for substrings that match a pattern, making them a powerful way to work with strings. For basic substring searches, you can use String class methods such as indexOf(). Methods such as indexOf() work when you know the exact substring you want to find. For example, if you want to determine whether a string contains the substring cog you can use the following code:

```
var string:String = "Gears and cogs";
var index:int = string.indexOf("cog");
trace("contains substring? " + (index != -1));
```

The preceding code determines whether string contains the letters "cog." If the indexOf() method doesn't return -1, then it means that it found an occurrence of the substring.

When writing sophisticated programs, it's entirely likely that you'll want to search for substrings in a more abstract fashion. For example, consider if you wanted to determine whether a string contains the substring cog *or* the substring log. In such a case, you could simply test for both substrings using indexOf(). Yet as the number of possible substrings for which you want to test increases, so too does the complexity of the code necessary to test for every substring using indexOf(). If you wanted to test for all substrings that start with a letter followed by og, then you have to test for 52 possible substrings. More complex substring possibilities could require testing for hundreds, thousands, millions, even billions of substrings. This is where regular expressions simplify things greatly.

Regular expressions are a way of testing for substrings by using patterns. Regular expressions use standard characters such as letters and numbers as well as special metacharacters and metasequences to form these patterns. In this chapter, we'll look at how to build and work with regular expressions using ActionScript 3.0.

NOTE

Regular expressions are supported natively in Flash Player 9 with ActionScript 3.0.

Introducing the RegExp Class

ActionScript 3.0 uses the RegExp class to define regular expressions. There are two basic ways to construct a RegExp object. You can use the RegExp constructor or literal notation (that is, you can type it in directly as you would type a string or a number). Which you choose is mainly a matter of preference and usage. The constructor requires that you pass it at least one parameter specifying the regular expression pattern as a string. The following example constructs a RegExp object that matches any substring that contains between 4 and 8 lowercase alphabetic characters:

```
var pattern:RegExp = new RegExp("[a-z]{4,8}");
```

Note that when you want to define a regular expression pattern at runtime, you ought to use the constructor because it allows you to use a string value to define the expression. You can build this string using code, allowing you to create patterns appropriate for the situation at hand.

The literal notation surrounds the regular expression pattern by forward slashes (/). In the case of literal notation, the pattern is not a string and therefore is not surrounded by quotes. The following constructs a RegExp object that matches the same substrings as the preceding example. However, rather than using the constructor, the following example uses literal notation:

```
var pattern:RegExp = /[a-z]{4,8}/;
```

Note that when you want to add a backslash to a pattern that you build with the constructor, you'll have to escape the backslash because the constructor requires that you specify the pattern as a string and the backslash character has special meaning within a string. Many regular expression metasequences use backslashes. For example, the \d metasequence matches any digit. The following statement illustrates how to construct a RegExp object that matches any digit. Because the example uses the constructor, it's necessary to escape the backslash.

```
var pattern:RegExp = new RegExp("\\d");
```

Because the backslash character doesn't have special meaning within regular expression literal notation, the following is the literal notation equivalent of the preceding example:

```
var pattern:RegExp = /\d/;
```

However, because forward slashes have special meaning within regular expression literal notation, you must escape forward slashes. You can escape forward slashes with backslashes. The following matches the literal forward slash character:

```
var pattern:RegExp = /\//;
```

Working with Regular Expressions

You can work with regular expressions by way of the RegExp methods or by way of the String methods that accept RegExp parameters. The methods are as follows.

- RegExp.test()
- RegExp.exec()

- `String.search()`

- `String.replace()`

- `String.match()`

We'll next look at using these methods in the following sections.

Boolean Testing Regular Expressions

The `test()` method is a method of the `RegExp` class, and it accepts a string parameter. The `test()` method returns true if the string parameter contains a substring that matches the regular expression pattern. Otherwise it returns false. The following example uses a regular expression that matches one or more lowercase characters. As you can see from the comments, the `test()` method returns true or false depending on whether or not the regular expression matches a substring in the string parameter.

```
var pattern:RegExp = /[a-z]+/;
var string:String = "abcd";
trace(pattern.test(string));  // true
string = "1234";
trace(pattern.test(string));  // false
```

Finding Matching Substring Indices

The `search()` method is a method of the `String` class, and it accepts a regular expression parameter. The `search()` method returns the index of the first matching substring. The following example locates the index of the first word that starts with the letter *p*:

```
var pattern:RegExp = /\bp[a-z]+/;
var string:String = "There is no path to peace. Peace is the path.";
trace(string.search(pattern));  // 12
```

The `search()` method always starts searching from the start of the string. The global flag and `lastIndex` property have no effect on `search()`.

Retrieving Matching Substrings

The `RegExp.exec()` method and the `String.match()` method both enable you to retrieve matching substrings using regular expressions. However, the two methods operate in different ways.

The `exec()` method returns an array containing the substring matched. As discussed in the section, "Using Regular Expression Groups," later in this chapter, the array returned by `exec()` can also contain group subpattern matches.

Even when the global flag is set, the `exec()` method only ever finds one match at a time. The `exec()` method sets the `lastIndex` property of the `RegExp` object from which it was called to the index immediately following the most recent matching substring. This arrangement allows you to continue to apply the `exec()` method to a string, and it finds the next matching substring each time. The `exec()` method uses the `lastIndex` property to determine that index from which to start the next search. When no more matching substrings are found, `exec()` returns null and resets `lastIndex` to 0. The following code illustrates the use of `exec()` as well as `lastIndex`. When you run the code, you can see that after null is returned, the `lastIndex` property is reset to 0. Following that, the method searches from the start of the string once again. The following example outputs each word within the string, one at a time, along with the index of the last character in the string that was previously examined:

```
var pattern:RegExp = /[a-z]+/ig;
var string:String = "There is no path to peace. Peace is the path.";
for(var i:uint = 0; i < 12; i++) {
   trace(pattern.exec(string));
   trace(pattern.lastIndex);
}
```

The `lastIndex` property is a read-write property. That means you can set `lastIndex` so that it specifies the starting index from which `exec()` ought to start searching.

The `match()` method returns an array of all the substrings that match the pattern. Use the global flag to match all substrings. If you don't set the global flag, the `match()` method returns an array with only the first matching substring. The following example illustrates the use of the `match()` method.

```
// This expression will match strings that follow the rules of email
// address values.
var pattern:RegExp = /(?:\w|[_.\-])+@(?:(?:\w|-)+\.)+\w{2,4}/g;
var string:String = "emails: user@domain.com, user@server.com, email@example.com";
trace(string.match(pattern));
// user@domain.com, user@server.com, email@example.com
```

Replacing Substrings Using Regular Expressions

The `replace()` method is a `String` method that enables you to replace substrings using regular expressions. When using regular expressions with the `replace()` method, use the global flag if you want to replace all instances of a pattern or it will only replace the first instance. The following example replaces all email address with *<email>@<domain>.com*.

```
var pattern:RegExp = /((?:\w|[_.\-])+)@(?:((?:\w|-)+)\.)+\w{2,4}+/;
var string:String = "The following was posted by user@domain.com.";
trace(string.replace(pattern, "<email>@<domain>.com"));
// outputs: The following was posted by <email>@<domain>.com.
```

For more complex replacements, you can specify a function reference for the second parameter in place of the string. That function is then passed the following parameters:

- The matching substring

- Capturing groups (see "Using Regular Expression Groups") (Note that if there are no capturing groups then these parameters are omitted.)

- The index of the matching substring

- The original string

The function should return a string. The string the function returns is what gets substituted.

The following example uses a replacement function:

```
package {

    import flash.display.Sprite;

    public class RegularExpressions extends Sprite {

        public function RegularExpressions() {
        // The ?: sequences make the groups non-capturing as discussed in
        // the sections on groups in this chapter.
        var pattern:RegExp = /(?:\w|[_.\-])+@(?:(?:\w|-)+\.)+\w{2,4}/;
        var string:String = "The following was posted by user@domain.com.";
        trace(string.replace(pattern, replacer));
        // Prints out: The following was posted by user AT domain DOT com
        }

        // The regular expression doesn't have any capturing groups, so the
        // function only expects three parameters.
        private function replacer(match:String, index:int, originalString:String):String {
        var string:String = match.replace("@", " AT ");
        string = string.replace(/\./g, " DOT ");
        return string;
        }

    }
}
```

Using Regular Expression Flags

ActionScript lets you specify flags that affect how regular expressions work. Table 16.1 is a comprehensive list of those flags.

Table 16.1 Regular Expression Flags

FLAG	DESCRIPTION
g	Global
i	Ignore case
m	Multiline
s	Dot matches newlines
x	Extended notation allows spaces in regular expression patterns

You can specify flags when you construct a RegExp object. When you use the constructor, you specify the flags as a second string parameter. The following example matches all substrings of 4 to 8 alphabetical characters:

```
var pattern:RegExp = new RegExp("[a-z]{4,8}", "ig");
```

You can specify the flags with literal notation by adding the flag characters following the second forward slash, as shown here:

```
var pattern:RegExp = /[a-z]{4,8}/ig;
```

The order in which you specify the flags makes no difference. Specifying igms is the same as specifying sgim.

The Global Flag

By default, regular expressions match only the first instance of a pattern in a string. Obviously, there are cases in which it's beneficial to be able to match every instance of a pattern, not just the first instance. The global flag enables just that. Consider the following example. The pattern matches whole words. By default, it finds only one matching substring.

```
var pattern:RegExp = /\b\w+\b/;
var string:String = "There is no path to peace. Peace is the path.";
trace(string.match(pattern).toString());  // There
```

The preceding code finds just the first substring because the global flag is not set. The following changes the preceding example simply by setting the global flag. Notice that it then finds every word.

```
var pattern:RegExp = /\b\w+\b/g;
var string:String = "There is no path to peace. Peace is the path.";
trace(string.match(pattern).toString());  // There,is,no,path,to,peace,Peace,is,
the,path
```

NOTE

Both examples in this section return arrays. Because the first example does not have the global flag set, it returns only one element in the array.

The Ignore Case Flag

By default, ActionScript regular expressions make a distinction between lowercase and uppercase characters. For example, *A* and *a* are not considered the equivalent by default. The following code illustrates this. The pattern is supposed to match any continuous sequence of lowercase characters bordered by non-word characters (such as a space). Notice that the first matching substring it finds is the second word because the first word has an uppercase character.

```
var pattern:RegExp = /\b[a-z]+\b/;
var string:String = "There is no path to peace. Peace is the path.";
trace(string.match(pattern));  // is
```

Setting the i flag causes the regular expression to ignore the distinction between uppercase and lowercase characters. The following regular expression differs from the preceding code only by the i flag being set. The following regular expression matches the first word in the string.

```
var pattern:RegExp = /\b[a-z]+\b/i;
var string:String = "There is no path to peace. Peace is the path.";
trace(string.match(pattern));  // There
```

The Multiline Flag

The ^ character matches the start of a string, and the $ character matches the end of a string by default. Consider the following example in which the pattern looks for any sequence of lowercase and uppercase characters, spaces, and dots in which the substring is at the start of the string. Notice that the newline character (\n) delimits the substring, and even though the global flag is set, the regular expression finds only one substring.

```
var pattern:RegExp = /^[a-zA-Z .]+/g;
var string:String = "There is no path to peace.\nPeace is the path.";
trace(string.match(pattern));  // There is no path to peace.
```

The multiline flag causes the ^ character to match both the start of the string and the start of the second line, and the $ character to match both the end of the string and the end of the first line. The following example is identical to the preceding code except that it also sets the multiline flag. Notice that it now matches both lines from the string.

```
var pattern:RegExp = /^[a-zA-Z .]+/mg;
var string:String = "There is no path to peace.\nPeace is the path.";
trace(string.match(pattern));  // There is no path to peace.,Peace is the path.
```

The Dot Matches Newline Flag

The dot (.) character matches any character. However, it does not match the newline character by default. The following example illustrates the default behavior. The pattern matches one or more non-newline characters. Note that because the pattern does not match the newline character, it matches the substring only up until the newline character.

```
var pattern:RegExp = /.+/;
var string:String = "There is no path to peace.\nPeace is the path.";
trace(string.match(pattern));  // There is no path to peace.
```

The s flag causes the dot to match every character including the newline character. The following example illustrates the difference with the s flag.

```
var pattern:RegExp = /.+/s;
var string:String = "There is no path to peace.\nPeace is the path.";
trace(string.match(pattern));
/*
There is no path to peace.
Peace is the path.
*/
```

The Extended Flag

By default, spaces within patterns are interpreted literally. For complex regular expressions, that fact can make the patterns difficult to read by humans. For the purposes of legibility, you might want to add additional spaces to a pattern. If you want Flash Player to ignore additional spaces added for the purposes of legibility, you can set the x flag. Consider the following example that matches an email address:

```
var pattern:RegExp = /(\w|[_.\-])+@((\w|-)+\.)+\w{2,4}+/;
var string:String = "email@address.com";
trace(pattern.test(string));  // true
```

The pattern is complex and perhaps difficult to read. You can make it more legible by adding spaces, as follows:

```
var pattern:RegExp = /   ( \w | [_.\-] )+    @    ( ( \w | - )+ \. )+    \w{2,4}+    /;
var string:String = "email@address.com";
trace(pattern.test(string));  // false
```

In the preceding example, the x flag is not set, so the spaces are interpreted literally, and the test evaluates to false. The following example evaluates to true because the x flag is set so that the additional spaces are ignored.

```
var pattern:RegExp = /   ( \w | [_.\-] )+    @    ( ( \w | - )+ \. )+    \w{2,4}+    /x;
var string:String = "email@address.com";
trace(pattern.test(string));  // true
```

If you want to match a literal space when the x flag is set, you can use a backslash to escape the space, as shown here:

```
var pattern:RegExp = /a\ b/x;
var string:String = "a b";
trace(pattern.test(string)); // true
```

Understanding Metacharacters and Metasequences

Regular expressions are composed of standard characters such as letters and numbers as well as special characters and sequences called metacharacters and metasequences. These metacharacters and metasequences are what enable regular expressions to match abstract patterns. For example, using the metasequence \d, you can match any digit, which is more abstract than matching a specific digit.

The metacharacters used by regular expressions enable you to match specific parts of a string, group characters, and even perform logical operations. The list of metacharacters used by regular expressions is relatively short. The metacharacters are summarized in Table 16.2.

Table 16.2 Metacharacters Used in Regular Expressions

METACHARACTER	DESCRIPTION
^	The start of the string or the start of a line when the m flag is set
$	The end of a string or the end of a line when the m flag is set
\	Escape a metacharacter or metasequence so it is interpreted literally
.	Any character; includes the newline character only when the s flag is set
*	Zero or more occurrences of the preceding item
+	One or more occurrences of the preceding item
?	Zero or one occurrences of the preceding item

Table 16.2 *continued*

METACHARACTER	DESCRIPTION
()	A group
[]	A character class
|	Either the item on the left or the item on the right

The metasequences are sequences of characters that are interpreted in a specific manner by regular expressions. Table 16.3 summarizes the regular expression metasequences.

Table 16.3 Metasequences Used in Regular Expressions

METASEQUENCE	DESCRIPTION
{n}	n occurrences of the preceding item
{n,}	n or more occurrences of the preceding item
{n,m}	Between n and m occurrences of the preceding item
\A	The start of the string
\b	The border between a word character (a-z, A-Z, 0-9, or _) and a non-word character including the start and end of a string
\B	The border between two word characters or two non-word characters
\d	Any digit
\D	Any non-digit
\n	Newline
\r	Return
\s	Any whitespace character
\S	Any non-whitespace character
\t	Tab
\unnnn	The Unicode character represented by the character code nnnn
\w	Any word character (a-z, A-Z, 0-9, or _)
\W	Any non-word character
\xnn	The character represented by the ASCII value nn
\z	The end of the string including any final newline character
\Z	The end of the string excluding any final newline character

Using Character Classes

Character classes are denoted by square brackets ([]), and they enable you to specify a set of characters for one position within a regular expression. For example, the following regular expression uses a character class to match any substring that starts with *b*, followed by any vowel, and ending with a *t*.

```
var pattern:RegExp = /b[aeiou]t/g;
var string:String = "The bat lost the bet, but he didn't mind a bit.";
trace(string.match(pattern));  // bat,bet,but,bit
```

Most metacharacters and metasequences aren't interpreted as such within a character class. For example *{5}* is interpreted literally as the digit 5 and the right and left curly brace characters when placed within a character class. The exceptions are the metasequences \n, \r, \t, \unnnn, and \xnn. In addition, the -,], and \ characters have special meaning within character classes.

The - (hyphen) character within a character class can indicate a range of characters. For example, the following code defines a regular expression that matches any lowercase alphabetical character:

```
var pattern:RegExp = /[a-z]/;
```

You can define valid ranges of uppercase and lowercase alphabetical characters, digits, and ASCII character codes. If you use a - character such that it does not define a valid range, then it will be interpreted literally. For example, the following defines a character class that matches all lowercase characters, digits, and the - character:

```
var pattern:RegExp = /[a-z-0-9]/;
```

The] character closes a character class. If you want to match the literal] character within a character class, you have to escape it. The backslash character (\) is the escape character. The following example matches all lowercase characters or the right square bracket character:

```
var pattern:RegExp = /[a-z\]]/;
```

If you want to match the literal backslash character, you can escape it with a preceding backslash character. The following matches any lowercase character or the backslash character:

```
var pattern:RegExp = /[a-z\\]/;
```

Working with Quantifiers

The metacharacters and metasequences *, +, ?, {n}, {n,}, and {n,m} are quantifiers. They allow you to specify repetitions within patterns. Quantifiers are applied to the item preceding them. An item can be a character, metasequence, character class, or group.

The following example uses the + operator to find all the substrings that consist of alphabetical characters:

```
var pattern:RegExp = /[a-z]+/ig;
var string:String = "There is no path to peace. Peace is the path.";
trace(string.match(pattern));  // There,is,no,path,to,peace,Peace,is,the,path
```

The following code matches only the words that are 4 or 5 characters:

```
var pattern:RegExp = /[a-z]{4,5}/ig;
var string:String = "There is no path to peace.\nPeace is the path.";
trace(string.match(pattern));  // There,path,peace,Peace,path
```

Using Regular Expression Groups

Regular expression groups are denoted by parentheses. You can use groups for the following basic purposes:

- Add quantifiers to more than one character

- Add more control to logical or operations

- Remember subpattern matches for subsequent use in the code

Quantifiers apply to the preceding item. The preceding item might be a character, metasequence, character code, or group. The following example uses a regular expression that matches substrings with an *is* followed by one or more *s* characters:

```
var pattern:RegExp = /iss+/g;
var string:String = "Mississippi";
trace(string.match(pattern)); // iss,iss
```

The following example matches all substrings composed of one or more *iss* sequences:

```
var pattern:RegExp = /(iss)+/g;
var string:String = "Mississippi";
trace(string.match(pattern)); // ississ
```

The | character normally matches the entire pattern on either side of the character. For example, the following code uses a regular expression that matches either *re* or *ad*:

```
var pattern:RegExp = /re|ad/g;
var string:String = "red is rad";
trace(string.match(pattern)); // re,ad
```

If parentheses are used, then the | operates on just the characters surrounded by the parentheses as shown in the following example:

```
var pattern:RegExp = /r(e|a)d/g;
var string:String = "red is rad";
trace(string.match(pattern)); // red,rad
```

Parentheses also enable you to use backreferences. Backreferences allow you to reference a grouped substring within the regular expression. You can reference each group numerically from 1 to 99. The following illustrates a backreference:

```
var pattern:RegExp = /(\d) = \1/g;
var string:String = "1 = 1, 2 = 1 + 1, 3 = 1 + 1 + 1, 4 = 4";
trace(string.match(pattern)); // 1 = 1,4 = 4
```

In the preceding example, the \1 references the first group in the regular expression: the substring matched by (\d). The following is a similar example. Notice that in this case, the pattern doesn't match 2 = 2 because the grouped substring must consist of two digits:

```
var pattern:RegExp = /(\d\d) = \1/g;
var string:String = "20 = 20, 2 = 2, 3 = 1 + 1 + 1, 40 = 40";
trace(string.match(pattern)); // 20 = 20,40 = 40
```

The following example uses two backreferences:

```
var pattern:RegExp = /(\d)(\d) = \2\1/g;
var string:String = "42 = 24, 2 = 2, 3 = 1 + 1 + 1, 40 = 40";
trace(string.match(pattern));  // 42 = 24
```

You can use $1 through $99 as references to grouped substrings when using the String.replace()
method. The following example illustrates how to use these references:

```
var pattern:RegExp = /([a-z]+) function ([a-zA-Z]+)\(\):([a-zA-Z]+)/g;
var string:String = "public function example():void";
trace(string.replace(pattern, "The function called $2 is declared as $1 with a
return type of $3"));
```

When you call the RegExp.exec() method, it returns an array with the current matching substring as well as any grouped substring.

```
var pattern:RegExp = /([a-z]+) function ([a-zA-Z]+)\(\):([a-zA-Z]+)/g;
var string:String = "public function example():void { trace('example');}";
var substrings:Array = pattern.exec(string);
trace(substrings[0]);  // public function example():Void
trace(substrings[1]);  // public
trace(substrings[2]);  // example
trace(substrings[3]);  // void
```

You can also defined named groups using ?P<groupName> immediately following the opening
parenthesis. In this case, RegExp.exec() returns an associative array where the names of the cap-
tured groups are keys of the array. The entire matched string is still returned in the first index.
The following example is a rewrite of the preceding code such that it uses named groups:

```
var pattern:RegExp = /(?P<modifier>[a-z]+) function (?P<functionName>[a-zA-Z]+)\(\
):(?P<returnType>[a-zA-Z]+)/g;
var string:String = "public function example():void { trace('example');}";
var substrings:Array = pattern.exec(string);
trace(substrings[0]);
trace(substrings.modifier);
trace(substrings.functionName);
trace(substrings.returnType);
```

You can also instruct the regular expression *not* to capture a group. For example, you might
want to use a group with a quantifier, but without capturing the group. In such cases, you can
use ?: immediately following the opening parenthesis. The following example uses a standard
capturing group. Notice that the array returned by exec() has two elements because it captures
the subpattern.

```
var pattern:RegExp = /i(s|p){2}/;
var string:String = "Mississippi";
trace(pattern.exec(string));  // iss,s
```

The following code rewrites the preceding example such that it uses a non-capturing group. In
this example, the array returned by exec() has just one element:

```
var pattern:RegExp = /i(?:s|p){2}/;
var string:String = "Mississippi";
trace(pattern.exec(string));  // iss
```

Lookahead groups are non-capturing groups that can be either positive (the subpattern must appear) or negative (the subpattern must not appear.) Positive lookahead groups are denoted by ?= following the opening parenthesis. A positive lookahead group says that the specified subpattern must appear in that position, but it will not be included in the match. Frequently, positive lookahead groups are used to match patterns that are followed by a specific pattern. For example, consider a string that contains filenames with file extensions. If you want to retrieve the filenames minus the file extensions from the string, you can use a positive lookahead group as in the following example:

```
var pattern:RegExp = /[a-z]+(?=\.[a-z]+)/g;
var string:String = "Copy the program.exe and run.bat files. Move file.txt.";
trace(string.match(pattern));  // program,run,file
```

You can use positive lookahead groups for complex patterns that would be extremely difficult or impossible to match otherwise. Consider the example of an alphanumeric password that must be between 6 and 20 characters and must contain at least 2 digits as well as at least 1 lowercase and 1 uppercase character. The following example uses positive lookahead groups to accomplish that goal:

```
var pattern:RegExp = /(?=.*\d.*\d)(?=.*[a-z])(?=.*[A-Z])[a-zA-Z0-9]{6,20}/;
var string:String = "a1b2cd3e4";  // No uppercase
trace(pattern.test(string));  // false
string = "aBcdefg";  // No digits
trace(pattern.test(string));  // false
string = "a1B2cd3e4";
trace(pattern.test(string));  // true
```

Negative lookahead groups are denoted by ?!. Negative lookahead groups work just like positive lookahead groups, but they define subpatterns that must *not* appear. The following example uses a negative lookahead group to match all filenames (with file extensions) that don't have the file extension *.txt*.

```
var pattern:RegExp = /[a-z]+(?!\.txt)\.([a-z]+)/g;
var string:String = "Copy the program.exe and run.bat files. Move file.txt.";
trace(string.match(pattern));  // program.exe,run.bat
```

The following example rewrites the preceding regular expression slightly so that it matches all filenames except those that have file extensions of *.txt* or *.bat*:

```
var pattern:RegExp = /[a-z]+(?!\.txt|\.bat)\.([a-z]+)/g;
var string:String = "Copy the program.exe and run.bat files. Move file.txt.";
trace(string.match(pattern));  // program.exe
```

Building a Mad Libs Application Using Regular Expressions

In this example application, we'll use regular expressions to build a Mad Lib application. Mad Libs are the fill-in-the-blank word games that prompt the user to specify words without knowing the context of the words. The words are then used to fill in the blanks of a story, often with humorous results.

The Mad Lib application we'll build consists of the following elements:

- `MadLibTextElementData`: A data model class for each text element, whether plain text or substitutable text.

- `MadLibInputItemData`: A data model class for each of the word blanks that stores both the original value from the text file and the user-provided value that is substituted for the original. `MadLibInputItemData` is a subclass of `MadLibTextElementData`.

- `MadLibData`: A data model class for the entire story. The data model consists of several arrays of `MadLibInputItemData` and `MadLibTextElementData` objects. The class loads the data from a text file; after the data has loaded, it dispatches an event to all listeners. `MadLibData` is a Singleton class (see Chapter 4, "Singleton Pattern," for more information).

- `MadLibInputItem`: A control that allows the user to input a word. `MadLibInputItem` objects use `MadLibInputItemData` objects as their data models.

- `FormScreen`: A view class that renders the form of `MabLibIinputItem` controls for each of the word blanks from the `MadLibData` instance.

- `ResultScreen`: A view class that renders the story with the user-substituted words.

- `MadLibs`: The main class that renders a `FormScreen` and `ResultScreen` instance, and uses buttons to allow the user to toggle between the screens.

Additionally, the application has to load text from a file to use as the Mad Libs text. To start, create a file called `madlibstory.txt` in the deploy directory for the application. Then add the following text to the document.

```
There was once an old <type of building>, that stood in the middle of a deep gloomy
wood, and in the <type of building> lived an old fairy. Now this fairy could take
any shape she pleased. All the day long she flew about in the form of a/n <something
that flies>, or crept about the country like a/n <something that moves on land>; but
at night she always became an old woman again. When any young man came within a
hundred paces of her castle, he became quite fixed, and could not move a step till
she came and set him free; which she would not do till he had given her his word
never to <something you like to do> again: but when any pretty maiden came within
that space she was changed into a/n <something that goes in a cage>, and the fairy
put her into a cage, and hung her up in a chamber in the castle. There were seven
hundred of these cages hanging in the castle, and all with beautiful <something that
goes in a cage> in them.
```

The words and phrases that appear within <> are the word blanks. The application uses regular expressions to substitute those values.

Creating the Data Model Classes

As described previously, the Mad Libs application uses several data model classes. The first class we'll define is the data model class for each text element used in the application. A text element could be a substitutable or non-substitutable portion of the application. Define the `com.peach-pit.aas3wdp.madlibs.data.MadLibTextElementData` class as follows:

```
package com.peachpit.aas3wdp.madlibs.data {

    import flash.events.EventDispatcher;
    import flash.events.Event;

    public class MadLibTextElementData extends EventDispatcher {

        public static const UPDATE:String = "update";

        private var _data:String;

        public function get data():String {
            return _data;
        }

        public function set data(value:String):void {
            _data = value;
            dispatchEvent(new Event(UPDATE));
        }

        public function MadLibTextElementData(value:String = "") {
            _data = value;
        }

    }
}
```

This class simply holds the string value for a text element, whether substitutable or non-substitutable.

Next, we'll create the data model class that is specific to substitutable text. This class is called `MadLibInputItemData`, and it extends `MadLibTextElementData`. This class stores one additional piece of data: the label to use for the input. Define `com.peachpit.aas3wdp.madlibs.data.MadLibInputItemData` as follows:

```
package com.peachpit.aas3wdp.madlibs.data {

    import flash.events.EventDispatcher;
    import flash.events.Event;

    public class MadLibInputItemData extends MadLibTextElementData {

        private var _label:String;

        // The default label includes <>. Use a regular expression
        // to return the value between the <>.
        public function get labelFormatted():String {
            var pattern:RegExp = /[a-z ]+/i;
            return _label.match(pattern)[0];
        }

        public function get label():String {
            return _label;
        }

        public function set label(value:String):void {
            _label = value;
```

```
      }

    public function MadLibInputItemData(value:String) {
      _label = value;
    }

  }
}
```

Next we'll create a class to serve as the data model for the entire Mad Libs application. This is the most complex of the data model classes. It should store collections of instances of the other data model classes. The class should then define an interface that allows access to those collections using iterators. Define com.peachpit.aas3wdp.madlibs.data.MadLibData as follows:

```
package com.peachpit.aas3wdp.madlibs.data {

    import com.peachpit.aas3wdp.collections.ICollection;
    import com.peachpit.aas3wdp.iterators.ArrayIterator;
    import com.peachpit.aas3wdp.iterators.IIterator;

    import flash.events.Event;
    import flash.events.EventDispatcher;
    import flash.net.URLLoader;
    import flash.net.URLRequest;

    public class MadLibData extends EventDispatcher {

      private var _items:Array;
      private var _textElements:Array;

      private static var _instance:MadLibData;

      public static const UPDATE:String = "update";
      public static const INPUT_ITEMS:String = "inputItems";
      public static const ALL_ITEMS:String = "allItems";

      public function MadLibData(enforcer:SingletonEnforcer) {
      }

      public static function getInstance():MadLibData {
        if(_instance == null) {
          _instance = new MadLibData(new SingletonEnforcer());
        }
        return _instance;
      }

      // Load the data from a specified location.
      public function load(file:String):void {
        var loader:URLLoader = new URLLoader();
        var request:URLRequest = new URLRequest(file);
        loader.addEventListener(Event.COMPLETE, onData);
        loader.load(request);
      }

      // Return an iterator of either all the text elements
```

```
        // (inclusive of the input items) or just the input items.
        public function iterator(type:String = ALL_ITEMS):IIterator {
          if(type == INPUT_ITEMS) {
            return new ArrayIterator(_items);
          }
          else {
            return new ArrayIterator(_textElements);
          }
        }

        // The onData() method is the listener that gets called
        // when the text data loads.
        private function onData(event:Event):void {

          // Retrieve the data from the URLLoader.
          var text:String = String(event.target.data);

          // Define a regular expression that will match all
          // the substitutable text.
          var expression:RegExp = /<[a-z0-9 ]+>/ig;

          // Match all the substitutable items.
          var items:Array = text.match(expression);

          // The _items array stores references to the
          // MadLibInputItemData objects. The _textElements
          // array stores references to all the text elements,
          // including the input items.
          _items = new Array();
          _textElements = new Array();

          // Make an array of all the text element text.
          var textElementsText:Array = text.split(expression);

          var index:uint = 0;
          var item:MadLibInputItemData;
          var newItem:Boolean;

          // Loop through all the matched items.
          for(var i:uint = 0; i < items.length; i++) {

            // With each iteration initially assume the
            // input item is new.
            newItem = true;

            // Create a new MadLibInputItemData object.
            item = new MadLibInputItemData(String(items[i]));

            // Loop through all the items already stored
            // in the _items array. If the current item
            // label is equal to that of an existing
            // item in the array, then use the existing
            // item, and don't add the new item to the
            // _items array.
            for(var j:uint = 0; j < _items.length; j++) {
              if(item.label == _items[j].label) {
```

(CODE CONTINUED)

```
              item = _items[j];
              newItem = false;
              break;
          }
      }
      if(newItem) {
        _items.push(item);

        // Listen for UPDATE events from the
        // item.
        item.addEventListener(MadLibTextElementData.UPDATE, onUpdate);
      }

      // Add the text element for the non-
      // substitutable text.
      _textElements[index] = new MadLibTextElementData(String(textElementsText
      [index]));

      // Add the text element for the
      // substitutable text.
      _textElements.splice(index + 1, 0, item);

      // Increment the index by 2 since each
      // iteration adds two items to the
      // _textElements array.
      index += 2;
    }

    // Notify listeners that the data model has updated.
    dispatchEvent(new Event(UPDATE));
  }

  private function onUpdate(event:Event):void {
    dispatchEvent(new Event(UPDATE));
  }

  }
}
class SingletonEnforcer {}
```

Creating the Input Control

Next we'll create a class to use as an input control. The Mad Lib application consists of two screens: one that accepts user input and one that displays the results of the input combined with the story. The MadLibInputItem class defines the input control elements used on the form screen. This class uses MadLibInputItemData as a data model. Define com.peachpit.aas3wdp. madlibs.controls.MadLibInputItem as follows:

```
package com.peachpit.aas3wdp.madlibs.controls {

  import flash.display.Sprite;
  import flash.text.TextField;
  import flash.events.TextEvent;
```

(CODE CONTINUED)

```
import com.peachpit.aas3wdp.madlibs.data.MadLibInputItemData;

public class MadLibInputItem extends Sprite {

    private var _label:TextField;
    private var _value:TextField;
    private var _data:MadLibInputItemData;

    public function MadLibInputItem(data:MadLibInputItemData) {
        _data = data;

        // Add a text field to display the input label.
        _label = new TextField();
        _label.autoSize = "left";
        _label.text = data.labelFormatted;
        addChild(_label);

        // Add an input text field for the user value.
        _value = new TextField();
        _value.type = "input";
        _value.border = true;
        _value.background = true;
        _value.width = 200;
        _value.height = 20;
        _value.x = 200;
        addChild(_value);

        // Listen for TEXT_INPUT events.
        _value.addEventListener(TextEvent.TEXT_INPUT, onText);
    }

    // When the user updates the text, update the value stored
    // in the data model.
    private function onText(event:TextEvent):void {
        _data.data = event.target.text + event.text;
    }

    }
}
```

Creating the View Classes

Now we'll create the two screens used by the application. Each uses MadLibsData as the data model. However, each displays the data in different ways. The first class, FormScreen, displays just the inputs for substitutable text. Define com.peachpit.aas3wdp.madlibs.views.screens.FormScreen as follows:

```
package com.peachpit.aas3wdp.madlibs.views.screens {

    import com.peachpit.aas3wdp.iterators.IIterator;
    import com.peachpit.aas3wdp.madlibs.controls.MadLibInputItem;
    import com.peachpit.aas3wdp.madlibs.data.MadLibData;
    import com.peachpit.aas3wdp.madlibs.data.MadLibInputItemData;

    import flash.display.Sprite;
```

(CODE CONTINUED)

```
import flash.events.Event;

public class FormScreen extends Sprite {

    public function FormScreen(data:MadLibData) {
        data.addEventListener(MadLibData.UPDATE, onUpdate);
    }

    private function onUpdate(event:Event):void {
        // If the screen hasn't already drawn itself, then
        // add input items for each of the elements from the
        // data model's INPUT_ITEMS iterator.
        if(numChildren == 0) {
            var data:MadLibData = MadLibData(event.target);
            var iterator:IIterator = data.iterator(MadLibData.INPUT_ITEMS);
            var item:MadLibInputItem;
            var y:Number = 0;
            while(iterator.hasNext()) {
                item = new MadLibInputItem(MadLibInputItemData(iterator.next()));
                item.y = y;
                y += 25;
                addChild(item);
            }
        }
    }

}
```

Now we'll create the screen that displays the results of the user input. This screen displays both the non-substitutable text as well as the user input text in place of the substitutable text. Define com.peachpit.aas3wdp.madlibs.views.screens.ResultScreen as follows.

```
package com.peachpit.aas3wdp.madlibs.views.screens {

    import flash.display.Sprite;
    import com.peachpit.aas3wdp.madlibs.data.MadLibData;
    import com.peachpit.aas3wdp.madlibs.data.MadLibTextElementData;
    import com.peachpit.aas3wdp.iterators.IIterator;
    import flash.text.TextField;
    import flash.events.Event;

    public class ResultScreen extends Sprite {

        private var _text:TextField;

        public function ResultScreen(data:MadLibData) {
            data.addEventListener(MadLibData.UPDATE, onUpdate);

            // Add a text field to display the story.
            _text = new TextField();
            _text.width = 400;
            _text.height = 400;
            _text.multiline = true;
```

(CODE CONTINUED)

```
            _text.wordWrap = true;
            addChild(_text);
        }

        // When the data model dispatches an UPDATE event, update
        // the text correspondingly.
        private function onUpdate(event:Event):void {
            var data:MadLibData = MadLibData(event.target);
            _text.text = "";
            var iterator:IIterator = data.iterator(MadLibData.ALL_ITEMS);
            while(iterator.hasNext()) {
              _text.appendText(MadLibTextElementData(iterator.next()).data);
            }
        }
    }

  }
}
```

Defining the Main Class

We have yet to create the main class that puts the application together. In this class, we create instances of the two screens and use buttons to toggle between the screens. You'll need to ensure that the AAS3WDP library is in your project's class path for this to work. Here's the main class.

```
package {

   import flash.display.Sprite;
   import flash.events.Event;
   import flash.events.MouseEvent;
   import com.peachpit.aas3wdp.madlibs.data.MadLibData;
   import com.peachpit.aas3wdp.controls.BasicButton;
   import com.peachpit.aas3wdp.madlibs.views.screens.FormScreen;
   import com.peachpit.aas3wdp.madlibs.views.screens.ResultScreen;

   public class MadLibs extends Sprite {

      private var _data:MadLibData;
      private var _formScreen:FormScreen;
      private var _resultScreen:ResultScreen;
      private var _formButton:BasicButton;
      private var _resultButton:BasicButton;

      public function MadLibs() {

         // Tell the data model to load the data from the
         // text file.
         _data = MadLibData.getInstance();
         _data.load("madlibstory.txt");

         // Add the two screens. Only add the form screen to
         // the display list.
         _formScreen = new FormScreen(_data);
         _formScreen.y = 25;
         addChild(_formScreen);
         _resultScreen = new ResultScreen(_data);
```

```
            _resultScreen.y = 25;

            // Add buttons for toggling between the screens.
            _formButton = new BasicButton("Mad Lib Form");
            _formButton.addEventListener(MouseEvent.CLICK, onFormScreen);
            addChild(_formButton);
            _resultButton = new BasicButton("Story");
            _resultButton.addEventListener(MouseEvent.CLICK, onResultScreen);
            _resultButton.x = _formButton.width;
            addChild(_resultButton);
        }

        private function onResultScreen(event:Event):void {
            if (contains(_resultScreen)) return;
            removeChild(_formScreen);
            addChild(_resultScreen);
        }

        private function onFormScreen(event:Event):void {
            if (contains(_formScreen)) return;
            removeChild(_resultScreen);
            addChild(_formScreen);
        }

    }

}
```

When you test the application, you ought to be presented initially with the form screen with input controls for each of the substitutable elements from the story. After you've entered a value for each input control, click the story button to toggle to the ResultScreen view. Then you will see the story with the new words substituted for the original placeholders.

Because the application uses regular expressions to parse the text data, you can quite easily change the story and/or the substitutable elements. Regardless of how you edit the text in the madlibstory.txt file, the application will parse it and interpret any text in between the <> as substitutable text.

Summary

Regular expressions are a powerful way to find substrings that match a pattern. In this chapter, you've seen how to construct RegExp objects and use them to match substrings by using the RegExp and String methods that support regular expressions.

INDEX

N